Cry or Laugh

Cry or Laugh

Volume Two

Life in the UK following resettlement as a survivor of the children's transport from Germany in 1939

Sylvia Hurst

SYLVIA OF DURHAM PUBLISHERS

First published in 2017 by Sylvia of Durham Publishers
5 Sheridan Drive, Stanley, Co Durham, DH9 6YX

Distributed by Gardners Books, 1 Whittle Drive, Eastbourne, East Sussex, BN23 6QH
Tel: +44(0)1323 521555 | Fax: +44(0)1323 521666

www.amolibros.com

British Library Cataloguing in Publication Data
A catalogue record for this book is available from the British Library.

ISBN 978-0-9933897-1-9

Typeset by Amolibros, Milverton, Somerset
This book production has been managed by Amolibros
Printed and bound by T J International Ltd, Padstow, Cornwall, UK

To my parents and Grandmother Hedwig
Victims of the Holocaust

And to the children of Germany
Victims of Brainwashing

Contents

Foreword

This is a true account of refugees and other people.

The speech is mostly verbatim.

When I was writing, I heard it again, and I could see it again, as if I was there. Good or bad 'happenings' are correctly reported.

I have changed some names, not those of the family members.

The book begins in 1939 in London when refugees arrived to escape Nazism.

Sylvia Hurst,
Spring 2016

Sylvia Hurst passed away, peacefully, on 28th July 2016, in County Durham, may she finally rest in peace.

PART ONE

Liverpool Street Station, Reception Hall

I had arrived. The hall was poorly lit, I could hardly see the rows of tables. The loudspeaker announced, "Attention, please. Find the table with your initial, your surname. No talking."

I sat on the bench next to my table, F, waiting.

The trolley came around, bringing us tea in paper cups, the serving girl said, "Your family will collect you from here, you'll have to wait here."

A tall lady wearing a pink straw hat stood at the large top table, attending to the queue of people, handing them small folders. I thought these must be families who have come to collect their children. The lady had girl helpers, I suspected volunteers, who took the people to the tables, handed over their child. "Good girl, be a good girl, this is your family. Goodbye, God bless."

The hall slowly emptied. It was hours now, no one had come for me. Plenty of time. I was the last one, all the children on my table, F, had been collected. There were only a few children left in the hall. I went to the top table. "No one has come for me."

"You have to be patient!! Go back to your table." Now I was the last remaining child. I got anxious, went again to the top table. "They will come, surely. No, they have not cancelled."

I was waiting, waiting. What happens if no one calls for me? I watched the door. A couple with two children had come in. A tall man, a fat lady, his wife. She went to the top table. "I am so sorry we are late. We came as soon as we could, had to close up our business. Sorry, have you been waiting long?"

"I am glad, you have finally arrived." She took the lady to my table. "This is Sylvia Fleischer."

The lady looked me over. Obviously I was not what they expected. "Bist a possem?"

"Yes, I am Sylvia Fleischer." She repeated again, "Bist a possem?"

"Please speak to me in English, I understand English."

"Bist, an orphan? You come from the orphanage?"

"Yes, I lived there, I went to college in Hamburg. I was a student."

She touched my blond hair, it was very blond and corkscrew curls. Then she called across to her husband, "Abe, she's not a Schikse, she speaks English."

Pink hat, wanted to close up, and go home. She handed over my small folder. "It's late."

The family took me outside, to their car. It was a very small car. "Is this all your luggage?"

"Yes, we were only allowed one suitcase."

The husband put my case in the boot. "Croc," he said, "crocodile." I realized it had been the wrong thing, taking this case, my mother's best suitcase.

I stared at them, my family. I could only see the lady's strange hat, with a large diamante brooch stuck on it. She was very fat, obese, that's what they call it. She had a big nose. Ugly.

The children were beautiful, the girl had ringlet hair, how can this woman have such lovely children? Yes, the husband is handsome, tall.

"Get in, get in." I could see only the woman's funny hat, the diamante brooch.

Ah, he drives fast, very fast, I looked out of the window, but I can't see anything. He drives like a racing driver. I have to hold on, where there is a loop, on the side, leather.

Large, wide street outside, now small houses, a cul-de-sac. We stopped. I was still shaking. The children laughed, having enjoyed the race. We were home. "Take her up," said my lady to a pale young woman.

Turning to me, she said, "I am Rachel. You call him Mr Abraham." She said to the children, "Wash yourselves. What do you want for tea? It's late."

"Can we have salt beef?"

"No, that's for tomorrow."

"Latkes." What was latkes, never before had I heard this word – what kind of food? The potatoes went into the mincer, we had the same for mincing meat, at home. On the cooker was a large pan, with oil. Mrs Rachel worked very quickly, very efficient. The latkes cooked rapidly.

I soon found out – crispy potato cakes. Very rich. We sat around a large table in the kitchen. American cloth, white. Thank you, no sugar in my tea. "Ruth, Reuben, Rachel, Ra Ra Ra." She laughed at her joke.

"I'll help you to unpack." I was to share the bedroom with the young woman. Her maid. "She's cleared two drawers for you."

The contents of my suitcase seemed to be of great interest to Mrs. Rachel. She handed my underwear to me. Some items were examined. "Pure silk."

"I'm allergic to wool, I have to wear this underneath."

"Hoity-toity." The drawers were not large enough to hold everything. Some of my stuff had to stay in my suitcase. "What's this?"

It was a small reticule, made of tiny pearls, with a silver filigree firmature. I explained: "Fragonard, a girl on a swing."

Mrs Rachel looked puzzled.

"An eighteenth-century painter." A very precious birthday present, it had belonged to Mother, she had given it to me.

I was tired, it had been a long day. I was glad to slip into bed, without washing or cleaning teeth.

It was late when I woke up, after 8 o'clock. There was a cup and plate for me on the kitchen table. A loaf of bread, a sliced loaf. Red jam, margarine. I could not find the family. Possibly in the building at the back, across a yard. This was not a good way to start work and worried me greatly. I found them in the workroom and Mrs Rachel showed me my workstation immediately. I was obviously here to work, not as part of the family. She told her friends she had asked for an orphan, but she got a student.

"Ah, there you are, did you sleep well?"

"Yes, thank you."

"I'll show you your work," said Mrs Rachel.

The work rooms were cloudy, steamed up. A man was stirring a large pot over a gas fire.

On the ceiling were several lines, hat-like shapes were pegged on to them. "Oh, it's a hat factory," I thought, not many people working here, counted three, plus of course Mrs Rachel. She took a shape off the line. "I'll show you how to block them, they are called hoods."

Metal shapes, like flower pots, different sizes, marked on them, on the shelves, also other shapes. The hoods were placed over these metal shapes which had gas light underneath. Steam rose, after a while the hood had become a flower-pot-shaped hat, quite nice.

"Be careful, don't burn yourself." Mrs Rachel went back to her sewing machine. "I sew the hat bands in, it's tricky because it's round," explained Mrs Rachel.

A bell went at 12 o'clock sharp, not our bell, outside, also a hooter. "Lunchtime!" We went into the kitchen. The maid had prepared sandwiches from the salt beef. The children ran in from the street. They never spoke to me, they seemed embarrassed and just grinned at me.

"Washing," called Mrs Rachel. They washed at the kitchen sink. I also washed my hands at the kitchen sink. "All of us, we work here. My husband, he works in the office." She pointed to some steps leading to a half-landing. "He also does the deliveries, the post is too expensive. You'll get used to the work. Just now, the trade is not good." She shook her head: "Don't look so worried, there's enough to put food on the table. Orders are down, it's because people say there will be a war."

I knew I had to earn my keep. Besides I am learning a trade.

The house was very poorly furnished. The parlour had leather furniture, which had cracks, it was rarely used. The sitting room settee was covered in creasy cushions. Odd chairs and a trolley. The floral wall paper in the bedroom I shared with the maid was a little mouldy on top, the joins were badly matched, perhaps the maid had done papering as an improvement.

"We have the only bathroom, the only one in the street." Mrs Rachel was very proud of this. The bathroom was for the family. I washed at the kitchen sink, took my turn in the morning.

On Saturday, people came to visit, relatives, neighbours, sat in the parlour. I was introduced: "This is Sylvia. I asked for a girl from the orphanage, she would not be spoiled. I asked for a possem, what do I get? A student. She has silk underwear. I must say she works okay." She told this story to everyone.

The visitors had asked me many questions about my background, how I got to London: "Please speak to me in English," for I could only follow their conversation with some difficulty. I assumed it was Yiddish, I had never heard Yiddish before, it contained many German words. It was not spoken by our Jewish community at home, not even by the Polaki. These were Jews who had settled in Goeppingen. That was between 1880 and 1890, on their walk from Poland or Russia, to escape the pogroms, they walked from one synagogue to the next one. It was an honour to help, not a charity. There were jobs in the Jewish factories in Goeppingen, doing well. These people deserved a better life. Why go to the United States when we have jobs for them here, locally. They did not speak Yiddish, their children spoke good German.

Father said, "Yiddish is not a language, it is like pidgin English, they speak that in the East."

I was tri-lingual, German, French, English. My family came from Alsace-Lorraine, in France. We had a factory in London, before World War One. English relatives. Why did these not give my father the guarantee to come here? Father had explained to me that Aunt Frances refused, saying her own family came first, her priority, she had sixteen siblings, brothers and sisters. The London factory was still there: Adolphe Rosenthal in Margaret Street, near Oxford Circus, London W1. The aunt was now over eighty years of age. Her nephew Jeffrey Frank ran the factory.

"I don't know much about the Rosenthal Factory. Perhaps it belongs to her nephew now. She calls herself Rossendale." Mrs Rachel was intrigued. She said, "Next time I go up West, I'll have a look at it, you say Adolphe Rosenthal?"

She reported her visit to her husband. "Well, I had a look around, noticed there was a sign at the door. 'Sample machinist wanted.' I went in.

"For the sample machinist?"

"The fore-woman made me sit on a machine, gave me a small bundle. Obviously I did that to her satisfaction." "Ok, do you know it's for our factory in Leicestershire?"

"No, I didn't, I can't, I have family here, I can't move."

Mr and Mrs Abraham had a good laugh.

The family had booked their annual holiday in Margate. Most factories closed in August.

"Sorry we can't take you, we haven't booked for you. There is no room in the car, no room for luggage, sorry. We cannot take you," she repeated.

I had arrived in London on 27th July 1939. I had been with the family only ten days. They obviously trusted me. They trusted me to stay alone in their house. How did they know I was trustworthy? But what could I steal there? Surely not those horrible hats. I would not burn the house down, the main gas had been turned off in the work room.

"What will you do?" they asked. I answered, "I could clean the work room." It certainly needed it. The maid had also been given holiday, her annual holiday, proudly, "With pay," said Mrs Rachel. "I am a good employer." Paid holidays were not the norm at that time.

Mrs Rachel had left me some food, tins such as baked beans. Several tins of pilchards, ugh, pineapple, that's nice. All tins were stated as having been approved by a Rabbi, were kosher. I couldn't care less, kosher. We had not been kosher at home, not for generations. Few of the local Jews kept the kosher cuisine.

Milk was by daily delivery. They had an account at the bakery. The bakery sold meat pies, kosher pies, also some pastries. Only one, don't be greedy, Sylvia.

I carefully had swept the workroom, washed down tables and cupboards. But the dirty walls had me beaten. I swept them with a hard broom. No good, it made no difference. They needed painting. I remembered having seen some tins of paint in a cupboard. I had been looking for the loo; it was a broom cupboard, and storage place for the household rubbish which had accumulated. The tins were difficult to open, I broke a finger nail. "Why don't they keep the rim clean, it gets stuck?!" And where are the brushes? Here, oh dear, all hard. I soaked them, tried to separate the bristles. They fell apart.

When I mixed all the left-over emulsion paint together, it came out a 'shitty' brown. I also had found a small tin of gloss paint, red. That might help. Hopefully there will not be a chemical reaction, emulsion and gloss paint together. It came out a nice beige, with the white added emulsion.

I thought, I have no experience in decorating, it can't be all that difficult. I am good in drawing. New brushes are absolutely essential. Where from? On my way home from posting my letter, the one I sent home to give my address to my parents, I had noticed a small general store in the street. Yes, there was in the window a display of articles for decorating. I went in. "Have you brushes six or ten centimetres?" The young boy serving looked perplexed. I realised why, and quickly calculated, three or four inches, please.

"Oh, yes."

"It's for Mr Abraham. Do they have an account at the shop? I have no money."

"The schikse's here, Abe's schikse, she wants the brushes on tick," he called out.

"Not schikse," I said. "Refugee."

The boy's mother came from the back of the shop. "Oh yes, you're the possem," she said.

"From the orphanage." It seemed the whole street knew Mrs Rachel had taken in a refugee.

Whatever old newspaper I had found, I spread out on the floor. I was a messy painter. After a while I got the hang of it. The paint spots came out, if I washed my clothes immediately.

My father had said before I left home, "Make yourself known to Aunt Frances."

Now was the time. My decorating, such as it was, was finished. Where was Gerrard's Cross? Mr Abraham had an A-Z in his office. He did the local deliveries. I found the village, not very local, it could be reached by train, the proper train from Paddington. I hoped it wouldn't cost much. I have to change my ten marks into English money. I needed money for stamps and for the travel to see my aunt. To write home, Mrs Rachel had given me a sheet of their business paper and an envelope. She put three stamps on it. "I don't know how much for Europe." Where would I change my Reichs Marks? At the end of the street the fancy building looked like a bank. It was a bank. I took my passport with me, in case they thought I had stolen the German bank note. I received sixteen shillings for my Reichs Mark. Ten Reichs Marks was the total money refugees were allowed to take with them. The rest of 'their fortune' was confiscated by the Nazi Government.

The bus to Paddington Station did not cost much. The train ticket was cheap. The man of the ticket office shouted when he gave me instructions about the platform. Why did people think all foreigners are deaf? I tried to telephone Aunt Frances. This large contraption, this large box with A and B and Return and Press, and, and, and. I did not understand the instructions. Besides my train was due to arrive.

Gerrards Cross Station, I had to get out here.

I asked passers-by the way, to Manor Cottage, Windsor Road. People were kind, explained: go through the village, then a straight road. It was at least five to six kilometres from the railway station to Manor Cottage. A nice house, set back in large gardens. The house names were on the gates. No numbers.

I had arrived in the afternoon. "Oh dear," I said to myself, "I've come at the wrong time." There was a tea party in progress. My aunt's lady friends. I was directed to sit on a small chair at the back of the room. "You should have telephoned," Auntie said. "A distant relative."

"I am sorry, I tried, it was too complicated, the phone box at the railway station."

"So, really, you live in Whitechapel? Surely not. Since when?"

"In the East End, Jubilee Street." A discussion took place about refugees. I could follow their talk, most of it. I was quiet, apprehensive. They did not ask about my parents. I was wearing ankle socks. One of the ladies noticed red spots on my legs. Auntie took her stick, lifted my skirt for inspection. They talked about prevalence of bugs in the East End. They go from house to house. It came to me, it was bug bites. I had thought my spots were caused by the nasty red balloon sausage (polony), the lady had specially bought in for me. Germans eat sausage. On the continent the butchers made their sausages daily, only the cheaper ones contained preservatives, sodium nitrate. Those horrid balloon sausages, they had made me itchy, spots on my legs, so I thought.

Bugs. On my bedroom wall I had noticed two flies, different from the German ones. I couldn't see their wings. Would they copulate? I was waiting, but no. When I clapped my hands, they scuttled away. Those were the bugs.

Gerrard's Cross August 1939

In front of her guests, the ladies, my Aunt felt honour bound to offer me hospitality. She had two empty guest bedrooms. "You are to come next week, when your family returns from their holiday."

"Yes, Auntie. Thank you, I'll write before I come."

When I told the family of the visit they were not surprised. "It's only right, you are a relative."

I took a taxi from Gerrard Cross Railway Station. My case was too heavy to carry a long way, it cost me most of my remaining money.

At Manor Cottage, the housekeeper met me at the door. "I am Miss Margaret. Let me have your case." She took me to a small building, the servants' quarters, the servants' bathroom. She gave me a piece of red carbolic soap. "I have to fumigate your clothes."

Now I was washed and again fit for human society.

I felt my presence was suffered, I felt like an intruder, an unwanted nuisance. "She is doing her duty to that refugee girl, a 'distant relative'. As long as she does not make extra work."

I was introduced to Aunt Anna: "My sister Anna, she is not very well." She stayed in her bedroom most of the time, a former dressing room was now her sitting room, too small to be called that, but it gave her some privacy. She had many ailments, the doctor was often called.

I thought, she suffers from boredom. She cheered up when the young doctor called. She must have been, once, quite good-looking. Regular features, white hair, a dainty lady, so different from Auntie, who was very tall with heavy features, an impressive large figure.

Immediately upon my arrival, I wrote a letter to let my parents know that I was now living at Auntie's. I also wrote a nice thank-you letter to my English family. "Olnut will post them for you," said Auntie. Olnut the gardener lived in the village. "On his way home."

I found my thank-you letter in the waste paper basket, torn up. I challenged her. "I forbid you to write to them, to have further contact with those East End Jews. I will not have those East End Jews here, God knows what they would bring."

"They've been good to me."

"Free labour. No contact do you hear?"

It was now mid-August. Everybody was speaking about the coming war, but not believing it, not wanting to believe it. We listened to the Prime Minister's announcement, repeated several times on the Radio, September 3rd 1939. I was frightened, Nazis again.

I tried make myself useful. I was kept busy doing the flowers, writing pretty labels for the jam the housekeeper had made, running errands to the village, which was a good two miles away. Walking the dogs, laying the table, mending the linen, including some difficult-to-repair lace, cleaning the silver, picking up the windfalls in the garden, and the berries. These were ripening just now. Just the things for young ladies.

The aunts were forever criticizing my appearance. I wore my blond hair shoulder length, it was fine, blow-away hair. "Not neat, tie it back, you're not an actress." "Have you not got a better brassiere? Your bosom is sticking out." "It's young," said Aunt Anna, "it's the fashion." "You are wearing ankle socks, hardly suitable for your age." I had been saving my precious silk stockings for important occasions. "Have some Lisle ones." The aunt gave me several pairs. These were heavyweight and wrinkled at the ankles, even if I tried to pull them up, quite hard. Oh well, good enough for taking the dogs for walkies.

I noticed that the lovely pearl-embroidered, small reticule was missing from my luggage. I was not allowed to contact the London 'hat' people because the aunt had forbidden it.

Shortly after I had arrived at the house, the house parlour-maid gave notice. She was joining the Forces, the new ATS. I inherited her job. Au pair. My weekly pocket money had been one shilling, now increased to half a crown. My only expenses had been postage stamps, no mail now to Germany. I also bought, occasionally, a small bar of chocolate, Cadbury cost twopence, when I was shopping in the village.

There was no social life for me. After all, Auntie's ladies were ancient. Somehow I was always sent out of the house, shopping, or I was with the dogs when people came. One lady introduced her granddaughter to me, early twenties. "It's her birthday tomorrow, you must give her a present," said Auntie.

"I hardly know her!" What could I give her? One of my handkerchiefs had an elaborate lace border, it had been a present to me.

"That's not enough," said the aunt, "find something else."

I could not find anything else. I had nothing, I reluctantly gave her my very loved little book from the Insel Verlag of the Sistine chapel in Rome, good colour reproductions. What did the girl give me in return? German measles. I was ill for a week.

I was dead-heading the roses, a job I loved. The neighbour's son, my age, called over the fence. "Are you better now?"

"That was two weeks ago, I've been well for ages."

"You missed my party, it was a good party." I did not receive the invitation. The Aunt had lost it!! Yes, lost it. She did not want me to meet the neighbours.

Mrs Rossendale, not Rosenthal, the churchgoer, Church of England, pillar of her local society.

I was that refugee girl. Is she a relative? I might talk, no one even knew she had been a governess who had married well, the brother of my grandmother. Her husband was dead, long ago. I might talk. Is this why I never met anybody? I would have liked to go to the neighbour's party. She had also said to me, "Don't discuss your affairs with people, they don't want to know."

The work of house-parlour maid was easy. There was little to dust, the countryside had clean air. Someone came in to help Miss Margaret with the laundry. Sheets sent away. I must say, she was a very fine cook, as good as our Liesel at home. Miss Margaret had to serve us at the table, she did not like that. She was a cook-housekeeper. Sylvia, the now au pair, was served at the table with the aunts, by her.

Olnut the gardener was nearing sixty years old, call-up for males was up to forty-five years. One felt very patriotic: grow your own food. The garden was four acres, one acre was woodland, more like shrubbery, with some birch, beech, hazel, low growths, a favourite of visiting rabbits. Miss Margaret called, "Olnut, shoot one, now, today, I want it for lunch."

They decided to keep chickens. Baby chickens, in boxes, could be bought at Slough Market. Miss Margaret offered to take me. It would be interesting to watch the auction. From the dozen babies we expected good laying hens. We got eleven cockerels. "They will make nice Sunday dinners," I said.

The turkey for Christmas was walking around the garden. It was an enormous beautiful beast, a pity to kill it. A Christmas tree was carefully dug up from the garden, put in a large pot, watered daily. I was allowed to decorate it. It was to be replanted after the holidays. There had always been a vegetable patch in the back garden. Now much increased, it supplied friends. Their donations went to war charities.

I knew Christmas presents all round were expected. What could I give to the aunts? I found some balls of wool in the mending basket, enough to crochet multi-coloured striped covers for hot water bottles. For Miss Margaret I bought a box of Cadbury's Milk Tray, for Olnut some tobacco. What did I get? Six handkerchiefs, plain ones. I doubted if they had even been bought new, probably hiding in the back of a drawer. The atmosphere was not festive. 'Jingle Bells' came on the radio several times a day. Gracie was Auntie's favourite. Conversation had to stop, one had to listen in respect. Our Gracie. This wonderful artist from Rochdale.

There was a lot of snow, February 1940. I kept the path clear, helping Olnut.

An enormous trunk had arrived from Switzerland, three x four foot, metal, it said, one of three. Where were the others? The trunks had been used by our family for export of corsets to the United States, returned with goods to a warehouse, then returned empty to our factory in Germany. Now only one had arrived, one of three, my parents had sent us our luggage. Towels, blankets, Turkish towel bathrobes, several of these. Arnold's precious knife sets – catering equipment, Arnold's whites and checked trousers. His catering outfit. Brother Arnold had been asked to escort the old Aunt Anna from Frankfurt, to join her sister in England. The old lady was frightened, she had never travelled alone, and now she was asked to come to England by plane. She refused. Who could bring her? There was no one. Then Aunt Frances remembered, there was a grown-up boy, twenty years old, a son of the German Fleischers. He could bring her. She would give the guarantee for this young man, find him a job. Brother Arnold has impeccable manners, he was well-liked by the older folk. He escorted Aunt Anna to England. A job had been found for him in Hinkley in Leicestershire in a slipper factory as a trainee machinist, the work permit had been obtained. Why not a job in London in the family firm Adolphe Rosenthal? Why not there? Arnold was always interested in food, had completed a three-month chef's course in Munich. He had learned high-class catering, hopefully this would get him a work permit abroad. Catering staff generally were excepted, could get visas.

There had been an excess postage charge for the trunk. To be paid for. "You have to contribute," Aunty said. The aunt stopped my half-a-crown pocket money for several weeks. She said she would keep the trunk for me, when I looked in the trunk, it was empty. She kept the contents.

Arnold's catering uniform was given away, he would not need this. His beautiful, very expensive knife-sets, very special, made their way into the kitchen table drawer. Their quality was commented upon.

The linen went into Auntie's store cupboard. I was given one of the Turkish towel bathrobes. "You have a dressing gown, what do you need a bathrobe for?" One was given to Arnold when he came to visit. He had to save the fare money himself. And I kept Susan's robe for her, hopefully she could visit. She lived in London with a doctor's family. My sister Susan was aged fifteen years.

People were afraid, expecting air raids. Nothing happened. People called it Sitz-Krile (sitting down now), or Blitz-Krile.

Children, especially London's children would be safer in the countryside. Whole schools were evacuated. Parents were rarely consulted. For the mass exodus of evacuees, all available accommodation had to be found. It was claimed for 1.5 million people. The Women's Voluntary Services called at all the houses in Gerrards Cross. How many spare bedrooms in Manor Cottage?

They said, "We are billeting you with three children, same sex."

"Whatever made you think we can look after these children? I am eighty years old, my sister Anna is eighty-seven and my housekeeper is in her sixties – she has arthritis, has some difficulties in moving. Impossible."

"We understand. So sorry, Mrs Rossendale, would an Air Marshall be acceptable?"

"Sylvia, you have to give up your room, move your things into the ballroom." I had wondered before what this building was, it looked like a late addition, judging by the low, long windows, built around 1930s, very different from the main building. I had tried the door, being nosy, it was locked. Manor Cottage was Victorian.

I was to sleep in a ballroom! It was large. There was parquet flooring, a dance floor. In the corner was a bar, now empty of glasses. A small sink, a hot water maker. Next to the bar was a small section that looked like a library, this was more like a walk-in cupboard, or box room.

A very large overstuffed settee, covered in green velvet. A number of small, spindly chairs. We called these 'wallflower' girls, where girls waited for a possible dancing partner. This was the total amount of ballroom furniture. On my inspection of the library/box room, I found the bookshelves were eight feet high and four feet wide. They were on castors, easy to move. Sylvia, the designer, decided to create a bedroom, a decent bedroom, for herself. It measures, when finished, nine x ten foot.

This is how Sylvia did it. She selected a window wall. The bookcases became the new two walls, a gap was left instead of a door, covered by a curtain. These she had removed from the short ballroom windows, two widths of forty-eight inches, the correct height. The large curtain rings were slotted on the broomstick, supplied by Olmut. He secured it on the top of the bookcases. It worked. Jumping about on the bed created from the settee, she was surprise how comfortable it was. The bar had a sink, a water heater. All mod cons!

The aunts and Miss Margaret were surprised. "The girl is a designer, a decorator, an architect."

"May I have some of my own blankets?" "Would it be possible, could you spare me a small table, a chest of drawers?" No decorating was required. The backs of the bookshelves were of blockboard, the grain of the wood was attractive.

I had known that my aunt's only child, a boy, had died of

appendicitis. Not much later her husband died. She was still grieving. Her doctor suggested work, work, it might help you, when you are fully occupied. She joined the factory, Adolphe Rosenthal. In a short time she took over. I am told she was very efficient.

The following is second- or third-hand information. The ballroom was built. Her Italian Chauffeur was an excellent dancer. I looked at the stern mountain of a lady with a new light.

Refugees – Save the Children

England had taken in 10,000 children, to save them from the Nazis. The Quakers had approached Parliament, the rescue of the children, mainly Jewish, was arranged. Newspapers, radio appeals. Special meetings, Save the Children. The Jewish Board of Guardians joined these life-saving calls, but they were more interested in finding kosher homes. These were not a priority. Jews in Germany, Austria, mostly had given up religions, food, laws, having considered them outdated.

Tribunals were set up to examine these children, and also the other immigrants to see if they were a danger to the security of Britain. Most of these immigrants were unknown. Therefore they were interviewed before being sent to the Isle of Man. The guest houses had been taken over by the Government.

Not so for the Fleischer children. We could prove we were not a danger in England. My family had arrived in 1871, when my grandfather, Samuel Fleischer had founded a branch factory to Rosenthal and Fleischer in London, London Wall, WC1. The brother of my grandmother, Eurilie, had settled in England, and his wife's family had been nationalised, their children born in England. The tribunal decided we were 'Friendly Enemy Aliens, Category C'. I received my call-up papers when I reached my eighteenth birthday, same as if I had been born in England.

I had told the judge at the Tribunal that my father had been arrested twice, put in a concentration camp, Dachau. Were my parents still alive? I did not know.

The Aunt took me to the Labour Exchange in Slough, Gerrard

Cross, which was purely residential. What is suitable? Not factory work, not the Land Army, she doesn't ride. Yes, to look after the evacuees.

"There is a vacancy in Princes Risborough, Loosely House, the children are from London," said the Clerk.

War work

The aunt took me to the interview at Loosely House. Our taxi waited for us. I wondered what the fare would be.

To look after the smaller children, wash them, dress them, feed them. "Yes, I can do that, I've done this before."

"You have to sleep in the Dormitory with the other helpers."

"All right."

To start as soon as possible: "We're short staffed. We have no single bedrooms left."

The Dormitory was on the top floor of the house. Beds had little space between them, suitcases were kept under the beds. One wash basin in the corner. For the cleaners, called maintenance staff.

I start work at 7 a.m. I went downstairs, found the notice board. Two sections – Maintenance and Childcare.

The Rota

I found my name, my duties were the same, like the ones of another carer. We worked in pairs. She'll show me what to do. Our allocation was toddlers. Those children looked so pale, had almost grey complexions. They came from a poor district of London. At mealtimes they behaved themselves, ate ever so quickly, did not throw the food around. I thought most probably it was better meals than they got at home, they even enjoyed their nasty greens!!

My own breakfast had been a surprise. I had never had an English breakfast before. Only what they called Continental one, even at Auntie's. Another surprise was: I met the other carers, girls from the call-up, or volunteers. I had been placed in the dormitory of the cleaners, the kitchen helpers, recruited from mothers of the children because no bedroom had been available for me.

Well-educated young ladies, all were snooty girls, class distinction. Except one girl, she made me feel welcome. She was very tall, not beautiful, but oh so glamorous, positively glowing.[†]

Every day the kids received "Cod liver oil. It's good for you, it will make you grow, make you clever," I said.

My spoon was of no interest to a little boy. "I don't like you."

"But I like you."

"No you don't." He spit it at me, luckily it landed on my overall.

"What's your name?" I asked.

"Enri."

"Well, Henri, you don't do that spitting anymore."

He said, "My mummy would clout me about my earhole."

I fetched my roll of elastoplast out of my pocket. I cut off a piece of the sticking plaster, then I stuck the piece over my hand. The children were watching. I pointed to my mouth, started to retrieve the plaster, oh pretending ever so hard to get it off my hand. I sighed and grimaced, finally I got if off.

"Spitting, sticking, spitting, sticking," sang Henri.

The children were amused, laughed. I remembered when I was little how I had hated cod-liver oil. At the office I explained, "Could we not give them a sweet."

"A bribe?"

"No, a reward." There was no longer trouble with cod liver oil.

Some children had separate bedrooms, we called them the special bedrooms for 'dirty' children, needed for some children on arrival. When you have lice, impetigo, scabies, eczema – you will need special treatments. Lice are clever, they like new heads, very infectious. The SRN nurse called once a week, more if needed.

The carers could give simple treatments. Most new arrivals had lice. There is a fine lice comb, new to me. There is a special cream, and the stand-by – Gentian Violet. Gentian Violet was magic, a few

† Footnote – her name was Constanze Higginson. She had worked before at BBC Radio. Years later I read in the headlines of a newspaper 'Radio Girl marries Russian Prince, of the Romanoff family'.

grains dropped into water turned into a lovely pink colour. Look at it!! However, the best treatment was the wholesome food, the fresh clean air, sufficient warm clothing, proper boots and shoes. The carers cared, and people were kind. Absence from drunken parents, unfortunately often their home had not been a happy place. How good was Loosley House in Loosley Row? It was a good place, a former Rothschild mansion. It depends a lot on the character and on the ability of the person in charge, the manager, the matron.

The chief cook acted also as a chief housekeeper. She is Canadian, a very tall middle-aged lady. She was a good cook, considering the catering allowance was small. She let you know that she was college trained, proud of it, let you know she is in charge by giving orders like a sergeant major. Two of the children's mothers assisted her, preparing vegetables, washing up, she supervises the cleaning, done by the other mothers as well.

Floors are washed daily with disinfectant. When the children return from their walks they bring in much dirt, especially if it had been raining.

Most of the food and also the cleaning materials were delivered from nearby Princes Risborough, but somehow there was always something extra needed. The carers were asked to collect it, and this in their afternoon free time! Taking turns, to cycle with that ancient bicycle, kept in the shed, down the steep road. When it was my turn, I was frightened because this old contraption had no brake. Could I stop it before getting to the main road? The A4014 was always busy, the cars whizzing past. And then to return to push it up the steep hill.

My dormitory companions from Loosley Row were a pleasant lot. They called me love, or deary. I had never been addressed as love before, it was nice. I was fascinated by their conversation, their frank talk. "My old man, when he is sober, I get his wage packet, more often than not." "It's cushy here, one can save all one's wages, what do I spend? Fags, a snorter, nothing much else. Even my kids' clothes are free, in that store, the do-gooders bring them in, a bloody good choice, well they have the lolly, yes I can pick and choose – lovely quality, from the best stores."

It was an education for me, it improved my vocabulary. They were a friendly lot, at first a bit suspicious of me, because I was from the carers, the other lot, but I was soon accepted.

The Loosely Row house had been requisitioned, like many other large buildings in the countryside. Did it belong to Mrs Waite, the lady who seemed to be in charge, working in the office? The Waites had a beautiful large bedroom and a small sitting room. They used the Entrance Hall, which had a table in the centre for their meals. It was served to them on a tray. Mrs Waite lived alone during the week. Her husband spent only weekends at home. He drove home from work in London, he had the petrol, he must have an important job. Doctors, midwives, senior personnel had the petrol allowance and the VIPs.

Mrs Waite questioned me about my background. She became very interested about my ambitions to become a designer. "I'll show you my clothes." These were kept in the large fitted wardrobe. "Molineux is my dressmaker." I knew he was a top couturier. I told her my mother also used the Couture houses. I attended a course run by the Couture House Bendit in Berlin, to learn pattern-cutting, how to design the paper pattern.

"Can you really do that?"

"Yes, I can design as well and I can copy all clothes, by measuring them."

"Could you make a pattern from these?"

"I think so." She gave me a fancy blouse. "Quite easy."

"Do it then, here you are."

I set to work the next afternoon, in my free time; she gave me some fabric, not as good as Molineux, but passable. My pattern was perfect, my blouse was a Molineux copy. She loaned me her *Vogue* magazines, always finding a little work for me in my free time. I enjoyed talking fashion, 'talking shop'.

I admired the Waites, they had given up their beautiful large house, lived now in this much reduced area. I found in the sideboard in the hall Damask tablecloths, silver candle sticks. Exactly what we had used at home. I decided at least when he came at weekends he should be able to eat again properly. At 7.30 p.m., same time we had eaten at home. I laid up, put fresh rolls on the table, which I had warmed in the Aga. I busied myself in the kitchen, ignoring the Canadian cook's displeasure. Yes, a starter like egg mayonnaise, or crudités. This is a

French fashion. We always had additional salads, stuffed tomatoes, mushrooms on toast, "for the Waites" I explained to the cook. All from the kitchen larder, by me.

"Go ahead, no skin off my nose," said Cook. I wondered what this meant, I could not find this expression in my pocket dictionary. Mr Waite selected a bottle of wine from his wine cellar store. Just like my father. And she wears couture clothes, just like my mother. Flowers on the table, I arranged these at home too.

One morning Mrs Waite called me into her office. "Sylvia, we have discussed this, would you like to work for me, personally. See to my clothes, design them for me."

I was shocked: this is not war work. "You're kind, but this is not war work, no thank you."

I stopped everything I had done for her because I had admired them, but kept up the dinner table work at weekends, as this was for both of them. Now I had time, my afternoon free time, no dress designing for Mrs Waite.

They had called me the Museum Hound at home. We had books, many art books. I knew the Rothschilds Mansion, a place quite near, and it had a fantastic art collection. I decided to visit on my free afternoon.

It was a bit awkward to get there and find it. Bus? Walking? It's further than I thought. I had wasted time getting the information, I'll try again next week, I must leave earlier. It was getting late. I waited at the bus stop. A lady came up to me. "The last one has gone." What could I do? "Is there a taxi?" Ok, I was worried now, I waited for a taxi.

Where is the police station? They'll help me. "None here, it is in the next village, why don't you have a cup of tea?" A small cake, not very appetizing. I walked to the next village. It was now quite dark. I told them, I must get back, I missed the bus. The nice policewoman suggested I stay the night. "Mrs Brown does accommodation, reasonably priced. Then you can take the bus tomorrow." I telephoned Loosely House, told them I was stranded.

"What time is the bus?"

"About 7 o'clock," he consulted the timetable, "yes, 7.10."

"That's too late, I start work at 7 o'clock." I was worried.

"Girly, don't fret, we'll drive you there, we'll collect you at 6.30," said a policeman. They did. Driven by another nice policeman, in plain clothes. He was very nice, called Bob. We chatted. "If you like, you like the countryside, I'll call for you on your next free afternoon."

"Oh, that would be lovely, yes please!!" Something to look forward to.

He did call for me, waiting in the lane outside, and the next afternoon, and the next one, and the next one. The countryside was beautiful. Always brought me back on time. He has the petrol, he must be important. Mrs Waite quizzed me, "Where did you go? This is a restricted area, you are an alien." She phoned my aunt, reporting. The aunt came.

"What are you doing? Making yourself cheap?"

I did not know what she meant. Yes, we had kissed. I did not tell her. "It's beautiful, there are rare flowers in the meadows. I saw a tree, 300 years old!"

"Be careful, you could be arrested, it is a restricted area."

He had bought me a small book on wild flowers, "a pressy". I did not tell her that he was a policeman.

After my refusal to become Mrs Waite's ladies' maid, personal servant, my work routine was changed. "War work, essential war work," said the Canadian Cook. I had said I preferred war work. I was a cleaner now. All day and every day. On my knees. They became very sore, from the disinfectant. Starting to bleed, I have sensitive skin. I put a plaster on my knees, it was no good, the water soaked through. My friends from the dormitory said, "You must see the doctor, love. You have insurance, it won't cost you."

I cycled to Princes Risborough, the doctor said, "A bad case of housemaid's knee. This work must stop. It's getting infected. I'll write you a sick note, if you like." I did not think a note would be helpful.

"Please, may I have other work?" I asked the Canadian lady.

"I have not got any, I have no other. What are you doing here anyway? You are a German. I don't like the Germans."

"I don't like them either, that makes two of us," I answered. "My father was twice in a concentration camp."

I bought a long-handled scrubbing brush in the village, also rubber gloves. She did not allow me to use them, saying, "They all will want rubber gloves." What could I do? Change my job. That's the only thing I can do.

I told my nice policeman, Bob, the difficulty: "The Canadian 'moo-moo' won't let me use the long-handled brush."

"Get another job. You'll be better off in London, that's where the clothing industry is. Oxford Circus. Why don't you go to London on your day off? Find out, take your drawings."

I knew there were factories manufacturing ladies' clothes, in London, near Oxford Street, in the W1 district. I look it up in the phone book. Ever so many were listed. I decided on my free day which was once a month, I would visit London, taking my drawings, my pattern-cutting folder. Perhaps if I am l lucky, I would land a job.

I took the early morning train from Princes Risborough to Paddington Station, then by bus to Oxford Circus. Bob had given me a map of London – marked in red the Oxford Circus Underground Station. He also marked Bloomsbury Street, saying if I had time I should call on them. I did not have time, so I wrote to them.

I was amazed, every building in the streets next to Oxford Street was a clothing factory; most of them occupying only one floor. Up and down the steps, I had prepared a little introduction speech.

"No thank you," and after only a few words, they closed the door on me. Only three factories allowed me to show my work: "Very nice." "You draw well." "Not our style." I had not counted, but it had to be at least twenty, or even more places I had called on.

At least there was some interest, two young men took my folder with the pattern-cutting instructions away. Returned with a middle-aged, grey haired man. "When can you start?"

As Assistant Designer. Yes! "I have to give notice, one week's notice."

"Why are you leaving?" "It's in the country." They did not enquire what was in the country. They gave me their letter-heading, "Suits and Mantles", with their address.

"I'll be here, I don't know the time, in a week." God be thanked. I had thought I would never find something. How much would they pay me? It was late afternoon, many hooters, factories sometimes closed early. I had not eaten all day, not had a cup of tea. I treated myself to ‘Tea n Bun’ which was a milk bar. They advertised many types of milkshakes, those fuzzy things in a glass. Not knowing what they were, I didn’t risk it, but repeated my order for ‘Tea n Bun’.

I was happy all the way home, even in the squeezed-alive compartment of the train, rush hour. Are the buses better?

“Serve them right, the cow, go for it,” said my friends, my bedroom companions.

I had left my long-handled brush with a ribbon tied onto it, to the Canadian lady. I had given notice in writing. My friends, my companions, told me what to write. They were very helpful, protective.

Where would I stay in London? Refugee children’s movement in Bloomsbury Street. They must have addresses. I don’t want to stay with private people. Not too far from Oxford Circus. I wrote a letter, saying I had found employment, could they suggest accommodation, it must be cheap. It must be clean. Not the East End, I don’t want that.

My policeman friend, Bob, offered to drive me to London. “We will call first at that Children’s place. I’ll have to see you get settled.”

I called at Bloomsbury House. They suggested Leinster Square, off Bayswater Road, a private hotel, we have several people there, eleven pounds and ten shillings, breakfast and supper is included. Buses? “Yes, on the bus route, a few minutes from your hotel.”

Bless my friend, Bob the policeman, he found the hotel easily in the A-Z, delivered me, with a kiss and a hug.” Sorry, London is too far away, I don’t know when I can see you.” It was the last time I saw him.

I shared a narrow single room with another girl. The sparse supper was a mangy main course. An orange or apple, no pudding. At breakfast, tea or coffee, make your own toast, margarine, plum jam, nothing else. One is allowed two slices of bread. “You can have another two slices for lunch, you take them now.”

I queued up at the bus stop in Bayswater Road. The Conductor called out, buses were full up, “Can only take three.” People were pushing. I had started out very early, arriving in good time for work.

Suits and Mantles – a new job near Oxford Circus

"You work with me, come along," said the middle-aged grey haired man.

"Yes sir." He took me to a long table. "Have you done any grading?"
"What's that?"

"I saw some in your folder. Have you got it with you? LATERAL DIVISION, that page."

"Oh yes," I said. "That's how the body measurement increases, when you get fat."

He said, "Out standard size here is size 14, in centimetres, 96-98 thereabout."

"That's 38-40, our size."

"Quite right. You make my patterns bigger, size 16, so that we can offer a range of sizes. Understood! When I have to do the grading, I come home late. My wife tells me off. She complains, 'You don't even get overtime.' I tell her, "Staff don't, only workers."

A thick roll of brown paper, like packing paper was spread out. He laid a pattern on it. "You draw around it. What school did you go to in Berlin?"

"It wasn't a school, it was a Fashion House, Haute Couture, an Atelier, called Bendit, Passauer Strasse. They ran courses for people who wanted to emigrate."

"Tell me about it. More."

"I was only fifteen when I went, but they didn't know that. They said I was one of the best pupils they had ever had. Most of the people attending were old, at least thirty, almost all men, sales people, they wanted to know more about textiles. Oh, some were ever so stupid, had never used a ruler, or a set square, before. I had to help when they got all muddled up. They couldn't work it out – the pattern."

On the wall hung a row of bundles, patterns, size numbers on then, he took one. He laid it on the brown paper, "See, this is a 14, a 16 I want, can you do that?"

"I'll try, I will just draw around it?"

One of the young bosses joined us. "How are you getting on?"

"She was telling me about Berlin."

"Carry on, carry on, I won't disturb you any longer." He went away.

It was easy. I enjoyed it. My first day was a success. I'd come on the right day, with the right goods. That expensive training course in Berlin, it paid off. My salary was twenty shillings, very good. Still, I had to be very careful with my money.

Lunch time. My hotel – it was only a boarding house, allowed us to take away two slices of bread for our lunch. 3d. There were my fares, twice a day. To Oxford Circus. If I alighted one stop before, Bond Street, I could save 2d pence. It mounted up. 10 x 1d saved per week.

Near Oxford Circus I studied the window of the delicatessen nicely laid out, with artificial parsley around the dishes. What was the cheapest, the best buy? Luncheon meat. I did not know what this was, it was marked pork. Garlic sausage, French style. Garlic sausage, German style, Kosher sausage – all the same price, a little dearer than the luncheon meat. Hardboiled eggs, with the shell on. Would they sell small quantities? I needed something on my two slices of bread.

My fellow residents at the Boarding House were friendly, talkative. Told me about Roxy, the local cinema in Westbourne Grove, only five minutes' walk. They showed the latest films, and on Monday, Tuesday, Wednesday you could get in for fivepence, in the front rows.

Yes this was a much better life than scrubbing floors or being a ladies' maid! Unfortunately the good times did not last long. My firm, Suits and Mantles, could no longer get supplies of the woollen material. This was now needed for uniforms, war effort. My young bosses decided to close up the following month: "We will give you holiday pay, pro rata."

Oh dear, I was on the job hunt again. I was only offered machinist jobs. Better than nothing. I tried it, had never used this very fast machine before. I stitched my finger. "I am a designer, not a machinist." "Sorry, girl, see the nurse," I was told.

If one lost one's job, one had to report to "Bloomsbury House – the Refugee Children's Movement for the KINDER. English Societies are there to help one. Address: Bloomsbury Street, get out at Tottenham Court Road." I studied a map. They had given me my Boarding House address, I went. I had my interview with the Welfare ladies.

I sat in a room for a long time, with other kids, they looked frightened, did not talk.

I was interviewed by an old lady. I was severely ticked off for not informing them before of my stay in Loosely Row, they only had Auntie's address. "You had a full-time job? That's nice, as a machinist?" She glanced at my bandaged finger. Could be anything, a jammed door.

"I am a designer, I am no good as a machinist."

She studied a folder, my details. "You had some training in Berlin and then went to Fashion School in Hamburg."

"Yes."

"Have you a Master Certificate?"

I felt like saying: Master Certificate! You don't know what you are talking about! Three years apprentice, then two years journeyman, and after a further five years you can sit your Masters. This old thing doesn't know anything!! But I only said, "No, madam."

"We are starting a training course for the clothing industry, here." She took me to the basement – the room had two domestic and six industrial machines. "We are looking for a teacher. Now they want machinists, uniforms, parachutes, that sort of thing, war work."

I was appointed as their teacher. I look older than my age. Better tie my hair back, wear my navy blue jumper, and navy skirt. Hours 10 – 12, 2 – 4, Monday to Friday.

She took me to the office: 'Accounts' on the door. I got one month's wages in advance.

"You start teaching on Monday." I did not enjoy it, there was lack of discipline, those kids started talking, they did not know each other – "Where do you live?" "Have you ever used a sewing machine?" I clapped my hands, like a school marm. I had prepared a very large scale picture on how to 'thread up'. My knowledge came from the Singer shop in Westbourne Grove, W11. I had duplicated the information and made an explicit enlarged drawing.

"No talking. I'll talk, I get paid for it."

There were stacks of offcuts, materials supplied by clothing manufacturers. For practice.

I got used to teaching, they got used to me, they got used to the machines, the fast ones. They did not stitch their fingers either!

Category C: I am a friendly enemy alien

There were five of us, teenager refugees working in Bloomsbury House. We met in the Accountant's Office, Miss Avon, at pay-out time on Fridays. We had been given small jobs, our wages were small, but just about sufficient to keep ourselves and pay our way.

I came from Goeppingen, Wurttemberg, a small town near Stuttgart. I had been given a 'Class' to instruct girls how to become machinists for the clothing trade, for the war effort. I did not consider myself good at the sewing machine. I was a designer or pattern cutter. That was my aim.

There was Sonia Kane, from Vienna. She was a health fanatic. She ran the keep-fit classes, where the youngsters came three times a week. She was very tall and good looking.

There was Ermintraud von Drohonhausen, from Karnten, Austria. She liked to be called Trudy. She later designed the posters and notices. She was a very good artist, mostly animals, but there was no opportunity for this now. She had been sent to school in England by her grandfather in Vienna. The fees could no longer be paid because of the war so the school sent her to Bloomsbury House.

Then there was Walter from Frankfurt, who had been given the job as postman. Bloomsbury House was formerly Bloomsbury Hotel, a second-rate hotel which had been taken over by the Jewish Refugee Administration, in Bloomsbury Road, London, WC1. Walter distributed the mail, went around on his trolley to the hundred rooms, or so it seemed, did postage and deliveries. He also made tea.

There was Ilsa from Berlin, who worked for a Harley Street doctor as receptionist/secretary. She was the only one who had a full-time job outside.

Miss Avon was in charge of the accounts department. She paid us every Friday, in cash, our wages. Miss Avon was a very tall, thin English lady. With a pale face, saturnine features, central parting of her sparse hair. She always wore dark, tailored suits. She was charming, treated us well, not like a foreigner or stupid child, which most people do when one is in an inferior position. Yes, she treated us with respect. Every Saturday she invited us for lunch at the Tottenham Road, Lyons Corner House. She said she wanted to make sure we were getting one hot English meal per week. A roast, vegetables and potatoes, including Yorkshire puddings, unknown to us, but a very delicious treat. Then apple pie and custard, also unknown. I knew crème patisserie, crème brulèe, crème chantilèe. This custard was hot, delicious.

The happenings of the week were discussed, but we never spoke about our background, not to each other. One just did not do that anymore, not even at the dinner table. We enjoyed our Saturday meals.

One Saturday Miss Avon said to me: "I am afraid we are going to lose you, your class."

"What do you mean? What is happening to my class?"

"Oh, we have a replacement, the class continues. We have had a letter from the Denmark Street Labour Exchange, which deals with catering staff. They have made an appointment for you to call next week, Tuesday. They may have a full-time job for you."

I went to Denmark Street Labour Exchange in London, Soho, W1. I sat in the entrance hall for a long time, then the fat lady in the cubicle called me. After taking my name, address, age, she gave me a menu, asked me to read it. It was in French.

"Do you understand it?"

"Yes."

"Translate it, explain the dishes, if you know them."

I could see she did not know what I was talking about. She did not understand the menu. I explained we had, at home, a Herrschafts Kochin, that is like a female chef. They know the French cuisine, and also other European dishes. Our Liesel had been with us for years. We had lost her because of the Nuremberg Laws – no female staff under forty-five – in Jewish houses.

"You are to see the staff manager of the Cumberland Hotel, that's at Marble Arch, say it's for the Grill Room." The Grill Room was very short of staff, she explained, the younger English waiters having been called up. The kitchen staff would only accept orders in French, pretended not to know English.

"Come to think of it," she said, "I doubt if the customers understand the French menu, some of them. This is your job," she smiled. "Now you are a qualified waitress, French and all."

"I don't know anything about being a waitress."

"Yes, you do," she said, "did you not have to lay the table at home?"

"Not during week, I was at school, but weekends, yes. White damask tablecloths every day, correct order of cutlery, two wine glasses, tumbler for water." Yes, it was not so different in the Grill Room.

I went to my appointment with the staff manager. He made me wait a long time outside the office. I got nervous. Finally, the bald, short, ugly man took my address and other details. He gave me a printed double-sided sheet. "Sign here."

"What am I signing?"

"Come on, come on," he somehow was annoyed that I wasted his time reading it. "Can you read English?"

"Yes I can, and French and German."

"Clever, aren't we?" he said.

The form was printed in very small type. It had words I did not understand. I asked, "What is that about Trade Unions?"

"It means if you are joining them, it would mean dismissal. We don't allow Trade Unions here, no. This is your contract."

"What are my wages?"

"After deductions your take home pay is eleven shillings per week." This is not enough to live on. The rent for my room was 11s/6d. "You are not meant to live on that. You get paid from the trunk." A trunk is a large suitcase. I asked what it meant. He explained that is where your tips go, everybody in the Grill Room gets a share of the trunk, the managers as well, the under-managers, the head waiters and the rest of the staff, all get paid from the trunk.

The contract was two pages long. "What am I signing?" I asked again.

"It is not important, just sign. We don't want any rebels, making trouble. And you are not to talk about what you hear from the customers. We want your discretion, and we want your hygiene, that's what it means."

I was dismissed.

"Tomorrow, 10 o'clock, ask for Del Rosso."

Staff had to work from 10 a.m. We prepared the Grill Room, laying up, polishing, filling salt cellars, folding napkins (called serviettes), until the Grill Room closed at 11 p.m. At home when we had guests, I knew how to fold the napkins into fancy shapes.

Del Rosso, the manager, called me over to his desk. "You are now a commis – that is the name given to apprentice waiters. You are MM. I'll put you to help with different waiters, until you know the ropes."

When the Grill Room was ready, we were allowed a cup of coffee. We opened at 11.50 a.m., closed at 3 p.m. "When do we eat? What do we get? What food?"

"Well, you have plenty of time, after 3.30, eat at home," said the Head Waiter.

I had been given a duplicate note pad, it had perforated sections. My number was MM, printed on it. "You put your orders on the kitchen spike, MM Petit Pois, MM pommes nature, MM for the vegetables." Another spike for the meat, called the MAINS. Silver service. Mains and veg separate. "When the food gets cold, or lukewarm, you heat it on the gas ring on your station. Your buffet." This was called your station.

War-time regulations allowed only three courses, starters, main with veg, dessert or cheese. The portions were generous.

If one liked the customers – if they were not snooty – if they had ordered different starters, different sweets, one could serve their three-course meal as a five course, by suggesting of halving the portions in tow. For the solider on leave with his best girl, give them a treat, a more festive meal.

The menu did not state service was included. One expected ten per cent, more if possible. Even the extra money given to you personally had to go into the trunk. No stealing from the trunk. Denmark Street Labour Exchange had sent the new staff. These refugee girls came from good backgrounds, good houses, meaning upper middle class, used to servants.

Del Rosso was the manager, the staff seemed to fear him. No one contradicted him, not even the kitchen staff.

Denmark Street Catering Labour Exchange had sent eight refugee girls for the Grill Room's shortage of staff. Knowledge of a French menu and our upper-middle-class background had qualified us as waitresses.

We had no time to socialize, one was too tired on one's day off. One slept, three days on, one day off.

Erica's family had owned Kampinski, the best hotel in Berlin. Hilda was the daughter of a former High Court Judge in Dresden. Liselotte's family owned the Salamander shoe factory in Bad Camstadt. Ruth's family owned the Schiller store in Prague. Wanda's father was a publisher in Vienna. Mitzi's people produced toys, she said of poor quality, which sold well, and of course there was myself and my sister Susan, who formerly worked as a Doctor's au pair.

Del Rosso did not like me, I think it was my blow-away hair, which kept escaping from the obligatory headband. He said to me, "Why can you not be smart like your sister?" But Susan had always been neat and tidy, even as a child.

The head waiter at the door gave the 'good tippers' to his favourite waiters. The refugee girls were left with 'stiffs', maiden ladies, clergymen, people with small children, who forgot to tip the expected ten per cent, or hopefully more.

It was true: the tips were collected in the waitress trunk, MM box. Each waiter had to hand them in. The whole staff was paid from the tips, including the management.

The kitchen staff would not accept any orders given in English, not chips, pommes frites. They were professionals, fully trained, so they claimed. Of diverse nationalities: Swiss, hotel-trained, were the elite, French next, Italian just so-so, and English, for the vegetable preparation only.

Continental restaurant staff had come to England after attending Hotel Schools. They hoped to get superior positions, once qualified in English, often they came from hotel families. The Swiss were stuck up, the French tried to get a date with us, the Italians were deferential, coming often from poor districts of Italy or Sicily.

However, the English waiters, those tall, middle-aged fellows with their hunched shoulders, were our enemies. They pinched our dishes, waiting at the hot plate in the kitchen. Vegetables were also silver-served. Marked MM with paper, to go with my entrée. They just exchanged MM vegetable for their own number, to save time, for quicker (their own) service.

I had been nicknamed Baroness by the kitchen staff, because of my Parisian French accent, possibly derived from my mother's finishing school. It embarrassed me.

Every morning Del Rosso put up the list of what the various trunks contained. MM was not good, also the other refugee waitresses' results were poor, or perhaps we were not servile enough.

Dr Atherton

Sometimes customers wanted to talk to the young ladies: Where do you come from? Any news of your family? This was upsetting and we said we were not to discuss personal details, please. We were proud of our background, please, not now. I also had regular customers. A Dr Atherton who came alone or with his family, he asked for me, my table. He seemed to be interested in my family, he had travelled widely. He asked what I wanted to do after the war. When I told him I wished to be a dress designer, he asked to see my work. He seemed to be impressed. To become a dress designer was a pipe dream – girl, be realistic, to be a dressmaker would be the best, if I could even achieve that. Dr Atherton said there were several people who would like to meet me. He thought I was talented, perhaps he could help me. I wondered what is this man, a doctor, a busybody? Or just a do-gooder, like the ladies who patronized the children from Bloomsbury House.

"Meet my family, here is my address. Cockfosters is on the Northern line of the Northern Underground. We were bombed out," he explained, "so an old friend let us have the Lodge, and also consulting room at the Main House, at a peppercorn rent. Do you play tennis?"

"No, only table tennis, not even that now."

He laughed. "There is a nice garden, if the weather is right we can have tea outside."

I was apprehensive, he could see that. "I'd like you to meet the old lady who owns the estate. She likes visitors. It's rather far out from London, the city I mean. My wife does not come to London, she stays at our house in Sussex."

I had no social life – three days on, one day off. Too tired to do anything. It would be nice to meet people of my own age. I don't play tennis, but perhaps I could learn, have a go at it. "Bring some of your work, nice designs, I liked them, they were different," so said the doctor.

On my next free day I went to Cockfosters. The old lady was in a wheelchair. "You must be hungry, you missed tea." She rang a little hand bell, asked her elderly maid to bring me a sandwich, and some of the Madeira cake – is there is any left? She asked me questions about my background.

"Oh, Alsace-Lorraine, is it now German or French? I had a French governess, it's nice to speak a little French, I must be rusty. Louise doesn't do languages, not any, pity that." Louise was Dr Atherton's daughter.

"I am almost blind, Louise reads the newspapers for me, every day. And we do one or two chapters of a good book." She laughed. "Or not so good book."

"I like murders and historical romances. They take a liberty with history!! I suppose most people wouldn't know."

She was fun, this old lady, I was going to like her. I promised to visit her often. The Atherton family was waiting for me at the Lodge, they offered me a glass of sherry. Decent sherry, hard to obtain now. "I don't play tennis," I apologised to the two sons. "You can help us in the garden, the weeds are crying, 'Yippee'!"

The sons tended the garden in a fashion, pruned the roses but wrecked them and almost killed them! The lady who owned the estate loved to be taken there in her chair, so she could smell the different kinds of flowers.

"Yes please, I know the difference between plants and weeds. No, I don't want gloves."

I had been invited for tea. Louise had prepared the evening meal. The table was laid for four persons. Obviously I was included. To me tea is afternoon tea, not an early dinner, like for the working classes. Snob, yes, I am an upper-middle class snob. The stew was not very nice, the meat was hard. The salad from the garden made up for it.

Louise said, "I looked at your designs, they are too extravagant for me, too showy."

This did not surprise me. Louise was a mousy-looking girl, a beige girl. Her father had asked me to design a wardrobe for her. Where could she buy interesting clothes? The Jewish manufacturers had transferred from Berlin to London, were now well-established. They produced nice clothes, Louise's dress was like a sack, no shape. Fit for the bin, I thought. Her edge-to-edge coat was probably made from a woollen blanket, only closed with one button. Made by herself? Possibly button holes were too complicated. Make do and mend was a popular radio program. Mousy hair, pale complexion, no make-up. A nice quiet young lady.

Clothes became a problem. They became a ration item, clothing coupons were at the back of one's food ration book. Four coupons for a blouse, four for a skirt, seven for a dress, a coat was ten coupons. A wedding gift, most welcome, were clothing coupons. White weddings were rare, the guests could not have fancy clothes. Most people spent their coupons on a suit. These looked masculine, with square padded shoulder, straight knee-length skirts with a pleat for walking. Mother or grandmother's white wedding dress, with fine veil, was fetched out from storage, a treasure to be treasured.

So my help and advice to Louise was a 'no, no'. There was a surprise for me. Mrs Atherton had sent for me six eggs, two jars of raspberry jam, home-made from their house in Sussex, very kind of her.

Ration book was marked one egg every fourteen days, one slice of bacon every week, meat to the value of one shilling, this would get one two small lamb chops, or half a pound of minced meat. One week, four ounces of butter and two of margarine, and the next four ounces of margarine and two of butter, and once a month half to a pound of sweets and chocolate, depending upon the price and quality. Also, a quarter-pound of tea a month, and a pound of sugar a month. The instant coffee wasn't very good, and I used to swap my sugar for tea.

Dr Atherton went home every weekend, as a doctor he was allowed the petrol. Restaurants seem to get the meat. Was it from the Black Market?

It was years later, we had lost touch. It must have been him. There was a picture in the newspaper. "Doctor accused of murder by family. Body to be exhumed." These were the headlines in the *Daily Telegraph* and the *Observer*. These were my papers, delivered to the door.

An elderly blind lady, living in Cockfosters had died. Her relatives ask the police to exhume her to find out which poison was used. The estate is considerable, the relatives ask for the Will, which must have been made when the lady was drunk, to leave the family nothing. The doctor's family receives everything after taxes and expenses. The family receives nothing, had been cut out of the Will.

Herewith details of the interviews by the papers.

The doctor was accused of murder by the family. They asked for the body to be exhumed, they asked for the doctor to be struck off the register. They say the old aunt was drunk every night. The family was cut out of the Will. The Doctor said, "No comment." He was disturbed by the papers, he suggested, "Contact the deceased's lawyer." The lawyer would not discuss clients, not even dead clients.

There are several interviews given in the papers, of the maid, and of the nurse who had called every day.

Before the Will was written, there is a letter which stated:

"My own family never came near me, did not visit for over ten years, and then only on one occasion to discuss a difficulty with the water main. It must have been at least twenty years since I last saw them, not a soul had visited me. The children of Dr Atherton have been my family and therefore I feel they should be treated as such. I was fortunate to have their company in my old age."

Finally, Dr Atherton was interviewed; he said the considerable fortune is disputed. He stated, "We have been living at the Lodge after my London flat had a direct hit. I also had consulting rooms at the main house. Her family claims I poisoned her and that the Will was made when she was drunk. This is libellous and will be proved so. I never prescribed more than Aspirin and a small glass of brandy at night-time to help her to sleep."

The paper interviewed the old maid. She said: "I have been with my lady for a long time, I came during the First War. I can't do very much now, because I have arthritis. I do the cooking and what my lady needs personally. A cleaner comes twice a week to help me out. The nurse comes every day. The young gentlemen have been very helpful. They do our shopping. Since the gardener was called up they do the garden, in a fashion. One of the young gentlemen was not called up, there is something wrong with his foot. The younger one still goes to university. Louise is a good girl. She comes every day to read the newspapers to my lady. They laughed a lot. I gave a little brandy to her every night. We also sometimes have a glass of red wine, she likes Burgundy, never more than one glass, with the meal. The Doctor has a consulting room on the ground floor, not used much. Since he was bombed out. He is a lovely man. She's left me some money and any furniture I want, if I move away."

"How much?"

"It's none of your business."

There was also a statement of the nurse, SRN. She said:

"We have been expecting it, it's old age. It comes to all of us. She got very weak. She was doing well for her age, got over the flu last year, we were worried then. She told me more than once that the Atherton children were more of a family than her own. If it was not for them, she would been desperately lonely with no one to visit her. It was only right that and fair if the children acted like a family, they should be treated like her family. They used the tennis court in summer, they brought their friends. I can assure you, she got no more than Aspirin, I would have known. Well, when somebody is rich, there will always be jealous people, but to get her dug up, that's going too far. And to ask to have him struck off the Register. It will show what is right. God forgive them. It will prove he is innocent."

I read the newspapers several times, both of them. I kept them, somehow I have lost them – I thought he was a nice man but you never know. Of course, he was innocent.

Meeting Miss Avon

With the Christmas mail arrived a letter from Miss Avon, hoping I could join her for lunch, on Saturday. At Lyons Corner House. A reunion. I was looking forward to this. I had not seen Miss Avon for years. We have to meet in the vestibule, a table upstairs had been booked for a traditional Christmas lunch.

I arrived a little early, but Dolores was already there, looking very elegant, made up like a film star. "Hello Dolores," I said.

"Sssh, sssh, I am Sonia Kane – Dolores is my stage name."

Miss Avon arrived, in a sombre black suit, as usual, except for that carnation buttonhole.

"For me! How wonderful," she accepted the large bouquet from Sonia. The silver ribbon bow said Constance Spry, a famous florist. I gave her my pressie, which was one of my blouses. "I'll open this later," she said. The blouse was in cream Swiss georgette, trimmed with point de venise lace, a swiss guipure.

Now Ilse and Walter joined us, they both gave Miss Avon boxes of chocolates. "We will carry them upstairs for you."

Trudy arrived last, she gave to all of us our Christmas cards. She said, "My own work, you know, I am a famous painter now, puppies and kittens."

The service was slow. We had plenty of time to talk to Miss Avon.

"I am so looking forward to hearing all your news, tell me all that you have been doing."

Walter said, "I am articled to a firm of lawyers now. You know my father was a lawyer in Frankfurt. One of the do-gooders in Bloomsbury House had arranged it, paid the fee in secret and she wanted to remain anonymous. I am the junior, the 'very' junior, I still do the post and make the tea. Not so different from before! Kidding aside, I have a lot of studying to do, I am very grateful."

Sonia Kane, looking so beautifully dressed, related that she worked in a club at Knightsbridge. Very expensive, this club, good clothes are essential.

We studied our Christmas cards which Trudy had given to us. They said 'Greetings for the Season'. Trudy said she had found this firm at the East End, the name and address was on the back of their own cards. She had gone there on spec. They liked her work, but it was only occasional work – greetings cards. It was a Jewish firm. Who said the Christmas Card trade was mostly Jewish? "I paint china plates. Buy them in white, then fire them to make it permanent, commemorative plates for weddings, twenty-firsts and suchlike. They don't pay much, the stores, but it is regular work. I employ two people part-time, a girl and an old man to help me."

Ilse said," There is not much to tell, I am still with my doctor, in Harley Street."

Miss Avon unwrapped my present. "Oh, this is wonderful, I have never had such a beautiful blouse before."

"It's from our workroom," I said. "I am trading as Sylvia Russell (Kensington). Miss Avon, there is a small label in the back of the blouse, 'Sylvia Russell', like a cash name tape. I don't get the publicity, the stores cut out my label, and put their own in, to maintain the 'lie' the blouses were made in their workrooms. I also design for film stars. I have premises in Notting Hill Gate."

"In the artistic section of London! You always said you would be a designer," said Miss Avon.

The traditional Christmas lunch was very good. We toasted our success, in a perry. This was as nice as champagne, which I did not like. I much preferred the Rhine wine or the Alsace Traminer.

Ilse took the same bus home to Notting Hill Gate. We were no longer on speaking terms. She still lived in Lime Court, Linden Gardens. She had moved away to the back of the bus. I thought she had behaved dreadfully. For my sister Susan's birthday I had given her a beautiful metal belt. It was made in sections, floral and scrolls, most probably North African design. She was delighted, showed it around in the hostel where she lived now. The other girls much admired it, so much, that Susan was afraid someone might pinch it. She had given it to me for safe-keeping. I hung it on my wall, it looked really nice.

When Ilse came to visit me, for a cup of coffee, she asked if she could borrow the belt, she said it would look just right on her new red dress.

"Bring it straight back," I said. But she didn't. I phoned her and reminded her, "You promised, it belongs to my sister, I had no right to lend it to you."

"I want to buy it off you," she said.

"It's Susan's, I can't sell it." I went up to her house. I was angry. "Please, give it to me now." She closed the door in my face. I rang the bell. It was a B and B in Linden Gardens. The porter let me in. I knocked at her room. I said through the door, "I am not going away, I will sit here on the chair until you give me back the belt. I am not going away." I knocked on her door. "Please, Ilse, it was not my property, I should not have lent it to you." The door opened, she almost smacked the belt into my hand. We didn't speak again.

The Sonia Kane story is rather amusing. It involved my boyfriend Charles Bradshaw. I had met him when Sheila Coghill, who lived in my house, had coffee in the Linden Café. Charles had come to read the specialist magazines which were hanging on the sticks on the wall. This was a great attraction to many people, the Linden had all the daily newspapers, but also mags on engineering, dog-keeping advice, and clothes for sale as good as new. People could sit for hours, over a coffee and read. The Linden was also popular with the artistic crowd, and the beautiful people.

Charles was introduced to me. I was surprised to find out he was interest in theosophy, he knew about Rudolf Steiner as well.

So we became friends. He took me on his motorbike. I was frightened at first. Charles also had a Lee Francis car. That meant nothing to me, I am not into cars. I should have been impressed. Well Charles came for coffee, after the ride. He stayed. He was a gentle lover, caring. He insisted that I go to a doctor and get protection.

One evening he said he was meeting friends at a club, would I like to come. "It's a fantastic place, it's fun, put your best clothes on, very high class. If we are lucky, Dolores might dance. Dolores is the owner."

I put on my white jersey dress, with the gold belt, and my gold sandals. A little gold clutch bag. Charles showed approval. He was not dressed up. Wore his checked shirt. He said, "It's only the girls who dress up, gents can come just any way they want to."

The club was in Knightsbridge. Two negro boy statues were next to the staircase, everything was red, plush and gilt. The bar was on the first floor. The 'upstairs' were part of the premises.

"Oh, Sonia," I called out, and Charles introduced me.

"Meet Dolores." The club belonged to Dolores, formerly Sonia Kane.

Dolores came from the Caribbean. Charles explained, "She is not very dark, she could pass for white." (I would not betray her secret.)

"There are a lot sugar plantations," explained Charles. "The English aristocrats own them."

Dolores took me aside. "Being half caste is good for business." She introduced me to her two greyhounds, beautiful beasts. "I walk them very day in Hyde Park. That's good for business. When the gents talk to me I'll give them my card, from the club." In my mind's eye I could see this very picture, her and her two hounds.

We met Charles' buddies. Had our drinks, at exorbitant prices. No one seemed to mind the prices.

"Are you going to dance tonight, Dolores?" The elderly, very corpulent gentleman sidled up to her. He explained to Charles that he had specially come up from the country.

"I would like to see her dance, yes, I would like to see her do the dance of the seven veils, I'd give a lot, Dolores. I am told you have the most beautiful torso in London, I'd give a hundred pounds."

Dolores tapped his protruding tummy, "Fat boy, fat boy, when you lose this, you might have a change. It's no fun for me like this."

"Yes," he sighed, "it would be worth it."

One morning, early, I had a phone call from Dolores.

"You have to help me; I am stuck here in the Ritz. Usually the Honourable orders my breakfast and leaves the taxi fare, a good taxi fare. I must have been drunk; I came here only dressed in my veils. I can't get home in this, no clothes. Will you go to my flat and bring me a coat and some money?"

"Why don't you ring your friends?"

"I have not got their number. The key is in the hedge next to the entrance. I could remember Sylvia Russell (Kensington), you're in the phone book."

"Look, I cannot go into a flat and burglarise for money and clothes. I will bring you some money and a coat of mine, in a taxi."

When I arrived at the Ritz, the Commissionaire was very understanding, he accompanied us to the back entrance. Even so, Dolores looked ridiculous in my coat, her 5 foot 9 inches to my 5 foot 2 and a half inches. I delivered her at her flat. She got a shop to deliver a bunch of flowers. She forgot about my taxi fare, which was quite steep.

Dr Stein

I accompanied Elisabeth to Rudolf Steiner House for a lecture on Race, given by Dr Walter Johannes Stein. He had been a close collaborator of Rudolf Steiner, the founder of the Anthroposophist movement. She told me that Dr Walter Johannes Stein was a universal genius. He gave lectures on different subjects – history, religion, evolution, medical plants. He had collaborated with an Austrian lady, called Louise Meitner, about splitting the atom. Both came from Vienna. He had taught in the Waldorf School in Stuttgart, the largest private school in Germany, until the Nazis closed it.

I was interested in Race, not only because of my recent work in the club for American black soldiers. We Jews had suffered the persecution because of race and religion. The chosen people? Chosen for what? Who had invented 'chosen'?

Firefis (fire son) was the son of Hazelside and Peter John. How could that be? Wolfham von Eschenbach's Grail Story in Austria, and Peter John of the 2nd Century AD in India. Firefis was black and beautiful. An inner individual development for achieving the Holy Grail.

The Negro American soldiers varied much in appearance and speech. Some had copper-coloured skin with European features, some were quite black, it frightened me even to look at them. Three generations of western education, one forgot that their grandparents had been slaves. After the lecture, I approached Dr Stein, to tell me if Firefis was symbolic.

"Why don't you come home with me, meet my wife and have tea with us?" I never received the answer to my question, but I did to many others. Dr Stein became my mentor, my second father. To Mrs Stein, I was her little dressmaker. She came from a Dutch aristocratic family. To her coloured people were the lower orders. I argued with her. How did I dare to argue with my betters? With the lectures, my knowledge of the History or Comparative Religion, helped by intent study of Eastern Art, improved rapidly. I became a member of the Oriental Ceramic Society, Mr Bernhard Leach recommending me, when at an exhibition he overheard my late husband and myself discussing the great potter Hamada, from Japan.

In my spare time I designed glamour garments for the starlets. I managed to retrieve various odd lengths of lame, brocade, velvet and lace, and I believe wearing these nice clothes helped them to be chosen at the auditions for extras or small parts. I only recently discovered that often they sold these garments and got a good price for them! And this after playing hard-up and making me wait for settling their account with me!

This situation was rectified when the TV companies paid me direct, settling their monthly bill promptly. I had now graduated to working for stars, main actors. The big name stars also settled directly, more often, when they liked to keep the garment for their own use.

There I was producing high class couture garments and millions were starving. I felt almost wicked, so I decided to ask Dr Stein what I should do.

He said it was most important to keep the standard up, "And you are doing that, you produce fine work." I was reassured.

My friendship with Dr Stein lasted for many years, until his death in 1957. He became my second father, my mentor. How fortunate I was.

[Footnote: Dr W J Stein had worked together with an Austrian lady, called Louise Meitner on splitting the atom. To break the uranium atom into two smaller atoms, Barium and Krypton.]

Engineering in Hounslow

I was no longer a waitress.

Catering was no longer considered war work, not essential work. I received notification from the Labour Exchange. They wanted me to train in bench-fitting. This is another name for making tools, precision work.

The Government Training Centre was in Hounslow, one had to clock in at 7 a.m. I had to catch the first train from Notting Hill Gate Underground Station at 5.30 a.m. There was a twenty-minute walk from the station, over a common, a footpath, which very often was muddy after rain.

Trainees were each allocated a machine and a template to follow. For me that was the easy part, after all I had been trained in pattern cutting. The guide, the head of the machine dug into the steel, a dust storm! No masks had been given for this extremely dusty work. I suffer from hay fever, I started to sneeze, I couldn't stop it! For a while I was sent to the rest room, back to work, sneeze again.

We learned how to cut shapes correct to a thousandth of an inch. Then all our work was thrown away. What a waste! It would have been encouraging if our 'masterpieces' were used for the war effort.

Sneeze, sneeze again. They decided to sack me. Was my sneezing catching? The staff was not so sure. I was grateful to be sacked.

I reported to the Labour Exchange, who found me a job near Oxford Circus, on a direct bus route, start 8 a.m. We were dismantling 'junction boxes' with soldering irons, so that the boxes could be re-used. The small factory was light and clean, formerly for a clothing manufacture. Our pay was one shilling and two pennies per hour. This meant I had just under forty shillings per week, after paying insurance stamps. There was no bonus, even if one achieved more than the quota expected. Thirty-nine shillings – this was not sufficient to live on. If I took the bus to Bond Street, one stop before Oxford Circus, I saved one penny, this was six pennies per week. Return fare was twelve pennies per week, it adds up.

I took on an additional job as a waitress, Friday night, Saturday lunch, Saturday night and Sunday lunch. These were busy times. In this small café in Edgware Road. They did not ask for insurance cards. I could keep my own tips as there was no trunk. I also got a meal, whatever was left over. If there was leftovers at the close of night, the chef packed it up for me, leftovers were not served to customers the following day. My finances were now settled, however doing two jobs was tiring.

Professor Levy worked on the Beverage Report for the new coming National Health Service. He had his lunch every day in the Lyons Corner House at Tottenham Court Road where you could have a reasonably priced lunch or snacks quickly served. I also lunched there when I worked in Bloomsbury House. He had kept in touch with me when he discovered that my cousin the Regierungsrat – Dr Konigsberger and wife had been his Bridge partners. They also had lived in Charlottenburg, Berlin. His wife said to keep an eye on me. "Young girls alone!" Mrs Levy was very good-looking, an actress before her marriage. They phoned me: "How are you keeping, etc.," about once a month. The professor and his wife were shocked, when I told them about doing two jobs. After all, I had to live. I needed the extra money.

"We must find you something better, more suitable. What would you like to do?"

"Well, I would like to work for the American Red Cross." I liked the uniform, I had heard the pay was all right. He said he would see what he could do. At that time he worked together with a Professor Sargent Florence, whose wife was the personal secretary to the American Ambassador in London. That's how I got my job at the American Red Cross, recommended by the American Ambassador. I worked there until after the end of the War. It took until 1946 before the American soldiers and officers had been repatriated.

I was interviewed, first day at the Embassy, then at the Headquarters of the American Red Cross. Only vacancy at present was in the Club for coloured soldiers. How do you feel about this? I had not met any coloured people, seen yes, Indians in the street, but never any black people.

"Because of the way we have suffered from race prejudice, I certainly don't have any race prejudice," I answered.

The job was to work in security – the safe, the store and where the soldiers kept their belongings, their duffle bags. I was not good on luggage, it was very heavy, but there were porters. There was storage for the duffel bags, and it was the porter's job to climb up and get those bags, but sometimes I had to get them myself if they were doing other jobs, and I considered myself a climbing monkey!

Well, the black soldiers liked me, talked to me, called me Goldilocks. They invented further stories about Goldilocks and the three bears, about three puddings, not about the porridge, or sweeping the hut and not finding the broom. Baby bear wanted to have cake with icing. They called me Ma'am respectfully, some of them. We laughed a lot. And they invented more stories about the three bears. The reception ladies did not approve of me. They were serious, middle-aged ladies. Reception was next to my store. First I had been frightened, when the soldiers had such black faces. Then I did not see it anymore.

A very famous musician had come from the States to spend a couple of days in London, before entertaining the troops. I cannot remember, was it Humphrey Littleton? This comes into my mind.

He spread out a plan, places of interest, marked in red, important to see. "The Tower of London, London Bridge, black and white houses – yes, Liberties, their windows."

The reception ladies said, "Unfortunately we are busy." They couldn't take him around.

I said, "I can take you".

"Thank you, young lady, that would be very nice." He said, "I promised to look into the coloured club, before going to Europe to entertain the troops." He had been given a soldier in uniform to chauffeur him around. Liberty's store was just around the corner, so he suggested we should walk as it would be interesting to see the town, and the soldier parked the car, and then walked with us.

I had started to put on my outdoor uniform.

"No, do not wear that, otherwise they will think it is an official visit."

He had a discussion with his driver. We took one of those red double-decker buses for a glimpse of the Tower and London bridge.

"No more time, I promised to play for them at the club," said Humphrey.

The club gave us peanut butter sandwiches, these had sausages on them and strawberry jam. I thought this very peculiar, but this was what the Americans liked.

We joined a group of black students, sitting at a large table. They were, all of them, law students! Except one. That's not what Africa needs, I thought. They need doctors, engineers, road builders. The one who did not study law told me that he and his family wanted to manufacture shoes. The hides were cheap, cattle were driven across the parched fields, no grass, no water. They die, the hides are sold cheaply. We had an interesting conversation. I said I thought coloured and black ladies liked fashion shoes, not boots. Italy makes lovely fashion shoes and other leather articles. Look for magazines. Feragamo is their famous designer. He took notes. Several white girls sat at another table. I did not like their looks, they wore nasty, flashy imitation jewellery, satin blouses, low cut, very short skirts.

"I have to go home now. Which buses go to Notting Hill Gate?"

"Stay for the dance!"

"No, really I have to cook." I had promised to cook for Nursy, we shared meals.

"I am going that way, I live there, with my cousins, in Farm Place." These were the small, even miniature houses in the back of Notting Hill Gate Station. We set out together. He started a conversation by telling me how important he was at home, how important his family was, how he was studying Law. "Come, have a cup of coffee, meet my cousin."

I replied, "I must go home, I have to cook."

"Only for coffee."

"All right."

His cousin was not in. He started to make coffee, it was horrible, Camp Coffee from a bottle, and condensed milk. Then he tried to embrace me, tried to kiss me. I struggled: "No, don't. I am going now." He stood in front of the door, I could not get out. I banged on the wall. The cousin had come home. To my great surprise he threw onto the bed a set of bedlinen.

"I want to go home," I shouted.

The student said, "I picked her up from the Club, there were other white girls. She was talking to us."

"I want to go home," I shouted.

Thank God, they let me go home.

The black soldiers had told me it was better in London. In the States there was strict segregation, one had to sit in the back of buses, use the other entrance, exits. I agreed it was all wrong, and needed changing. I said, "If you are good enough to fight for a country, and to pay the taxes, this is all wrong."

The reception ladies did not like me, perhaps they thought I was talking politics, or was too condescending.

They somehow got rid of me, the cloakroom girl, the Goldilocks. I was transferred to the Columbia Club, a white club, at Marble Arch, a similar job, security of property, but on an eight-hourly rota plan. 7 – 3 p.m., 3 – 11 p.m., 11 p.m. – 7 a.m. in the morning. Same job, but very different. What had I done? I must have offended.

I worked together with porters. Their job was to help with the luggage and patrol the streets next to club and collect the drunk soldiers, so that their military US police should not arrest them – drunk and disorderly.

From 10 o'clock in the evening there usually was a queue at the store, depositing or collecting their duffel bags, to check their wallets in the safe, or other precious belongings they might have bought from jewellery shops on their leave.

Changing of shift made the queues longer. After midnight most of the soldiers had turned in, the communal sleeping quarters had eight to twelve beds.

When the porters brought the drunks in, if they were sober enough to understand we suggested they should deposit their wallets. "Here is a receipt with your number, give me your name, I'll enter it, in the morning you can collect. The safe is open from 6 a.m. for collections." We checked their dog tags in the morning to make sure they received their correct possessions. The drunk ones, blind drunk, were just put to bed. Receipts for money were put into their pockets.

Some of the soldiers were lonely, wanted to have a chat with a 'nice girl', tell them all about their family, their babies, their kid sister, or even Grandma. I said, "I am a bit busy now, it would be better later, in an hour. Why don't you go and have a coffee in the canteen."

"When do you go off duty?"

"About 7 o'clock in the morning, it is nearer 7.30, then I am going home – on the bus." Surprisingly, some turned up at 7 o'clock.

"Will you come out with me, there is a good show on, a matinee? Oh, please do." Mostly I did, not in my uniform though, wearing my best fancy clothes, the lace ones. The soldiers took the nice girls to the theatre, the restaurants, to shows. There were the nice girls and the whores.

Aunt Frances had written to me, suggesting that I meet her much younger brother, Major Manning. She was proud of him, he had been a captain in the Boer War. The former family name had been shortened from Manheimer to Manning. He was the Head of air raid wardens of High Gate, London. He invited me for lunch. I put on my favourite coat, red velour, which showed off my shoulder-length blond hair.

I met with his approval, an elderly man's approval. "Where do you want to go for lunch?"

There was a City Restaurant where they still served, slicing the beef from an old-fashioned trolley with a domed lid, in generous big slices. I had heard of it. I fancied that. He took me there, ordered sandwiches, explaining that a big lunch made him sleepy.

I gave him a résumé of the various jobs I had had. He was shocked, very shocked that I was not in the ARP. "Most of those houses around Marble Arch, they have flat roofs, for fire watching. Most suitable."

"Yes, I agree."

"What about it then?"

I joined the small section we had at the Columbia Club, I was put on the rota, two-hourly shifts, usually a night or early morning. One boy, one girl, on the roof. When an air raid was on, we wore thick tracksuits because we didn't want to spoil our uniform, with burn marks. "Here is your thermos."

When there was a raid, we climbed to the roof, the poles with the hooks are left on the roof, baskets of fire bombs, which were canisters with hooks on them, were dropped all over London.. What one had to do was to hook them with the pole and throw them into the street. "Hoy, hoy, there is one coming," we shouted. "Careful." We had small megaphones to help us to shout louder to make sure people heard us. But there were very few people in the road anyway, as most of them were in shelters by then. The air raid wardens and the police had escorted them to the shelters. The canister would then fizzle out on the road.

There was often transport difficulty during air raids because buses stopped running. The public waited patiently at bus stops, hoping, wondering how one would get home. Regulars, like catering staff, public services, cinema goers, congregated at the Marble Arch bus shelter; it had a roof, there was more protection from the rain. "Do you know if they are running?"

"Well, I've been here some time, there hasn't been one."

"I'm going to work."

"I'm going this way, too."

Men offered to walk one home, for protection, they said. I said, "To the door only, no cup of coffee!" This asking for a cup of coffee was a well-known ploy. I had learnt my lesson.

Some people were allocated petrol – doctors, district nurses, important people, senior officers. They offered lifts to the stranded public. I was in front of the queue.

A large car stopped. They called out: "Girlie, are you a business girl?"

"Oh, yes I am."

Did they know me?

"Are you sure?"

I repeated, "Yes, I have my own business. I do model blouses."

They laughed, "She does blow jobs, she models."

"No," I said, "I don't model, you have to be tall, five foot seven or eight inches."

The man in the back of the car called out, "I am only six to seven inches."

The people in the back of the bus shelter laughed out loud.

"I have my own business," I insisted.

"She has her own business."

It was hilarious laughter.

I had never before heard the term 'business girl' (a euphemism for prostitute).

What was so funny? Something was wrong. I tried to disappear into the back of the queue. "She doesn't want to know you, you're not her class." I knew what a pimp was. A man left the queue and asked the car, "Shepherd's Bush all right?"

"Yes, mate, jump in."

The bus had not come. It was getting late, I thought I'd better start walking.

A young soldier joined me. "Do you mind, may I walk with you?"

"All right."

"Where are you going?"

"Holland Park."

"Me, Acton. I have an old aunt there."

"She'll be asleep by now."

"No, she is waiting for me, she says she never sleeps, she does not believe in pills. You've got an accent, where do you come from?"

"I am a refugee." I did not like to admit GERMANY. People misunderstood. I am not a bloody German – my family originated in Alsace-Lorraine. "You have an accent too, are you Scottish?"

"And proud of it. It's too far to go home. On leave, I wish I could, I miss my family."

Arrested after Curfew

We walked along the Bayswater Road. At Lancaster Gate it started to rain, quite a heavy shower. We took shelter in the Lancaster Underground Station entrance. People sheltered there, slept on the platforms. I never went to a shelter, it smelled, it stank. People who went every night claimed they had 'reserved places'.

I was 'Category C', a friendly enemy alien, never interned, but subject to curfew. My curfew was extended to 1 a.m. because of my work. When it stopped raining, we continued our walk. Queensway, Notting Hill Gate, Holland Park Avenue. We arrived at my boarding house, where I had a furnished room. Several rooms had been let by two old ladies who lived in the basement. The soldier wanted to show me his pictures, of his family. I made admiring noises. We stopped at the front door of the garden wall. The dog-house was in the garden, I hoped the dog would not bark, waking the other tenants. A policeman was walking, patrolling the street. What was I doing with a soldier? He was showing her something, was it money? Was he giving her money?

"What are you doing here? So late in the street?"

"I'm just going in."

He noticed my accent: "Show me your papers."

I did.

"German, hm, hm. My brother was killed by the Germans, in the Army he was. What are you doing, out so late, curfew, there is a curfew?"

The soldier said, "I am going to Acton." He left quickly.

The policeman said to me, "You come along with me, breaking your curfew. I am taking you to the police station. I am arresting you."

It was now 1.30 a.m., I was allowed out until 1 a.m. Sheltering in from the rain at Lancaster Gate had made me late. I felt he had arrested me because I was German. His brother had been killed by the Germans. This was my fault, because I was German. I had broken the law, curfew law.

The police station was situated in Ladbrooke Road, the next road to Holland Park Avenue, a few minutes' walk away. The policeman handed me over to the sergeant on duty at the police station. "I found her in the street, with a soldier, past her curfew."

The Sergeant said, "Well not much over the curfew."

"I was coming home from work," I started to cry. "I live there, I was outside my house."

"Stop it, girly, I am not putting you in a cell. You'll have to see the Magistrate in the morning, no, it's today now. I'll let you go home if you promise to turn up, today at ten o'clock, at the Magistrates Court." He was nice, he seemed embarrassed.

They escorted me home. "Make sure you'll be there, here is the address." I told them I was worried, I had to be at work at three o'clock. He said he would ask the Magistrate to take my case early.

The magistrates were not pleased. Yes, the lady magistrate asked why I had not gone inside, I did not want to go inside, the dog would wake up the whole house. "I don't understand, she was at her house, though not inside. Fined one shilling, you can go now."

I paid the shilling.

On my way out of court, a policeman offered me money. "Have you money for a taxi?"

"There is a bus, I'll take the bus, thank you."

I heard him muttering, "Ridiculous, waste of time."

I was in good time for my three o'clock shift, so glad they had not asked me where I worked, glad very glad, the American Red Cross could not have been informed of my arrest.

Would my arrest be marked in my papers? No, my *incident*, that's what the police called it, unfortunate incident. I was frightened, severely frightened. It's over now, stop trembling. One can be arrested for nothing!! Sent to the Isle of Man. One can get deported, sent back to camps in Europe. Dreadful places, BUT I AM CATEGORY C.

News from the Red Cross

The Children's Movement, the Society in Bloomsbury House called the 'Kinder'. "We have some news, from the Red Cross in Switzerland." They informed us that most Jews were collected for transport last November. Stuttgart and especially Goeppingen was mentioned. They believed the transport went to Riga. Poland was also mentioned, I was upset. Susan was upset, we looked up Riga on the map.

I did my waitressing badly. I did not concentrate, forgot the vegetables. Susan said she was ill, had to go home, go to bed. I say to her, "Go to bed right away when you get home." Del Rosso said, "Get a doctor's certificate."

Susan's room was next to mine, I could hear her rummaging about, so I knocked on her door. We hugged each other. "Sleep now." Susan did not return to work the next day or the following day. Her suitcase was resting on her bed. I noticed tins of food in it, also packets of tea and coffee.

Susan said, "I am Sister Susan from the Red Cross. I am going to Riga, I am going to Poland to search for my parents."

"You're going to bed," I said. "Take this aspirin, you will feel better."

"Why don't you believe me? I'm going tomorrow, no I'm going right now." She put her coat on. "Get out of my way," she shouted. She did not listen to me, but repeated over and over, "I am Sister Susan."

The landlady came to see what the commotion was, saying, "It's late, you are disturbing everyone. You must be quiet."

"I am Sister Susan," again and again.

The landlady called a doctor. "She is very distressed, she can't stay here."

An ambulance came to take her to a hospital. I was not allowed to go with her. They transferred her to a psychiatric hospital in the country.

I telephoned to find out about visiting times. They were only once a week.

The hospital was in a restricted area. The Almoner told me I must get permission, I must apply, she would send me a letter stating that my relative was a resident.

When I got to the hospital, Susan said, "I don't like you, you put me here, the food is awful. They won't let me wear my own clothes."

She said to the nurse on duty, "That's my sister, she's come to take me home."

Nurse said, "Doctor will have to discharge you, I don't think that will be before a couple of weeks." It wasn't weeks, it was months before she was released from the hospital.

Susan could not work. I could not be responsible that she ate properly. Bloomsbury House put her in a hostel with other Jewish girls in Swiss Cottage. I worked irregular hours. When she was fit she had to report for work.

Susan's neatness was rewarded by the envy of the Labour Exchange Clerk, noticing the beautifully manicured pink nails. She found her the dirtiest job available in war work: engine cleaning, railway engine cleaning, needing a bath and thorough scrub every day.

Luckily the hostel, where Susan now lived, had a very large boiler for the bath cubicles.

The Refugee Kinder Committee had put on dances for the American Jewish Soldiers, stationed in London and on leave. Susan met a staff sergeant, a former medical student, Philip Nassau. He complimented Susan on her neat looks, like an American girl. Susan was the prettiest charming girl he had ever met, with violet blue eyes and a curvy figure. They got engaged. The very simple wedding meal was in the Trocadero Restaurant at Piccadilly Circus. When Susan became pregnant, Phillip managed to get her a seat on a return flight of a bomber to USA. He wanted his baby to have a USA nationality. Philip became a doctor, practising in Philadelphia, his home town.

I have included six pages from *Laugh or Cry*, to show why Susan had been so upset that she had a nervous breakdown.

We all agreed that as we were all earning well, we would not sue the German Government for our lost properties, as it would make Susan more ill.

We never talked about November 9th, 1938, this dreadful day, of burning synagogues, and collecting all Jewish males over eighteen years of age. Susan was then aged fourteen years. We felt people would not believe it – it was too horrible. This is a reprint from my book, *Laugh or Cry*.

The Pogroms of November 1938

On 7th November 1938 a seventeen-year-old Jewish refugee boy shot and killed the third secretary, Ernst von Rath, of the German Embassy in Paris. The boy's father had been recently deported to Poland, herded together with thousands of other Jews in box cars, which the railway normally used for the transport of cattle.

The assassin, Herschel Grynspan, had intended to shoot the German ambassador, Count von Welszeck; Herschel had asked to see the ambassador and did not know it was Secretary von Rath who came out to see him. Ernst von Rath was no anti-Semite; he was himself under 'supervision' by the Gestapo for his anti-Nazi attitude.

When we read about this in the papers, we knew it would be bad for us Jews.

"A German Jew? His name does not sound a bit German," said one of the domestic science students at the orphanage.

"Perhaps they made him change it," said another student. "I have heard they've forced some people to take peculiar names on their passports. They were so glad to get a passport out of Germany they let the Nazis put those middle names on."

One of the Nuremberg Laws had decreed that Jews must carry a Jewish middle name – most Jews took Israel or Sara. This was on the 'approved' list of names 'suitable for Jews', which had been concocted by the 'expert' Globke, from the Interior Ministry. The old testament names, like Jacob or Ruth, were not included because these had been 'Germanised' and were in general use in Germany. There was a whole list of names 'suitable for Jews', mostly they were figments of the imagination of Herr Globke – names like

Sharne (meaning all burnt up), Schlemche (meaning muddy), Feibisch and Sprinzi. These names sounded awful; the latter was a name I found in records of the eighteenth century, so Globke was something of an expert after all. Herschel (young stag) was a Jewish name but not in general use. I don't know if this was on the list.

"Perhaps it is not true at all, just propaganda," said a third girl. But true or not, one thing was certain, we were afraid. And then came 9th November.

9th November had been Grandfather Samuel Fleischer's birthday. It was also the anniversary of the Weimar Republic.

9th November was the anniversary of the Beer Hall Putch. The Nazis always celebrated the Beer Hall Putch. The storm troopers who had died in the Munich street fight had been declared national heroes, heroes who had been martyred in the sacred cause of delivering Germany from the 'traitors' of the Weimar Republic.

9th November is now the anniversary of the Cristall Nacht (night of the broken glass), the night of the burning of the synagogues in Germany – at least 267 were destroyed – the night of the beginnings of the pogroms.

I was not aware of anything unusual, that fateful night. I was asleep.

When I got up in the morning, I found the house deathly quiet. On my way to the washroom I passed one of the Kindergarten teachers.

"Good morning," I said cheerfully. "How silent the children are today… perhaps my watch is fast. What time is it?" "Sh…haven't you heard?" "Heard what?" Then she told me the dreadful news: the synagogues burned, the men arrested, the shops and stores burned, smashed and looted.

The children were told at breakfast that their school had been closed until further notice. "We live in difficult times. We know you all will co-operate by being on your best behaviour."

The silence in the house was broken only by the telephone, which rang very frequently. The phone calls came from all over Germany. They brought bad news: somebody's father, or brother, or relative had been arrested by the Nazis.

The older children and the students hung around in groups in the corridor outside Matron's office, waiting, terrified, for those phone calls.

Whose turn was it next? Some girls cried openly and some prayed. Others just strode off to their rooms. We were too afraid to even discuss it.

They arrested approximately 20,000 Jewish males. Within the span of a few days the SS had called at most Jewish houses and rounded up the men. They had even called at the house of an aunt of mine whose husband had been dead for two years. This shows that their lists must have been prepared far in advance. There was no escape. If you did not open the door, they knocked it down with the butts of their rifles. If you went into hiding, someone had seen you and gave you away. If you were caught hiding, you were usually shot, "trying to escape". You could not flee to another country; the passport had been confiscated by the Reich.

I also had my phone call.

My mother was in Frankfurt with the grandparents when the Nazis called to take my father away. It was in the early hours of the morning; two SS men had come.

Later I was told what had happened.

Father had awoken Arnold and Susan. Richard, of course, was away at the Jewish Orphanage in Esslingen. Father had gone over to the window and drawn back the curtains. "Look, the sky is quite red – it's the synagogue. I saw it from the laboratory upstairs. I got up a little earlier than usual because I had a lot do today."

He pulled his watch out, Father wore an old-fashioned gold repeater watch, he could not bear anything constricting his wrist. "Almost four-thirty now. I think I'll go and have a look at how things are going. I've called the fire brigade. They knew already, they were all out. I supposed by now they have the fire under control. I wonder what could have started it?"

Arnold and Susan were looking out of the window, speculating as to the cause of the fire.

"Do you think it could have been arson?"

"It looks worse," said Arnold. "I'll go upstairs. I can see more from there."

"Call me if you can really see something," said Susan. "I'm going back to bed." Sh…did you hear that? It sounded like an explosion. "I did not hear anything with you jabbering all the time. Perhaps it was the backfiring of a car." "Bit early for a car." "Lorry then."

Susan closed the window and went back to bed. After a while the bell rang.

Arnold called down, "Open the door, Susan, Father must have forgotten his key."

Susan slid downstairs on the banisters. In the vestibule, she quickly pressed the buzzer, then started to run upstairs. She did not want to be caught without her dressing gown. Mother always said, "carelessness", "catching cold", "no slippers on", etc.

Bang, bang, bank. Someone was hammering on the glass door. Susan peered over the banisters. She saw two SS men. Bang, bang, bang.

"It's open," she called.

They saw her. "Come here."

Susan became still, as if she had grown onto the stairs. She did not move. She stared.

"I said, come here, you brat."

They were slowly coming upstairs. Susan could not take her eyes off the revolver which the SS man was pointing at her. The other one was holding a briefcase. He opened it.

"Julius Fleischer. Your father. Tell him we want him. Be quick."

"He is not at home."

"When is he coming home?"

"I don't know."

They obviously did not believe her; they brushed past her and started to search the rooms, slamming doors as they did so.

Arnold came out of the laboratory. "What's going on?" He sized up the situation in a second and planted himself in front of Susan. Susan was silent. She was trembling. She looked younger than her age – she was fourteen then – particularly so because she had grown out of the striped pyjamas she was wearing.

Both Arnold and Susan were small; they took after Mother.

The SS men consulted a list. "No, I don't think so, he can't be the one. He's not eighteen. Not that one."

They searched very thoroughly – the closets, the cellar, but clearly didn't think anyone there was over eighteen.

"Let the boy look after the child," said the one with the revolver to his companion. Then he barked at Arnold, "We'll be back." They tramped downstairs. It echoed.

"I wonder where Father is. Oh dear," said Susan, "what are we going to do?" She sat down on the stairs. Arnold fetched her dressing gown. "Let's go and make some coffee."

Father was hardly through the door when the SS men returned to take him away. They must have been waiting for him.

"I'm just going to the police station with these gentlemen," Father said.

"For inquiries. I'll be back soon. You'd better go back to bed, both of you. If I am not home by breakfast, ring your mother. Not to worry."

It was Mother who rang first, at six in the morning. This was a good thing because later on in the day the telephone did not work anymore.

Arnold told her the bad news about the synagogue. She said the synagogue in Frankfurt was also burning. The grandparents were as well as could be expected. She did not want to leave them, but she would catch the morning train. Mother cautioned Arnold and Susan that under no circumstances were they to leave the house. No, she did not think they were burning down private houses. She was wrong: they did, though not in our town. "Promise me," she had said, "that you won't go outside the door. There are riots in the streets." She warned them to be sure to lock all doors and windows, but not to stand near them, and to draw the curtains because they were throwing stones. She would be home in the afternoon. She would get a taxi.

Later the details of the arson became public.

Hitler and Goebbels had been attending the festivities celebrating the Munich Beer Hall Putch in the Alten Rathaus in Munich, when they were informed of the murder of von Rath.

Goebbels, as Minister of Propaganda, gave the signal for the onslaught against Jewry.

The full machinery of information was used all over the German Reich to inform the various leaders of the District-Groups of the SA and the SS. The Group South West, the SA, Brigade 56 Ulm received the order to burn all the synagogues, and to transmit this order forthwith to their branches. This was done. The local chief of the fire services was told to turn off the alarm calls which called the local firemen at their houses. Later an order was given to protect only the Christian houses and premises adjacent to the synagogue. It seems that the local Nazis were asleep, as it was the two SA men from nearby Geislingen who committed the arson. They climbed in through a window, and with the straw and petrol they had brought with them, 'made a wonderful fire': they bragged about it later. The cupola fell in, the benches and the whole interior was burned out; only the outer walls remained. There was a small crowd watching, perhaps about fifty persons, mostly in uniforms, 'on duty'.

Opinions were mixed, about this outrage. One SA man said, "Tonight we really did a thorough job." Others said they were disgusted. When the Judge of the local Police Court (Amstgerichtsrat), Dr G Mueller, was heard to say, "That is no way to go about things." An SA man asked him "Is this not to your liking?" Dr Mueller replied, "Do you know who I am?" The man screamed at him, "It does not matter who you are, this is no concern of yours," and he threatened him with his loaded pistol, held at his chest. This Dr Mueller later became the Ministerial President of Baden-Wuerttemberg from 1953-1958. From 1958-1971 he was President of the Bundesverfassungs Gerichts. The Commandant of the Fire Service had also expressed his distaste for the 'action'.

The clean-up of the place where the synagogue had stood, cost 3,858 Reichmarks – to be paid by the Jewish community. On the green, there is a memorial tablet, erected in 1971.

My sister Susan was always neat and tidy, like out of a band box, whilst I did not care if my clothes were crumpled and had a spot, providing it was not too large and visible. Her hair was arranged in the latest fashion, whereas I had very fine blow-away hair, which was almost uncontrollable. During our childhood she had been an underling, meaning she had to do as told by me, who was the gross 'maul' (big mouth). I had the respect of the underlings, being top of the class in school and I even sometimes argued with the teachers if I thought I knew better. I had resource to our own library, better than the school library. Our own contained many unusual and interesting books, including art books with good coloured reproductions.

Some of the teachers retaliated, when no one put up their hand in answer of a question. I was asked and given lines for not knowing, as I possibly should have done. From all the girls in class I had by far the most lines to do, mostly caused by my inattention, and reading or even writing something else, secretly under my desk, during class times. Teachers considered me a pest, I was proud of being a pest. I could discuss any query with my father whom I considered all-knowing. Susan took a delight in scolding me for being untidy, having messy drawers containing my cosmetics, with spilling of powder everywhere. At night she hung up her dresses, folded her undies, whilst I had to retrieve and sort out my jumble of clothes.

"No wonder everything of yours is creased and needs ironing."

Susan sported the latest fashion in headgear, whether it was the turban or the baby bonnet introduced by the Paris Haute Couture or the soft felt hat with a brim like the one worn by the girls from public schools. I was satisfied with the Kangol Beret, worn standing upright like Deanna Durbin's, the American teenage film stars.

My sister Susan had arrived in London on 29th July 1939, on the kindertransport from Stuttgart. She was placed with a doctor's family in Wood Green. The doctor's nurse/ receptionist joined the Red Cross Nurses, his wife, who was also a nurse, took over. So Susan joined the family as an au pair. She was expected to look after the children, take them to school and do the housework. The doctor's wife complained that Susan did not clean very well, she said, "sloppily". After all, she was only fifteen years old and had not been used to it.

The little girls needed pleated school skirts, uniform was compulsory. These were expensive. Susan suggested that her sister could make them. I agreed, I knew that the Haute Couture stitched the pleats at the crease, this made them permanent, and they retained their shape, could be washed, no need to send the garment to the cleaners for re-pleating. The sample pattern from John Lewis, I sent this in an envelope. It was approved. It was not easy for me to press in the pleats, I did not have an ironing board. When I handed the bill over, for fabric, sewing cotton and the fare to John Lewis, the lady complained about my having added this. I said, "I had to make a special trip to town."

"You work in Oxford Circus, don't you?" was the response.

"Yes, I finish work at 6 p.m. and John Lewis closes at 5.30."

She said, "There is also a bus charge to Wood Green on this bill."

"Yes," I said, "you told me you needed the skirts urgently, for school, I had not intended to visit my sister so soon again." The fares did not amount to much, but she never gave me any money for my work, though she did give me a box of chocolates. The little girls told Susan that their mum had had these since Christmas.

Refugees were expected to work for free, Susan never received any pocket money. One had to be grateful to receive board and lodgings!

After the doctor was called up to the Medical Corps, there was no need for Susan. She got the sack.

Susan joined me at the Cumberland Hotel as a waitress.

The landlady gives me notice to leave, she says she needs both rooms, Susan's and mine. She had been very restrictive with hot water, only at certain times. I was not sorry to go. I find a new room, 8 Linden Gardens – in the Lyons Corner window, there are often adverts there.

There is better accommodation to be had. I wanted more comfort, hot water at any time, yes I want tea at any time. A gas or electric cooking ring to heat up the food I had bought at the Deli. I don't want to cook much , perhaps boil an egg, tomato soup is delicious hot, not cold.

Cards are in the papershop window of Lyons, at the corner – these adverts are interesting. Things wanted, things for sale, like prams or a home wanted for house-trained puppies. Jobs, such as delivering newspapers, apply within.

That is where I found my new room, at number 8 Linden Gardens. It seemed to be better, in every way to Holland Park Avenue, where the power points were cut off, except on weekends.

At no. 8 Linden Gardens, Mr Bennett had done himself a conversion of both his houses, no. 8 and 9. Linden Gardens was a cul-de-sac. Formerly the residences of the middle class, it was now a boarding house, bed-sits, with superior and good-sized rooms with high ceilings, all with constant hot water in all rooms.

My room had a large walk-in wardrobe, shelves on one side, suitable for my crockery, cutlery, food tins and most important, the vegetable and potato basket. My fruit was kept in a bowl on my chest of drawers. The Bennetts lived in the basement – halfway down from the street level. The communal bathrooms and toilets were kept spotless, mail was in lockable pigeon holes, a good landlord. He even took telephone messages. Landlords could be selective in their choice of tenants. There was a housing shortage because of the bombing of London.

My cousin, Elisabeth, a children's nurse, lived at no. 4 Linden Gardens, at Miss Plant's house.

The Ries family's father had worked in our branch factory at London Wall. He had married the boss's daughter, my Aunt Paula, so Elisabeth was a first cousin. Her brother Herbert was born in England.

This had made him an Englishman! He was allowed to bring near relatives not as refugees, but as near family, mother and sisters, Elisabeth and Rita; Elisabeth popped around, for a chinwag, or coffee

– not too strong, please. She had not visited me for two weeks. I went to number 4, Miss Plant was a well-educated lady, got friendly with Elisabeth, both loved books, serious classics and especially poetry.

Miss Plant opened the door: "Miss Ries does not live here anymore." I was surprised. "She never told me that she was leaving."

"Come in, I will tell you. I think this is dreadful," said Miss Plant. "I noticed she had not come down, must be days, not picked up her mail. I took a cup of tea upstairs. You know she's been upset since she lost her job. She was a children's nurse. Little Anthony, the kiddy had been sent to the country, to be safe, with relatives. 'Nothing to get up for,' she told me. I did not take that for serious, you know Miss Ries is a lazy lady. She did not get up for her shopping, her food from Panzer's the Delicatessen, her Frankfurt sausages, or go to Panzer's café next door to the shop. I was shocked when I saw her. She looked awful."

"How long since you last ate?" "Don't know." She could hardly talk. I went down to make her some toast, but she could not swallow. Coughed. "I am not there to nurse tenants. I don't know, she needs help, let her brother's wife look after."

Herbert's wife had a rooming house in Prince of Wales Terrace, W8, the other side of the park. They should give her a room. He is stationed in the country in the Forces now, as an interpreter. He is bi-lingual, now a sergeant.

I was shocked, quite shocked. "So am I," said Miss Plant, "I have got the address of that place if you want it."

On my next free day I visited her. I was surprised to see she looked all right. Ward Sister said, "Regular meals, a good wash, no, good bath. The doctors are saying she can go home. Someone has to get her, to be responsible, see that she is safe."

Miss Plant said, "That Inge (Herbert's wife), she did it. I think she was afraid that Miss Ries could not pay, that's why she ended up in hospital. That Inge is money greedy. Luckily I have not yet let Elisabeth's room."

I said, "I could do the food side, give a meal, most days – yes, most days I am at home. If you agree, I have a suggestion. I telephone you, you tell her the food is ready."

This is what we did. It worked.

She completely recovered, was cheerful again. Elisabeth was a member of the Anthroposophic Society, she went to their Christian Communion meetings every week. Several members befriended her, a nice social life.

Her sister Rita lived in Chelsea, married to Val Mystyn, their own house. She never visited Nursy, and for Christmas she sent her a card with a two shilling piece taped inside.

Their mother, old Mrs Ries, lived in Marloes Road, W8, in a small bed-sit. Her suitcases were deposited on all the furniture, there was nowhere to sit. She was on social scrutiny. Both son Herbert and daughter, Rita, did not contribute to her upkeep.

Cousin Rita

My cousin Rita had emigrated, in early 1933, to England. She had been trained as a superior secretary, as she was bi-lingual, having been brought up in England in her early childhood.

She was of a strikingly beautiful appearance, very tall, with violet eyes and sandy hair. She met Valentine Mostyn, also very tall and very good looking. Together they looked like film stars. They got married. That gave Rita English nationality. I don't know if money (mitgift) was involved, but I certainly saw many of my grandmother's rare treasures when I visited them in their flat in Earls Court.

I recognized the chest with inlaid ivory figures, the battle of the Huns. It had fascinated me as a child, I tried to count the dead bodies portrayed on it. There also, standing around, were china objects which I remembered because Grossmutter had pointed them out to me as being especially valuable.

"Please, do be careful of my china," said Val. Not 'our' china. His china. I thought Val was a dancer, or an actor, the way he walked. I found out he that worked in an antique shop up West, in Bond Street. Rita was employed by a lawyer, doing legal and business translations. This very exacting work was well paid, so they bought a house in Chelsea, near the Kings Road. They lived in the lower maisonette, let the upper part.

I had been invited for dinner, arriving with my bunch of flowers. I was greeted, "Oh dear, we have eaten already." I thought they kept continental times, it was only 7 o'clock. Rita went into her kitchen: on a fancy tray, inlaid with fruit woods, she brought me my evening meal. Three cooked prunes, plus one slice of toast. I recognized the tray, Grandmother had her elevenses on it.

When our grandmother was chased out of her house, she moved to Stuttgart, together with her daughter, my aunt Paula. The flat was small. Much of her furniture and belongings had been sent to Rita. Jews could at that time still send belongings abroad. The Nazi major of the Goeppingen Town desired the 'Villa Fleischer' and moved in. His name was Mr Pack, 'lumpen pack' we said. (Lumpen means rubbish, or rags.)

Not wanting a repeat of Rita's skimpy evening meal – my three prunes – I invited them to dinner. "Val is busy, he is with his boyfriend, but I would like to come," said Rita.

"Where? Suggest a restaurant."

"There is one nearby, in the Kings Road. It is rather expensive."

"Fine, I'll meet you there at 7 o'clock."

There was a five-course dinner, all was very good. I did not manage the last course, the cheese platter, which also had grapes on it. Rita did.

Rita had warned me about it being expensive. It was, outrageously so, my God! I paid.

Nursy

Herbert and Inge sold their Prince of Wales rooming house, and moved into a luxury flat overlooking Holland Park.

Nursy has been very upset by Herbert and Inge. Their son, Peter, was shortly having his Bar Mitzvah and she is not invited. Inge said she would be ashamed to have her there, because she is dirty, her clothes are disgusting. They did not want their friends to meet her.

Nursy says she loves Peter, she really had her heart set on going.

Peter left his parents as soon as he could be independent. He has moved into the flat he inherited when his grandparents Bernheim died, in Kilburn.

When I met him, by chance, he told me he had not seen his parents for over two years, and he says, "I don't care if I never see them again. I don't like this family, Rita is just as bad. Nursy is the only decent one." He has no social life, he does not want it. His parrot is his only companion.

Nursy only wears navy blue, a sack of a dress – of course with little Anthony she had her starched white nurse's apron. For outdoor a three-button serge coat and her veil. As a qualified children's nurse from Germany, she is entitled to wear a veil.

Perhaps it is this veil which puts Inge off, it is similar to the one religious numbers wear in England. Perhaps her Jewish guests might think she is a nun.

The dress Nursy always wears is huge! This sack.

I tell Nursy I will make her a nice dress, a beautiful dress, from the midnight royal blue lace I have. "What do you say to that, Nursy? I will line the lace with silver-grey satin."

Nursy's figure is difficult, a very large bosom, almost no hips. I manage to produce a 'haute couture' garment for her.

Nursy telephones Inge, says to her, "I am coming, and don't you dare keep me away."

At the Bar Mitzvah party the people asked who is this woman in the lace dress. One of them suggests she has seen me in the Harrods model room. "It's the sister-in-law." "I thought she was a nurse, she is very elegant." The hostess, Inge, is of a very petit figure; her dress had to be altered for her, they made a bad job of it. I think it is a botch job.

I approach her. Thank you for your invite. Here is Peter's present. I say, "I think you need a new dress-maker, your dress does not fit you well. Look at Nursy, take a leaf out of her book. She looks amazing!"

I did not tell Inge I had made the dress.

My cousin Lilo

My cousin Lilo Guggenheim is attending a finishing school in Switzerland. She is taking a secretarial course there, this always combines with the traditional course for superior ladies.

Her parents had become friendly, when on holiday in the Riviera, with an English couple, who lived in the South of England, near the seaside.

When life became difficult under the Nazis, they offered help. Women and girls, aged over eighteen years old could apply for a work permit in England, as a domestic servant. Should Lilo want to come to England, they would give the guarantee and a letter of employment.

Lilo was required to do no housework, but had to help in their amusement arcade as a supervisor. The area became a restricted area, people were evacuated, the military took over.

Lilo had to leave. She had been classified Friendly alien, Category C, by the Tribunal, so she was not interned on the Isle of Man. A job was found for her, with a family. She had to look after the children. It was a hard life, as she had to clean the house as well.

A German lady had married Colonel Little, who had known the Guggenheim family from earlier times. They befriended Lilo. They lived in Thames Ditton, not far from London.

Lilo said she would like to become a nurse. This kind couple arranged it for her to be accepted at St Aliplages Hospital, near Greenwich for training. This area suffered many air raids. Patients had to be protected. There were a number of TB patients. Lilo was most afraid when she was called on to look after these, but gradually overcame her fear.

After four years training as a nurse, Lilo was fully qualified, to sit her final exams. Lilo did exceedingly well, so well, that she gained the Gold Medal. This was awarded to her in the Westminster Hall in London. It was not congratulations all round. Her matron was most put out. "The German girl got the Gold Medal!" Lilo therefore did not pass a practical exam, had to repeat time spent. "That will take her down a peg or two."

In 1946 Lilo's brother, Poldi, who lived in the United States of America, managed to get her a visa. The family was reunited.

Lilo became a nurse in New York Hospital, in a TB Ward. Unfortunately she caught this disease and was rather ill. She was sent up, for a cure to Lake Saranac, to the Trudeau Sanatorium, where she slowly recovered. There she met Melville Levin, also a TB patient, he was a young research scientist. The Trudeau Sanatorium was very successful, they had many complete cures.

They fell in love. They married. For several years they lived in Long Island, where Lilo had established her own dance studio. Then they transferred to Lake Saranac NY, New York. Mel was now an established scientist.

Saranac Lake had many wonderful wooded grounds, and of course there was a lake. The Trudeau Sanatorium had closed in 1954; by then different methods of healing had taken over to cure TB.

When Lilo was a child, the whole Guggenheim family had gone to Bad Worishofen, in Bavaria, for the cure. It had been successful, the family became a Kneipp addict. Invented by the Pfarrer Kneipp it had many followers. My father, Julius Fleischer, was the Chairman of the Goeppingen Kneipp Verein, since 1910. It was on his recommendation that the Guggenheim family had gone for the cure.

The Mayor of Camberg, the small medieval town in the Taunus Mountsin, the birth place of my mother, Irma May, had been to Worishofen, the Kneipp Spa, for a cure. He was so impressed that he decided Camberg should be well served if becoming a Kneipp Spa. When my father, the Chairman of the Goeppingen Kneipp Veriem visited Camberg – our family went every year to visit grandparents – he helped with advice and his valuable connections.

I wrote up the information as it was given to me by Lilo. She had arrived as an eighteen-year-old household help, the guarantee had been given by the couple who had met Lilo's farther in Nice on holiday. Unfortunately the gentleman wanted to pay attention to Lilo, who was a virgin (this was customary in our circles). So Lilo got in touch with another friend of the family, who found her a position as home-help, for pocket money, maid of all work, and then as this was unsuitable, as a trainee nurse in St Alfege's Hospital in Greenwich, where she earned the Gold Medal, as reported before; this was a great honour.

Fyl

Having done my weekly shopping in Panzers, I slowly walked home. I always looked through the large plate glass window, to see if any friends were having their coffee in the Linden.

Sitting at the window table was a young girl, I had seen her before. Her holdall was pushed under the table. I went in to have my coffee. "May I join you? They are very full today." She was still staring out of the window. "Are you looking for someone?"

"Yes, my boyfriend. He often comes here."

She looked very pale, ill in fact. After a while, I said, "I hope you don't mind me saying you look ill. You should be home in bed."

"Yes, I have been ill."

"Does he know you are waiting?"

"I don't think so. I am looking for a room, thought maybe he could help me to find a room. The ones I have tried have already gone, the ones from the notice board."

"Where did you stay last night?"

"Nowhere, the park, on a deckchair."

Looking at her dishevelled hair, poor clothes, nicotine-stained fingers, I was not surprised that landlords had turned her away.

"Rooms are hard to find, your boyfriend should help you. What is his name?"

"Philip Savile."

Shocked, I said nothing for a while. Yes, this was a shock. Philip Savile was the husband of Jane Arden. I knew them well.

"Does he know you have been ill?"

"Yes, I suppose so. I have been in hospital, when I came out my room had gone. The landlady had packed my holdall, everything."

"You phoned him?"

"There is no reply."

They often went to stay with Jane's parents in Wales. Philip drove an ancient Jaguar. Was he really this girl's boyfriend?

"How old are you?"

"I am seventeen." She was very well spoken. "My name is Fyl."

"You should go home to your parents."

"I can't, we had words. They don't like my friends, and me staying out all night."

I thought, she needs a hot meal, a bath, and a sleep. She should go home, make up with her parents.

Those young people, I don't know. It would be called interfering, being a busybody. But another night on a deckchair? Looking at her my concern grew, she can't spend another night on a deckchair.

"I can offer you a bed for the night, just one night. My flat is no-smoking. It is not far from here, in Holland Park. You understand, no smoking?"

Next morning when I rose, she was sound asleep.

When Mrs Champ, my domestic help, came, I told her.

She said, "God knows what happened. You know I don't like that art crowd."

Mrs Champ gave scrambled eggs, tea, toast to her.

"That girl looks really ill."

"She told me she had been in hospital."

She told us the reason. It was an abortion, a back street abortion, it went wrong. The ambulance took her to hospital. "I could not give them my parents' address." She started to cry, "I don't know what to do. I can't find a room. It's not the money, I have an allowance, since I passed my A-levels."

"Where did you go to school?"

"Darlington Hall, it's a public school"

I was still shocked. Philip Savile was one of the bright lights. His *Hamlet* was produced, and part of it filmed in Denmark. Had international acclaim. He did some directing in the United States. As a Rank Charm school boy he had starred in a B picture, playing a double role. "A double disaster." He grinned, "Forget that one!"

"What a shame," Mrs Champ said, shaking her head. "Those immoral men. She is so young. Worshipping a genius. If she was a year younger, he would be in prison."

I discussed again the situation with Mrs Champ. "Let her stay for a few days, until she is better. We should talk to her parents."

"I doubt she would allow that."

Mrs Champ said she would look in at lunchtime and give her a snack. She said she would ring me at my office if anything was wrong. She stayed, she recovered.

After a few weeks she seemed physically recovered. I asked her to phone her parents. I insisted. Fyl told them about Sylvia, about the flat, about my high-class business. Her mother wanted to speak to me.

"We were worried, her landlady said she did not know where she went, with her boyfriend possibly. I am glad she is safe."

I had books, all kinds of books, Fyl liked reading.

She made herself at home in my flat.

I told her mother I thought she needed new clothes.

"We did not like those either, those dreadful things she was wearing, we thought she looked like a ragamuffin."

I had not mentioned that she had been ill, neither had Fyl. Her mother rang back, to talk to me.

"We have discussed it, her father and I, she can have £100, but only on condition you go with her, to choose the clothes. Whatever you select for her."

The parents lived in a high-class apartment block off Kensington High Street W8. We collected the money, refused the cup of tea. "We are not staying, goodbye." Best to avoid further discussion, I was afraid of a scene. They need not know about the hospital.

At home I said, "Fyl, sit down. We have to have a very serious talk. It is about your appearance. You have a very good figure. Your freckles with your blue/green eyes look interesting. Sun-burnt with freckles just like the Nubian Princess, in my book on Thut-en-Kamum, you liked this book a lot. Do you remember the statue of the Nubian princess, very tall, delicately boned long arms and legs, very tall, just like you. You told me your family, grandfather and your father were in consular services in Egypt. When the looks are so special, so different, one's clothes must be traditional, to counteract it. You could be Egyptian."

"I like this," she laughed. "I'll say I am Egyptian."

Fyl and I chose very traditional clothes, a camel-hair coat from Jaegers, Regent Street. Lambs wool sweaters, now on sale, shirts blouses, like school blouses, to go underneath. Skirts, utility make, but of good fabric and good cut, plain shoes, courts, lace-ups, a simple mac for the rain. With care, the £100 stretched to cover all, as well as a nice handbag.

Fyl said, "I hardly recognize myself. Very bourgeois, upper class!"

"Well you are."

At the weekends I sometimes visited my family in Paris. I had no family in England, my sister Susan had married a GI, a sergeant, now a doctor in Philadelphia. Richard, my brother, had joined her. My older brother Arnold, lived in Toronto, Canada, he was an accountant, business advisor, doing very well.

There were special Airways fares, 'Weekenders'. Friday night London to Paris, to Monday mornings return. Only £10. So I could visit France. I walked through Holland Park, the air station was in Kensington High Street. I boarded the Airbus. I was collected in Orly by my cousins. They came in their rattle trap, so-called because the old car was so noisy, and roomy.

Cousin Eva and I were very close, much closer than my sister Susan and I. Her husband Jaques was like a brother. He was a ceramist, and a painter, very talented. Both had been in the Maquis. His father, Etienne Gril was a writer, very well-known, he had received the Légion d'honneur, Arthur Fleischer, Eva's father, was also a writer, they had worked together, and their children played together.

They lived in Mason Alfort, in the old family mansion which had been converted into eighty apartments. Gril senior had been the Postmaster General of France. No one lived grand anymore. Jaques and Eva had the ground floor apartment.

I went shopping with Eva on Saturday mornings to the local market. It was an experience! The fruit and vegetables were sun-kissed, absolutely gorgeous. There were also stalls with crockery, all studio-made, individual people made plates. They made lovely presents to bring home and at such small prices. We cooked together, her children were well behaved, played in the garden. Jaques and I talked philosophy, religion, yes, mainly religion, we were all non-denom.

With the time difference of two hours, on Monday mornings I left Paris at 8 a.m. and arrived in London before 8 a.m. in time to go to work, walking back through Holland Park.

Fyl was still with me at my flat. She said she tried out the 'rooms to let' and was surprised when landladies offered them to her. She told them she was Egyptian. No one minded her freckles and tan colour. She was so elegantly dressed, spoke with an upper-class accent.

Fyl told me, "I could have had any of the rooms, or flats. You were right, it was my careless appearance." And then she said, "I envy you your trips to Paris, I wish I could go."

"If you have a valid passport, you can."

Fyl was still looking for Philip Savile, but he was nowhere to be seen. Why did she believe he would marry her?

I felt she must get over it, this hero worship. She does not realise he had abused her, a young girl of seventeen years.

I discussed the situation with Eva and Jaques. "Send her to us, she'll forget him."

Fyl took the £10 weekend trip. They liked each other. Fyl was to stay with them, in Paris, to study at the Sorbonne. Her parents approved.

This was the beginning of a friendship which lasted sixty years, until Fyl, now called Carol, died in February 2015. She returned to live in Ardingley, Sussex after a few years. She had a part-time job teaching French and wrote a little, a children's books about a unicorn.

Trudy, from Austria

Often second sons went into the military. Trudy's father was given to reckless gambling, making debts, unable to pay them. His Colonel suggested a solution a marriage might solve the 'problem' better than shooting yourself. He suggests marrying a young Jewish girl, cultured, who was artistic. Well educated having been to Finishing School. The customery Mitgift (marriage portion) may be considerable as there is a title involved. Father or grandfather may be a banker, settle the debts. The family supports artistic circles.

Trudy's mother dies in Switzerland from TB, Trudy is sent to school in England. After the Anschluss of Austria to Nazi Germany, the money stops. Trudi is now a refugee, sent to work in Bloomsbury House. Her brother had joined the Nazi party, her grandfather is now retired, moved to his estate in Karnten.

In the Linden, Trudy introduced me to Gregory Malimacofski. "He is a writer, a poet. He writes verses on greeting cards for his uncles." Christmas cards were predominantly in the Jewish hands. "Actually I like some of these verses, they are really moving, but he thinks its degrading, this work. He quarrels with everybody. He is so angry." Trudy invites him for a good Austrian meal, you know Knodel, or Frankfurters, Lentils and Spatzle. He likes Mariella Knodel (apricot dumplings) the best, an Austrian dish. "He does most of the deliveries of the China commemorates, they are very heavy for carrying. The postage is too dear."

We sat in the Linden.

"Something has occurred to me, just now," said Trudy. "What are you doing with that small room, at Farm Place, are you keeping it?"

"My furniture is in there, of course I keep the room."

"Gregory has nowhere to stay, he bums around, a few days here a few days there with friends, on settees or sleeping bags. Would you have him, just for a few days?"

"He can have the room, rent free. There is no electricity, only gas light, and a small sink in the passage for water. The loo is in the yard."

Gregory moved into Farm Place, he has a chip on his shoulder, no, not a chip, an outsize bean!

He had lived previously with his parents in Peabody Buildings. This was a very cold apartment, no running water. He hated going into the street, to the standpipe for water. He was the best scholar for that year in the East End school, excellent in English. He got the one and only per year scholarship to the posh public school. His mother, the stupid cow, buys clothes for him at the Fifty Shillings Tailor. They are ill-fitting. He is a fat boy, stuffed full by his mother. The other boys laugh at him, the fat Jewish boy, the one who excels in English, in Literature, in History. He is a no-no in sports. Sports are important, so he runs away, hitchhikes home. His father is furious, he has to pay a fine for wasting the opportunity of a good education, this scholarship from the East End School.

The family moved to Fulham. At least there is now running water. The blackout curtains are still on the windows. No heating in the house except in the sitting room. His bedroom is freezing, not enough blankets on the bed. Almost no furniture – a table and six chairs in the sitting room, no sofa or easy chairs.

When he is fourteen he seeks employment at the Hyde Park Hotel, saying he is nineteen years old, he is a tall lad. The staff bedrooms are warm, lovely and warm! He learns to be a waiter, he does not like it. "Yes, sir, no sir, three bags full sir, the soup is not hot enough." He spends his free time, afternoons, at the Serpentine in Hyde Park. He loses his fat, puppy fat. People think he is very good-looking. Weight lifting improves his physique. Starlets working at the new TV tell him they need young men there, for crowd scenes. The work is not regular. He bums around, sleeps on settees. He is very angry, mainly about his family, his mother, the stupid cow.

He is annoyed, he writes letters to the newspaper. They print his letters.

He cannot understand why his father married the stupid cow. The father's family does not like her, she is not good enough for them.

He has not been home for months, that miserable, uncomfortable place.

His father's family are printers for greeting cards, Christmas cards.

"You are a poet? Can you write verse? Can you show sentiment? There is a part-time job here."

That is where he met Trudy. After a short courtship, they married.

Michael Kullman lives in the very large house in Ladbroke Road! They are white Russian emigrees, who managed to bring with them some of their considerable wealth. Mrs Kullman is a very active church goer, of the White Russian Church in Bayswater. She is a committee lady.

The services at the church are impressive. Full vestments, all that gold embroidery is worn by the priests. The incense. Gregory is impressed. He never liked going to the synagogue, he only went if the family insisted. He never liked anything in the East End, particularly his relatives, the ones with the greeting cards business. He only worked there a short time with Trudy.

Gregory's knowledge of Russian writers is vast. Dostovesky, the Prince Necedov is his favourite. Altogether his understanding of literature, including the Americans – Modern, and Modern English is also vast. He works on reading scripts for television. He advises on suitability of actors, scenes. This brings him in contact with actors and writers. People accept him, his perfect diction, elegant clothes. He is a white Russian émigré. Michael Kullman's friend, acceptable in the best circles. Gregory realizes he is as good as they are, better, yes better. He is considered a talents writer, a critic. The ladies accept him as their escort, more.

Trudy had over the years collected works of art, mostly china. She loves them, it reminds her of her home in Vienna. Now she is married, it becomes joint property.

Gregory gives Trudy's treasures to his conquests, they are perhaps one-day or two-day affairs. Her beautiful Ismic vase, a museum piece, he gives to Leila Karp, the Vogue shophound. A complete set of handmade China by the famous Austrian ceramist, Lucie Rie, now living in London in a studio in Bayswater, he gave to Esme, from the Chelsea Art School as a wedding gift. French perfumes and flowers are sent to girlfriends, out of Trudy's Harrod's account. Gregory entertains his friends in West End Restaurants, without Trudy.

The Christmas holidays are spent in St Auton, Austria. The number one hotel, the Post, had been fully booked, so accommodation was in the Hotel Adler. The food was excellent, all these dumplings and venison specialties. Gregory was annoyed, he spent his time sitting the Post Hotel lounge, when Trudy joined the 'Adler' ladies for ski. Gregory did not ski. There was no contact with Trudy's brother, he had become a Nazi after the Auschluss.

On the way home Gregory was furious, he had to be satisfied with Hotel number two. The Baur Au Lac was number one in the whole of Europe, but was fully booked, had accepted his booking for the next day.

"Baur Au Lac, that's where the millionaires stay, or aristocracy," said Trudy.

"You are aristocracy, Baronness Drohonhausen, are you not?"

"It will cost a fortune, we cannot afford this."

"I will make you bankrupt, that's all!" Gregory was laughing.

Trudy's enjoyment was spoiled. To stay in this lovely hotel costs a fortune! How could he?

Their bank accounts was not in the red. The Bank Manager thought Gregory's spending was excessive, far too high. The turnover does not warrant it. He called Gregory and Trudy in for a talk.

"I must advice you, madam, very strongly, to remove Mr Gregory's signature from the cheques."

So it was done.

Flower power, the general amoral behaviour seemed to be acceptable. Not to Trudy. She refused co-habitation, as it is called, her husband's right. Gregory moved out, into a 'den', a basement flat.

The Rank Charm School

The Rank Charm School had been grooming young people, hoping they would be successful in their acting career. The main subject was, of course, acting. This included also deportment and elocution, where experienced elder actors struggled to put some finish, polish is often hopeless with kids of no talent. But there were the odd ones, who reached for stardom.

Philip Saville was a successful director, on the stage and on the lately becoming well established television. He directed *Look Back in Anger* at the Twin Gate Theatre. He had played in a film a double role, two disasters, he said to me. His wife, Jane Arden, had written a play, *The Birthday Party.* I don't know how it came to pass that Charles Laughton wanted to play the father and the cheeky Jane Arden told him that she thought he was wrong for the part. The play was a flop, although people went to see Charles Laughton, who was of course the main attraction.

At the same time, showing at the Lyric in Hammersmith was a play by Harold Pinter. I went to see *Look Back in Anger*, and I can remember very vividly, that I identified with the leading lady and her ironing board. 1958 – you have to forgive, my memory is patchy, at The Gate Theatre entrance, Palace Garden Terrace.

Two cinemas, the Coronet had the latest release films. The other, the continental one, with European and films with were not for general release.

The Mercury Theatre with Director Impresario, Frederic Ashton, and Joan Littlewood, showed ballet, the undernourished little angels and their boys eating a meagre diet at the Lyons Coffee shop at the corner.

The Gate Theatre, Entrance Palace Gardens Terrrace with a bar and serving snacks, drinks during licensing hours, was popular with theatre and film actors, and later also TV people. This is bedsit land. The young people must be fed. Plenty of cafes, restaurants, bread shops serving twice daily proper meals. The flower people are happy, looked after, well fed, little money. The London Polytechnic in Regent Street ran special courses, to enable people who had missed out on education because of the war, to enable them to pass the entrance exam to a university of their choice.

Maurice enrolled, so did Jane Arden, and Jon Silkin, and others of course. At this time it seemed fashionable to claim working-class birth. Jon cleaned very well, he always believed in doing a good job. He organised his fellow cleaners, to join a union, his cleaning union. His employers promptly sacked him. I was told his union survived. He had started a poetry magazine, called *Stand. Stand* survived for fifty years, much respected. Sorry, I don't understand poetry.

Jon's next job was as a gravedigger for Hampstead graveyards. He told me he liked the fresh air. His attires were in a sorry state, no belt for his trousers, a string will do, but the seams had split. Sylvia to the rescue, with clothing coupons, at Pontings shop.

Working Class original! That's a laugh. Jane Arden (married Savile), father was a butcher, owned three butcher shops, plus a pie factory. He sent monthly cheques to Jane and weekly parcels.

Philip Savile's family were in the clothing trade, in the East End. Philip said he hated them, they ran a sweat shop. But he was glad of the money.

Jon Silkin did not accept anything from his family. They were famous lawyers. His uncle was Lord Silkin. This a secret – but well known. Don't mention it. He had gone to Dulwich College it was said he was expelled, hearsay.

Jerry Becker was a lovely man, he had recently arrived from South Africa, after a spell in prison. He complained about apartheid. He had been a teacher, now he writes and prints literature, to rouse people, back in South Africa, something must be done.

All these people sat in the Linden over a cup of coffee, talked. Sylvia listened. Sylvia is considered stupid, she is quiet.

It had been formerly usual to use a SHADHEN – a marriage broker to arrange Jewish marriages. However, from the nineteenth century it was no longer done. People said this was a pity. Homosexuals and bi-sexuals could be approached when they came to Vienna, they were keen to meet the English artists. Pity 'Mitgift' (marriage portion) could be used to buy a flat or a house. The Jewish girl was no longer Jewish, could travel with an English passport. Somehow the marriage à trois worked, he could keep his boyfriend, was safe from persecution, from prison.

Dressmaker

Mr Bennett had furnished his two properties just before the war started, all rooms had a basin with constant hot water, own gas supply with a gas ring. The large walk-in wardrobe had shelves on one side.

The single room on the first floor was furnished very basic. The table was just strong enough to take my newly acquired electric sewing machine. My release from war work had come through. Three years in the American Red Cross.

The residential club at Marble Arch had finally closed.

We, the English staff, celebrated in Hyde Park, a wonderful spring day, 1946, the blossoms were out.

I had put my name down at the local Singer shop in Westbourne Grove, the shop had taken my old treadle machine in part exchange.

Bed-sitting rooms, all mod cons, had been let to people in the acting profession, part-time actors, models, and mostly 'resting'. I was on shift work. In my spare time I had become a dressmaker. I fancied to call myself a designer. Well, I did the best I could, in this work of utility clothing. I had discovered Sylko, a pre-war cabinet full of colours, when I had been looking for matching cotton. It was a treasure, an old-fashioned store in Shepherds Bush. The Government had decreed that cloth had to be dyed in six standard colours. Even the styles offered appeared to be the same fabrics. There was also a price control. All was to be utility clothing.

I was firm, I would not do alterations, there were shops to do that work. No, I would not make underwear for a prostitute! If the customers brought in velvet curtains we would make a jacket or even a suit, but it was faded from the sunlight. I would see what I could do.

Talking to the little old lady, the owner of the small store on Shepherd's Bush Green, about difficulties of obtaining nice fabrics, as before the war, she told me she had put away fabrics, trimmings, buttons, lace. "Come one morning, I'll show you what I've still got, in the back, packed away." A treasure trove.

One of the tenants was getting married. I found satin to make a nighty, trimmed with black lace.

Margery Normile lived in the room next door to mine. I apologised for the noise of my sewing machine, asked did it disturb her?

"I can hardly hear it. May I see what you are doing?" I showed her the work in progress.

"Oh, that is lovely," she said. "I was best in sewing class, at school, I wish I could help you."

I said, "I can't pay much."

"It is the work I want, I am bored," she said. "Oversewing, finishing off is easy, you must do it neatly." Margery did it surprisingly well.

In 1946 I got my release from war work. The Columbia Red Cross Club had closed. For the last two years I had done dressmaking, yes, designing glamour clothes, in my spare time. The eight-hour shifts gave me free mornings or free afternoons.

I designed cocktail wear – very much in demand when you attended theatre performances or were invited to the posh restaurants. Full-length garments for evening were rarely worn now.

My fame as a dressmaker had spread. I was no longer unemployed, I was self-employed. Not really.

"Margery, I need permission to work," I said. She replied, "My family has a workshop in High Holborn. What about your stamps?"

So the Normiles from high Holborn "employed" me as a designer. I took my letter to the Notting Hill Gate police station, my cards were stamped. All in good order now.

Mr Bennet came to see me. He said people are asking for the dressmaker, this property is residential. "You will have to find yourself workrooms. I'm not throwing you out, you are a good tenant, but you cannot work here."

Margery and I went to the local estate agent, in Notting Hill Gate main street. They had a three-floor flat available in Kensington Park Gardens. The lease is for seven years, no restrictions on work, the usual, no music after 11 p.m., no brewing of alcohol (from an old church lease), no animals, etc. Margery said we should pay half each, the rent is reasonable. I paid the agent and the other costs. The accommodation was in Kensington Park gardens. Top floor, three rooms, no kitchen, no bathroom, one wash basin.

References – Bennetts gave us a good one. We moved in – I got some cheap, very cheap second-hand furniture, Margery got some from her family.

The most important item we forgot – *no telephone*. Essential for appointments, fittings, new clients. I found out that there was a two-year waiting list for the service of telephones.

Existing customers were willing to write, soon there was enough work for both of us. I said, "Mohammed and the mountain." I packed up the lovely evening dress I had finished for our best customer, a small bit-part actress. And my wrap-around draped evening skirt cocktail length, my own invention. It fit anyone, just move the button and waist band.

I put them both in a box, not too much tissue paper. Margery said, "Where to?"

"I'll try Kensington High Street, Knightsbridge, every shop is a clothes shop, they are pricey too."

"You had better go," said Margery. "Continental accent is an advantage in High Fashion – my cockney accent is a no-no."

"You have a charming accent," I said to her, but I had to agree.

I had prepared a little speech, "May I see the buyer?"

"Have you an appointment?" or sometimes, "No you can't." "She is not in."

I had called on all the shops in Kensington High Street. Now I was in Knightsbridge and I had not even opened my box. There were no more shops – I had now arrived in Piccadilly Circus, Swan and Edgar – "Office staff – appointments only. In writing." Simpsons I missed out, I knew they only sold coats and suits. No results whatsoever. "No thank you." They were mostly polite if you were well dressed.

Fortnum's – I was getting tired by now, "No, no, no." I thought I would have a cup of coffee in their restaurant; I deserved it, two hours and nothing. Now start again in Regent Street. Hupperts – two windows, one with knitwear, one with shirt blouses. All expensive, high quality. "May I see the buyer?"

An elderly grey-haired man smiled at me. "Well, young lady, what do you want to show me?"

You are number one, the first one, I thought, please God. Nothing to do with God. He took my box to the back, came back holding my wrap-around draped skirt invention.

"Yes, I like this, properly finished, how much is this skirt?"

"Four pounds."

"I cannot pay that," he said, "there is a price control, did you not know? I can pay only 72.3, no more, sorry, could you do it for 72.3?"

"Yes", I said eagerly, "I can cut it more economically if you buy several."

"Shall we say, half a dozen?" What about coupons, would you like me to give them in advance?" Four for each garment."

"Yes, please." He's nice, I thought, he's got a Viennese accent, he likes me.

"Come into the office." This was going down some narrow steps into the basement – quite steep. My first customer! "Bring it in with an invoice, even if the order is not complete."

I called first on John Lewis's Oxford Street, hoping they would stock the 1.45 cm width of black crepe satin-backed fabric. This would enable me to cut my pattern more economically. They did. Margery and myself managed to get the skirts finished in two days. Invoice? A name for the bill. Possibly Strakers – the stationers in Notting Hill Gate could help me with that.

"I would like an invoice please."

"Ah. An invoice book."

Pre-printed. I wondered if there were special ways of filling it in, I had 'slipped up' not knowing about price control. So I only filled in Sylvia and Margery and our address, coupons 6 x 4 = 24 coupons paid.

Mr Holzer, the owner of Huppert's shop was not in. Young Mr Holzer, bespectacled, said, "Deliveries downstairs." I braved the steep steps, handed my invoice book to the white-haired accountant or clerk, "Please could you help me?"

There are special numbers, as the garments were not utility. He made out a cheque, gave it to me. He smiled at me. Young Mr Holzer said, "They will cash your cheque at the till."

How very kind, to pay me right away – in cash.

"If you wait a minute you can have your box back." This was the folding-up box sold by Strakers, which I had used previously for the fancy clothes I had made for the actresses.

I had no other work, so I prepared a folder of the photos and magazines, cut-outs of the clothes I had made for my clients, mostly from the art world. They had recommended Sylvia and Margery, word had spread around. I was proud, there were three from *Vogue*, but not mentioning my name, nor describing the clothes. That lack of a telephone, it really was a worry. I had heard nothing from Hupperts, perhaps I'll take a bus and enquire what is going on.

I went into Hupperts. "Good that you called, we have written to you. We sold all the skirts at once, on the first day. Can you make some more? Just bring in whatever is ready. Here are fifty clothing coupons on account."

I am in the wholesale business now! Who is complaining?

On my next delivery, I showed young Mr Holzer my folder with my clothes. He seemed to be very interested in the Christine Norden one-off, an off-the-shoulder dress, broderais anglaise frills at the neck and peeping out from the petticoats, a very full petticoat, I had to ask for more clothing coupons, which she said the producer of the film gave her, with a grumble. Mr Holzer asked me if I could make a blouse like the off-shoulder dress.

I chose a spotted fabric from John Lewis. Luckily I had brought all of the stock of Anglaise trim from my Shepherd's Bush Green woman. This was my first blouse order. I called the style 'Victorian'.

"Your designs sell well, we put them in the window, the next hour they have gone," he said. "The people stand outside studying our window."

I was wondering if there were more 'haberdashery' shops selling pre-war goods. I found one in Berwick Street, W1. The woman said she had a warehouse full of old stock, and was glad to get rid of it – all that 'utility' stuff was in demand.

For some reason, Margery had disappeared – she was engaged to a Captain Beynon, a Welsh professional soldier. Why did she not tell me where she was going, was she on holiday?

There was a letter for me, left in the entrance hall of our premises. I could not understand it. It asked us to vacate our rooms forthwith. But we had a lease, paid for. I went to the estate agent. He told me it was because the house, our house, including our rooms, had been sold. Margery had sold our lease. They had paid her a very good price. "It was my lease as well," I said. "Not according to the papers, your name is not on it."

"I paid for half of it, and I paid for all of your fees."

The estate agent said, "We get a lot of this now, they give good money for the tenant or owners to get out."

"How much did she get?"

"I am not at liberty to tell you, but it was a good bit. They will have to take you to Court if they want to make you vacate."

They took me to Court. The Court gave me three months to vacate. "Rent free," they said, "this will make up for your loss of the deposit you paid. Your name was not on the lease."

I had a business, but no premises. This is a fine mess. I did not have a new address for Margery's family, they had been bombed out. Margery had seen to our employment stamps. She had left the cards in the drawers. And I had thought she had gone on holiday!!

We had no kitchen, just three rooms, there was a gas ring, there was electric power.

I had my evening meals in one of the many restaurants or cafes, in Notting Hall Gate.

These large houses had been converted into bedsits. Gas rings, but no kitchen. Anyway I could not be bothered to cook for me or Margery. The cafes also did breakfasts, no coupons, only for full meals.

One of them, The Linden, with the Art Nouveau oak furniture, did no main meals. It was my favourite place. I could read my newspapers, which were continental style attached to sticks, hanging on the wall. I got to know most of the regulars, the intellectuals, the artists, the actors, and the would-be actors, resting.

Sometimes there were adverts in the local papers, for rooms to let. I urgently needed these, I had to look every day; with the housing shortage they were gone immediately. The showcase at Lyons, on the corner of Notting Hill Gate, had sometimes rooms to let.

"You look troubled," said the elderly man I shared the table with.

When I worked as a waitress in the Cumberland, he often used the same late-hour bus from Marble Arch to Notting Hill Gate.

I confided in him. "I urgently need premises, to work and to live." His name was John Russell. He told me he was a consultant to a large medical supply firm. He said he often worked at night as a rat catcher.

"No, really?"

"Yes, I give advice, rats are a terrible problem now, since the bombing. Rats are very clever, you put the bait out, if it kills any, they tell their friends, or rat family, they advise them to keep off. I have told the company I work for we must find some poison that they do not associate with getting ill, a long-acting one, we are working on this now. War to the rats! Slow acting, give them haemorrhages of their guts, slow acting so they bleed to death, it thins the blood, makes blood clots, we are working on it. My company thinks it could have medical uses." It did – now called Warfarin.

He knew a lot, this old man. He said, "Kill one pest, it may be the main food source of another animal, eradicate one plant, again this may destroy something – we don't know what effect it will have on nature."

Mr Russell also told me that the company he worked for was into the research of Artificial Insemination and Immune Systems.

He mentioned research into the breeding of Apes/Monkeys (I cannot remember which kinds) with Humans.

Why did he tell me these things? I was shocked, frightened. Mr Russell assured me that the foetus would be aborted at four months. The research, he said, took place on a farm, or research establishment in the country, near Dorking. Mr Russell sometimes went to the country.

He also told me when he formerly worked in Africa, humans had intercourse with animals. I was frightened, shocked, but fascinated.

We had interesting conversations. I said, "I am on the flat hunt, I urgently need premises, to work and to live."

Next day he told me there was a vacant, very large room, in Strathmore Gardens, just around the corner, with a Mrs Bowman. Mrs Bowman offered the place to me, it would be vacant in four weeks. Pay monthly in advance, or weekly if you prefer. A gas meter, two-burner cooker. Electric for heating is included in the rent.

I was happy. A very large room. This Mr Russell seemed to know people, perhaps because he is a local man. He told me of business premises to be let by estate agents, different agents from the ones who had let me Kensington Garden Road, where I lived now.

What did I do with my furniture, such as it was? Mrs Bowman's house was fully furnished. Mr Russell knew a storage place, an old lady had an empty room but she wants ten shillings, a lot for an empty small room, but that's the housing shortage, she can get away with it.

The estate agent knew my former 8 Linden Gardens landlord, Mr Bennett. He gave me a very good reference. 135 Notting Hill Gate, in the main street. The brothers Pocket owned this property, they were jewellers, and had a pawn shop on the ground floor. Three golden balls hung outside. On the first floor was an old lady doing church embroidery, and on the second floor were two rooms free, to let.

I was back again, manufacturing, could again employ staff, but not yet. First I must get permission, as a friendly enemy alien I need official permission – I'll find someone to 'employ' me.

135 Notting Hill Gate. These were proper business premises. I can have a lease, yes, seven years, no conditions except not brewing alcohol – the old church clause, must have started a hundred years ago or more.

An acquaintance of mine, we had shared often a dinner table, Audrey Haydon, told me her sister had just come back from India. She was looking for a little part-time job. She had done secretarial work, she is well off, she wants very little money, just something to keep her occupied. We met, she offered to work for me, but officially she would employ me, as a designer – to cover my friendly enemy alien conditions.

Mr Russell claims I am his adopted daughter

I told Mr Russell the good news. He said, "You are too late, I have already given your details, and asked for permission for you to manufacture. I said you were my adopted daughter."

"What name did you give?"

"Sylvia Russell, you are my adopted daughter, or will be."

I said, "Not a good name, too many Russells, look, the phone book is full of them."

Sylvia Russell – Kensington, this is now the name of my company, Sylvia Russell (Kensington), sounds good!!

Hupperts were very pleased, they told me to bring along my new designs. Mr Russell told me he opened a Sylvia Russell bank account with the Midland Bank in Hammersmith. Why Hammersmith? He told me they know him, he had dealt with them before. It takes two buses to Hammersmith.

Huppert's cheques were now made out to Sylvia Russell (Kensington).

The Singer shop in Westbourne Grove put me in touch with Singer's wholesale Department. I chose two lightweight industrial machines. These could be delivered immediately, at my convenience.

My very good electrician had made a plan, a ring circuit for the second floor. All correct with the new regulations for safety. I put an advert for staff in the local paper, also in that showcase of Lyons, at the corner shop of Notting Hill Gate. Business firms could get telephones, no trouble there.

An Italian girl came for interview. She was married to an English soldier. He was studying on a special scheme for ex-soldiers. She could start any time and had been trained by the nuns to do good work, also she had a friend who was looking for work. Workroom equipment, office equipment, everything was 'hunky dory'.

Mr Russell was telling everyone that I was his adopted daughter. He said that would protect me from stupid gossip, he was right.

I said to him, "If I am your adopted daughter, may I say something, don't take offence, but your jacket is a disgrace." Many men prolonged the life of their garments by having patches of leather put on the cuffs and elbows. The make-do-and-mend shop did that for the tweed jackets so popular at that time.

"I tried to get this nasty spot out, must have been the gravy splashing. Actually I tried to buy a new jacket from Burtons but the fellow told me I had no coupons left."

I commiserated about this: "Someone must have pinched them from your ration book. Would you allow me to give you some?"

I had spare ones. "I have seen tweed jackets, a whole row of them at Pontings, all sizes."

Pontings was the cheaper shop in Kensington High Street. Barkers, Derry and Toms.

"I'll buy one for you. They are cheap there." It was a perfect fit, after all, I am a designer, I know about sizes. At the same time, I bought two shirts for him, his were clean, done by a laundry, but frayed. A daughter would be expected to look after her father. I addressed him as 'you', or 'Sir'. I could no longer call him Mr Russell.

I had been to the cinema, the Odeon at Marble Arch. I was having a cup of coffee, sitting at the bar of the Gate Theatre, where the actors could get their refreshments when rehearsing.

Mr Russell liked to get his all-day breakfast there. I asked, "Has he been in?"

"You have just missed him," answered the bartender. I recognized Joan Hickson, the actress, she came over to me.

"Are you Sylvia, the clever little refugee girl? Mr Russell told me about you. You are a lucky girl."

"How am I lucky?"

"He told me he set you up in business."

"Well, not exactly. He found me my new business premises. And I am grateful for that, because they are so hard to find." I know he tells people I am his adopted daughter, this is okay. But what else is he telling them? I continued, "But regarding setting me up, he never put any money in my business, not a penny." I was annoyed, finished my coffee and left.

Some days Mr Russell sat in my office doing invoices, wages, answering the telephones. He said he is 'just helping' his adopted daughter.

Well, I thought about this, a strange relationship, but better than people thinking he was my 'sugar daddy'. It was my money, for my work, Huppert's cheques covered all my outgoings. I accumulated stock in trimmings. I had tried haberdashery shops, but they were no good. My suppliers in Shepherd's Bush were coming to an end. I used Yellow Pages to look for wholesalers of lace in London. My list was long – industrial cords, shoelaces and all kinds of related goods. From about twenty calls only two were successful.

The shop in Berwick Street told me she was wholesale – retail. She had old stock of Broiderie Anglaise Allovers. Allover meant goods by the yard, fabrics she said she was glad to get rid of. Knowing I was keen to purchase, she charged me a 'good price', much dearer than my Shepherd's Bush prices.

Hupperts paid for all of my blouses regardless, 72.3 shillings.

I cannot remember the price of everyday goods. I cannot remember pounds, shillings and pence. Bread small loaf was two and a half pennies, potatoes half a penny, a pound of apples, one penny, at Portobello Market. I went shopping with five shillings. This covered my purchases for the week, with the exception of milk and bread.

Mr Russell told me it may take some time to register the business to employ me; I was a Friendly Enemy Alien, Category C. It takes five years to become British. I had applied as soon as the war was over.

Financially, much money was paid to me by Hupperts. Mr Holzer said my designs "sold like hot cakes".

Now I had three more girls on my staff. Two machinists. I expected them to machine five blouses per day, two finishers, to do the oversewing and the buttonholes. I did the cutting out, made the 'bundles', packed the deliveries into the cardboard boxes. Somehow I was not interested in money, only designing, producing good work, getting publicity. Occasionally a photo by 'Shophound' from Vogue, unfortunately without my label giving only the shop's name, but not mine.

I had my dinner mostly with Mr Russell (not tea!!), in one of the many restaurants or cafes in Notting Hill Gate. If Mr Russell joined me, he paid for both meals. People addressed me as Miss Russell, but not Hupperts, always Miss Fleischer, very polite: "You are a leading blouse manufacturer now, THE leading blouse manufacturer."

When will my permission to trade come through? Many people are starting up now, "You must be patient." I did not want my workrooms to be registered as John Russell, trading as Sylvia Russell Kensington.

Hupperts said I would be liable to charge purchase tax, I had reached the limit of free trading allowed, let alone if I supplied other people.

Mr Russell used his bank. He said they know him from before, the Bank is in Hammersmith Road, which took two buses. I needed more cash for business shopping. If there are special offers, one has to be quick. "Please introduce me to the manager, I don't want to inconvenience you, I realise you have other work," I said to Mr Russell. I often found him sleeping in our little office. He said it was his night work, the rats.

"All right, I'll take you, tomorrow for an appointment with the manager." But he did not turn up to take me. Nor at the next appointment he said he made. I was starting to worry; it looks like he did not want to take me at all. Where was he sending the purchase tax money? It was thirty-three and a third percent for the tax. It must be thousands that I owed, and I would be doing this illegally, I don't have permission to trade, or do I? No, I don't think so, I should have registered with the police, with the Customs and Excise. I am working until late, sometimes late evening, to 'bundle up' for the machinists. Hupperts take special orders for my blouses, these have to be ready in good time.

There was a loud knock at the door, it was after 11 o'clock. I went downstairs, the chain was on, I always put it on after 6 o'clock.

A policeman stood there, "Is everything all right? Can I come in? The light was on."

"Yes, yes," I said, "I want to get my orders ready. Do you want a cup of coffee?"

No, if everything is all right." He left.

The black-out curtains were still on the windows. Good-fitting, made for the air raids. I must pull them in future. The policeman had not asked my name, I must be more careful, I am not registered.

After Mr Russell missed the appointments he said he made for me, I decided to go to the bank myself. I asked for the manager. I introduced myself, "I am Sylvia. Mr Russell is not available sometimes, and I need money, for wages."

The manager said "It's nice to meet you, but I have no authority for transactions with you, get Mr Russell to arrange it."

I looked for the Sylvia Russell (Kensington) books, records of trading. I kept the books of Delivery notes – pre-printed by Slaters, and the purchases I had made for cash. I could not find the cheque book, the current one.

But I found the Insurance Cards for the staff were in the drawer – there was none for me. I went to the local Labour Exchange. "There is a job; can I have a card?" I put the card on the desk. Sylvia

Russell (Kensington), I filled in Designer/Cutter. Wages: to be arranged. I sent it to the Labour Exchange. After a week I called back at the Labour Exchange. The girl said to me, "Sorry you did not get the job."

"Are you sure?" I asked.

"Quite sure, look, the card came back 'not employed'."

I said, "Have you got any other work?"

"Only for machinists." She phoned for me to the Oxford Street Exchange, dealing with the Clothing Trade, they don't get the Designer jobs, trade papers. "The adverts are in those," she said.

"May I have my card back?" I asked.

"Sure , here you are."

So I am working illegally, not employed.

What about the Purchase Tax money I am owing? Also, I should have gone to the police to get my card stamped.

We were friendly with the other tenants in the house in Strathmore Gardens, we took each other's milk in, left on the doorstep, passers-by seemed to pinch it, you had to be registered with the milk shop/dairy. Pamela handed my milk to me.

"Thank you, Pamela."

"Why are you at home?"

"I had an upset, I don't trust myself with scissors."

"Come and have a cup of tea," she said.

"Yes, I am very upset, I am in trouble." I showed her the card.

"This is outrageous," she said. Pamela Chamberlain was a secretary. I did not see Mr Russell, when he came in during the week. The wage packets for the staff were made up. No envelope for me. I needed it to pay my rent, which was weekly. I apologised to Mrs Bowman, "Never mind," she said. "You're not running away."

I went for dinner at around 8 p.m. There was just enough money in the petty cash – I put a slip in.

Mr Russell joined me at dinner, I said, "My envelope was not there."

"Yes it was," he said.

"Give it to me on Monday."

"You are getting forgetful," he said.

"Monday will do," I replied.

Yes he did put it there on Monday, but I did not see him. Again he did not come in all week, but the wage packets for the staff were there, as usual. The petty cash was almost empty. Insurance Stamps, yes. Work had accumulated, I had sorted the orders. I stayed late at night. The staff knew what to do.

Our newspapers were lying on the desk. Articles about employment or suchlike were on a special page. This page was marked in red. Arrest of illegal workers, police find the catering trade employed people illegally. Surveillance about illegal landings on the coast, again marked in red.

I had read previously that illegal workers were taken back, if they had passports, to their country. If they had none, to holding camps for refugees, in Europe. The conditions were supposed to be worse than in the concentration Camps of the Nazis. The refugees had no water, little food, no latrines.

I went to the Austrian Club in Leinster Square Gate, near Paddington. They knew all about the conditions of the holding camps and had appealed to the Red Cross. It takes time. "Worse than concentration camps," they said. "The police just sweep you up and take you there, they don't ask questions, if you have no papers, what can you do?"

All I knew about my parents was that they had been taken to Riga; different reports, were they gassed, or just shot, or put to slave labour in factories? No, that was for younger people.

From France: later, much later, I found that twenty-three members of my family had perished in the Holocaust, later still that four members from Germany, including my parents – but my brother Richard survived.

I have no papers. Yes, I have, I am a friendly enemy alien. I have this information in my handbag. Where is it? I must find it, it is not in my bag. I am therefore working illegally.

They arrest first, then transport you away. Where are my old papers? I can't find them.

I was now very frightened of what Mr Russell would do. He had marked the newspaper in 'red', why?

I don't want to see him, I am frightened, I had trusted him. Oh God, what was I to do? He had tried to make out I was mental, losing my mind?

I knew he sometimes had breakfast/lunch in the private club

attached to the theatre at Notting Hill Gate and he sat near the window, on the first floor, looking out. Several times he accused me of forgetting messages, orders, misplacing things. The bar served coffee, tea, all-day breakfasts, drinks during licensed hours.

He can see the street, he can see me coming from my house at Strathmore Gardens. I must go another way. He'll recognise me, but not if I put my hair under my black crochet skull cap. Not if I put my new turquoise raincoat on, he has not seen that before. I'll go the other way to my office.

The staff are good girls. They answer the phone. Still no envelope with money for me. I cannot sleep at night – the worry. I have a bad cold. I cannot work. I cut out my orders at night, curtains drawn. I am going back, at night, to do the work. I cannot face it. He says I am getting forgetful, I don't know what to do. He did not put my envelope there later, twice now. I owe two weeks rent.

The purchase tax I must be owing would be thousands by now. I am defrauding the government – prison, then deportation, who will be believed? Him or me?

He is stalking me, *but I do not know this word,* lying in wait, will he call the police? He is Scottish, I am a 'bloody German Illegal'.

My mind was going around and around. I had picked up a bad cold, first my throat, then a cough. The aspirin did not help. The worry and the cough stopped me from sleeping. I needed something stronger, I called at the doctor's surgery, in the next street. I told him I had not slept property for weeks. He gave me pills, "One or two at night should do it."

I woke up, refreshed. I had taken one. But my problems had not gone away. Defrauding the government. I must owe thousands by now, if he has not paid it in. I had searched all the drawers, one was locked. There was another newspaper on the desk, again marked red, about illegal immigrants and deportations. Obviously he must have been told that I had called at the Hammersmith branch of the bank. The newspaper is a warning. There must be thousands in the Sylvia Russell account. If he disappears, I do not have his address. Fife, in Scotland, the guest accommodation of his consultancy place, firms kept spare rooms for their visiting fellows or advisors. I had told everyone that it is my business. That makes me responsible for the purchase tax. Thirty-three and a third per cent on all sales, must be thousands by now.

I could not deal with it, peace, peace. I wanted to sleep, so, yes, I take the lot, all the pills. God will forgive me, Jesus help me. I hold my little carved stone crucifix tight in my hand. Jesus, protect me.

I believe in reincarnation. I believe I might see my parents on the other side.

There are eight left. It will be enough. I cannot remember a prayer. God, please forgive me if it is a sin. I cannot face the Holding Camp. Holy Father in Heaven.

Three days later I woke up in Abbots Hospital.

I remember, I had locked my door, but Mrs Bowman's cleaner had a pass key to all the rooms. Hoovering once a week, tenants break hoovers, cannot be trusted with a hoover. She had found me. I am burning up, I am thirsty.

The nurse tells me, "We don't let the man in, you screamed ever so loud." He comes every day to enquire. The Almoner is kind, but I refused to talk to her, what could she do? I was several days in hospital.

A welfare worker took me home. Mrs Bowman told me she forbade him in the house, and she would call the police if he comes near me. Pamela Chamberlain had shown her the Labour Exchange Card – 'not employed'.

Mrs Bowman said, "I took the liberty to phone Hupperts, I told them you were ill in hospital, any correspondence is to be sent to me. I'll bring your letters to you."

I said, "I owe you about three weeks rent, I don't have any money."

"Never mind," she said," we'll discuss this later."

"There should be last month's cheque – to Sylvia Russell (Kensington)."

I don't have permission to work. I am still worried about the purchase tax.

The doctor came to see me, said, "It's over now, you need a good holiday. What about your family?"

"They're in France, no one here in England."

He asked was it boyfriend problems? "A pretty girl like you, there are plenty of fish in the sea."

"Oh, no," I replied, "Charles is nice, but he could not help me. I was afraid, very afraid. I am in serious trouble." Charles was my current boyfriend.

He said again, "No family, visit some friends then, perhaps there is somewhere you want to go, somewhere special?"

Pamela Chamberlain brought me some flowers, she said, "You did not give me a chance to help you, I thought it was outrageous. I told Mr Sims about it. He is the accountant at the firm where I work. Mr Sims is a special policeman. I believe he is quite important. Well, I am to tell you he fixed it with the local police. They will stamp your alien card, and they have put a block on the bank account in Hammersmith. Go, when you are fit, call on the police station in Ladbroke Road."

"This was awfully good of you, you're a clever girl, thank you, thank you."

Mrs Bowman said, "I've made an appointment for you to see my bank manager at Barclays, to open a new account. The other one is dormant." She brought my mail. A nice letter from Hupperts, saying they looked forward to new styles. Enclosed a cheque – how large, almost a thousand pounds, well six weeks. Mrs Bowman took me to the bank, I paid in the cheque.

"Here is your cheque book, only temporary. When the new one is printed, I'll send it. How much cash do you want?"

"I want to give the staff two weeks holiday pay. Close up on Friday, that's tomorrow. To thank them for their help, and then I am going also on holiday for two weeks. I need quite a bit of cash, to pay my back rent, plus two weeks when I am away, two weeks for staff. What do I need for travel? I need about £200."

Holidays. The doctor had said is there anywhere I wanted to visit? There was a recurring dream of steep steps. I found some which looked like the steps in my castle book, in Launceston. My boyfriend Charles came from Launceston, his house had been taken over by a girls' school for the war, but they are still there. He told me they had wrecked the garden, but the house would be repaired, when they left finally.

The whole house, all my fellow tenants, want to help me, come with suggestions for a holiday, even the doctor.

There are those steep steps in Launceston. Several times in my dreams. I wonder what it means? Remembering a former life. I show the photographs of the steps, from my castle book, to Mrs Bowman.

"Yes, I know these, they are in bad repair, perhaps they have done them up now. But you should see the old church, famous, every bit carved in the front, right to the top. The hotel is reasonable."

Charles Bradshaw, my current boyfriend – he was – has not come to see me, his estate is between Launceston and Lifton. He has 5,000 acres, it is entailed, and he said he has trouble to get money. At present he is building himself a small aeroplane in his garage, he needs a bigger garage. He said he would like to sell the house, but the executors won't let him. Donald, the partner of Carlotta Matkins suggests St Ives, the Artist Colony, they have a museum. Accommodation is half price now. It is off season, they drop the B & B prices, sometimes to half.

Cooks Travel Agency have a branch in Kensington Church Street. I give them my plan: Glastonbury, Launceston, St. Ives.

Why Glastonbury? A lively place. For the good of my soul. To thank for the help I was given. Dr Stein has often spoken about first-century Glastonbury. The Tin Trade. Joseph of Arimathea was a trader there, accompanied by young Jesus, his nephew, reported to be the Son of Jesus Christ. The Church exploits the story, makes out it was Jesus. They have also invented stories of finding the grave of Jesus Christ. Tourists flock there.

Cooks Travel Agency are very helpful, they explain we need trains, and buses. Accommodation. There may be several changes. They don't have the local timetable, but could give me the telephone numbers. "We will ask your hotel to assist you. Book for you."

Knight on a white charger comes to the rescue

I am off on my holiday, I arrive in Glastonbury. It is a tourist attraction, but the houses are shabby and neglected.

When I get there I ask, "Where is the famous well?" They say they didn't know there was one. But there is the Tor. It's quite a climb. And tonight we have the Cider Festival. Monastery Gardens? There is nothing to see, except the graves, but they have been proven to be a hoax, not the bones of Arthur and Guinevere. Tourist stuff.

The hotel is from medieval times. My four-poster bed has a dreadful mattress. The Monastery Gardens are well kept. A clergyman approached me, "Come with me, I will show you the Holy Thorn. Joseph of Arimathea brought it. Yes, it is a Syrian Thorn, still alive." It was his walking staff, for the tourist attraction. I don't know why he was talking to me. "Every Christmas I send a branch of our thorn to the Queen. It blooms at Christmas." He takes my hand, "Would you like it if I send you a branch?"

I pulled my hand away, I am frightened, I am frightened of men. "No thank you, no thank you."

The locals invite me to their Cider Festival, it is in the cellar of the hotel. That cider is so sour, so sharp, I cannot drink it. I say to them "I will keep it for my night cap." I leave with the mug. They tell me you can buy those in the tourist shop, they are Glastonbury marked.

I sleep late. A young man has a full English breakfast, he asks me do I want to the climb the Tor with him. He is a medical student, he wants to specialise in Lobotomy, it is then quite new. I think cutting up people's brains, how dreadful. The Tor is not interesting, but the view is good on this fine day.

The hotel informs me the next morning about the bus links up on the main road, to go to Exeter. Then by train to Okehampton, then another bus to Launceston. I am glad I have only a rucksack, it is very light, with only a change of underwear and socks, and a map.

I arrive in good time for dinner at the Launceston hotel, which is larger than I expected. 7.30 p.m. sharp. I have a wash. I am tired. Coffee is served in the lounge. Comfortable, large leather chairs. Coffee tables.

"Do you mind if I share the table?" The tall man sits down. "Would you like a brandy with your coffee?"

"No thank you, I don't like spirits."

I get up, excuse myself, I want to get my map which I had left upstairs. "Local map? Perhaps I can help you, I live here."

"In the hotel?"

"Yes, only for a few weeks. I am on loan."

"Loan for what?" I asked.

"To tidy up government departments. I can be ruthless when I want to be!"

"That must be interesting."

"Not really."

I return with my local map. Spread it out on both my arms. I had scars, they had cut my arms quite deep to give me saline and other tubes, at St Mary's Hospital, Abbotsbury Road.

"What's that?" he picks up my arm.

"I was ill in the hospital."

"You look so pale, tell me, what happened?" He looks concerned.

Why does he want to know my troubles?

"Did you cut your wrists?"

"No, I didn't." Why am I crying now? He gives me a large handkerchief, white, from his breast pocket.

"Sometimes it helps to talk about one's troubles."

I can't stop crying.

"Drink this." He puts a tumbler of orange juice in front of me, "Gin and orange."

It tastes quite nice. I say, "I was frightened, so I took some pills. I had locked my door, but I had forgotten that the maid has a pass key. Once a week she hoovers. The landlady does not allow the tenants to use the hoover, because they break it."

"For you to take such drastic steps, it must have been pretty serious. Tell me."

"I was afraid they would arrest me and send me to a Holding Camp in Europe. I could not face that. These camps are terrible, worse than concentration camps. And there was that man."

"There is always a man. You should have gone for help."

"No, I couldn't."

"That man, tell me about him. What's his name?"

"John Russell."

"My God, is he a Scot, from Fife?" He visibly went pale: "I know him."

"You do? What do you know about him?"

"I would not like my sister to meet him. Tell me what happened, you can trust me."

So I told him, all of it. He fetched some more gin and orange, it was not bad at all.

"This is a terrible story, about Mr Russell."

"I got help, after I came out of hospital. The nurse had told me I screamed the place down when he came to visit. They would not let him in after that, but he came every day, enquiring. The hospital did not let Mr Russell into the Ward. Mrs Bowman had also forbidden him from the house. I was frightened, I never want to see him again."

"Are you sure? You don't ever want to see him again?"

"Yes, I'm sure, yes, yes, not ever."

"Then I promise you , you won't see him anymore." He made me drink the gin and orange. After a while he said again, "Are you sure, quite sure?"

I said yes. "Yes, Yes." And at that time I felt, he will die. I felt it so strong. Knew that Mr Russell would die.

"Drink up."

"I can't drink all that." He had put two more tumblers in front of me on the table.

"You better go to bed, have a good sleep."

I woke up, late, around 10 a.m., went downstairs for breakfast.

"Breakfast is finished now," said the waitress, clearing up, "but you can have tea and toast."

"Thank you."

The receptionist brought me a timetable of the buses: "You'll have to change. The little bus will take you to the main road where there is a connection, to get onto the bus A30 for Penzance." I had forgotten all about my castle steps.

"Can I have my bill?"

"It's been paid."

"I don't want that, I want to pay, how much?"

"It's been paid, room and also dinner." I put the money on the counter. "I insist."

The gentleman had gone to work, about 8 a.m. I was told.

"You have to hurry if you want to catch the bus, the next one is in the afternoon."

I caught the bus, the morning one, the A30, London – Salisbury – Penzance. The long distance coach, like Cooks Travel Agency had told me.

The main line bus has comfortable leather seats, it is leather? Most buses have wooden slat seats.

I am thinking about my situation. Yes, I prayed for help, sort of not believing there would, or could be any help for me. My prayers were answered, I knew I was innocent, I had done nothing wrong, I had been stupid, too trusting.

Those people in my house, they helped me, Pamela Chamberlain, Mrs Bowman, Donald. They hardly knew me. And they insisted on a holiday for me.

But this is not the strangest thing, meeting that man in Launceston. Almost as if he was waiting for me. Who had sent him to talk to me? And how can a stranger promise me Mr Russell will never hurt me again? Who is that Keith? What is he doing in Cornwall? He said his job is tidying up. Too many staff in government departments. Sinecures, yes I know what sinecures are. This tall, very English-looking man, in his navy blazer and sandy hair, not a hair out of place, he had promised me what looked like salvation. Or protection. He seemed shocked when I mentioned John Russell's name.

The windows on the bus are dirty. I clean a large circle with some loo paper I always carry around with me. They don't always have it in toilets, sometimes only newspaper. Lovely countryside, cows of all colours, even two black ones. Then there are the sheep, little lambs next to their mothers, sometimes twins.

I am getting hungry, my appetite has come back, I couldn't eat for days, my stomach was sore. The pills. Next time I know better. No next time, please.

We arrived at Bodmin Bus Station. Twenty minutes to wait. The toilets are to the left, a café around the corner. Hurry, only twenty minutes. The bus empties, some people must have been travelling a long time.

The sandwich I had bought must be yesterday's, or even the day before. This doughnut may be better.

Arrival in Penzance. The St Ives bus is waiting, leaves in five minutes.

My hotel, the one Donald had recommended, is not far away, near the harbour. I am in time for dinner, time for a wash. Dinner, no choice: fish, with tartar sauce in little packets. Apple pie or ice cream? I am tired. I crawl into bed. No night clothes, I mostly sleep without, unless it is winter. My rucksack is small. Room just for a toothbrush, a change of socks and underwear, a pullover. My cagoule keeps me warm. Tomorrow I'll make out my itinerary.

English breakfast, generous portions.

First I look at the harbour, then the two beaches. Crab sandwiches for lunch. I have never had them before. Cobbled streets, I have sturdy low heels.

Postcard shops everywhere, with kiddies' beach equipment, balls, little buckets for sand castles.

I am not used to walking so much. So I go back to the hotel, have a little sleep before dinner. Lamb chops or fisherman's pie. I think this is yesterday's leftover fish. Rice pudding or ice cream.

Museum day. The place is surprisingly large. Barbara Hepworth, Ben Nicholson, some famous artists otherwise mixed up with local talent. I like Alfred Wallis the best, a fisherman. There is even a whole book about his work. I buy it.

A good-looking guy is in charge, looking after the place. "I belong to the St Ives Group," he says. "We take turns. Anything you want to know about the artists?"

I am most interested to know about Alfred Wallis.

"Can I see you tonight, for a meal?" he asks. "That would be nice." He sells me a little town plan of St Ives. "I've marked the restaurant, here with red. Also the catalogues on the exhibition. Is it too cold for a dip?"

"I don't know, but I'll buy a swimsuit." I try it on. An old-fashioned thing, black, with a low cut back. Front is all right. My boobs are not showing.

I arrived at the restaurant. He said, "I have been here for almost an hour, waiting for you."

"So sorry." I never know what time people eat here, they call it tea, high tea, dinner, meal. Fish again – but served with nice pink prawns. I insist we go dutch on the meal. He tells me about himself. He had been a dancer for many years. I tell him about the Mercury Theatre at Notting Hill Gate. "You don't look like a dancer."

"I was an Adajio dancer."

He laughs, "You mean like the 'nancy boys?' I would be too big for that." He shows me his muscles. Impressive.

"I danced with Carlotti for years, but you may not have heard about us." I hadn't. "Carlotti and Carl – she insisted on calling me Carl."

"I wanted out, she was getting old, ugly, she wouldn't admit it. Also too heavy to swing her around. Have a coffee with me, at my place, I'll show you my work."

"That would be nice."

His comfortable divan was inviting. I admitted to myself, I am not 'horny' as they call it, but I would like it if he cuddles me. Sort of affectionate. Then he tells me about his girlfriend, or is it ex-girlfriend now? He takes me back to the hotel. It is now after 10 o'clock. He says, "I'll see you tomorrow, I have a little boat. About lunchtime. Oh yes, that is 12 o'clock."

I say, "I will ask the hotel for a lunch pack." That would be lovely.

On my bed is a yellow envelope, a telegram, Mr Russell died in his sleep, please return, Bowman.

It is too late to find out what has happened. I cannot phone at this hour. The hotel says they will phone next morning, about 7 o'clock. They will phone about my arrival. The hotel books me a sleeper, on the night train, connection Penzance. They drive me to the station, we just make it, the connection to the Penzance train.

I have to share a compartment with an old lady. "My dear," she says, "you are shaking."

"Just found out someone has died."

"How old were they?"

"Over sixty years."

"That's a good age, perhaps they had a good life."

"Please, I don't want to talk now." I feel I am going to cry. Well, this old biddy, I hope she will shut up.

Those blankets are scratchy. No sheets, it is second class. I can't sleep. If he died with a haemorrhage, I know what happened. This rat poison he was working on. Keith promised me, "He'll never trouble you again." I just wanted him away, gone. I did not wish him dead. But I felt at the time he would die, I felt this very strongly.

Who had killed him? Someone must have poisoned his food. He had told me the rats would never know, would never suspect anything was wrong. So I am party to murder, but I just wanted him gone. Now I am a murderess. I wanted help, had prayed for it. Not this kind of help.

"My dear, don't rummage around so much, it keeps me awake."

"I am sorry."

The train arrives at 7 o'clock in Paddington. The attendant knocks, "I have a cup of tea for you. You can stay on until 8 o'clock, when the train gets into the station proper. We are just waiting outside the station."

There is Donald waiting. "That's kind of you."

"Mrs Bowman asked me to meet you."

"What happened?"

"I don't know, she'll tell you." We take a taxi home.

"Farm Place, that's where Mr Russell lived?" He had told me, he had moved in, just temporarily.

"Mr Sims and the police have arranged everything. Have a cup of tea."

I am going to the mortuary. The flower shop next door sells me a large bunch or orange lilies. He looks no different, just asleep. He's been dead now a few days already, three days after I met Keith.

The attendant approaches me.

"You must go now, it has all been arranged." I didn't ask, what has been arranged? I don't want to know.

I go to Farm Place, the rent for the room is due. The old lady says, "I let the gentleman have the other key, I hope this was all right. I never knew he was ill."

The room had been cleaned out. His belongings, if he had any, had been removed.

"You are keeping the room on?"

"Yes, yes. Do I owe anything for the gas?"

She says she had emptied the meter, and taken the wash bowl back. It was hers, she told me.

I had never used the room, only to store my furniture. When I arrived at first, I wanted to put down some lino. But the man would not do it, because of the large gaps between the floorboards. "You have to get a joiner to fill the gaps, I cannot lay the lino, with these large gaps." I had been afraid of mice or such, they eat anything if there is no food. My divan was almost new, I had made a cover and there was bedding, and other furniture. My present room was fully furnished, Mrs Bowman did not let unfurnished.

I did not know Mr Russell lived there. The guest room at his medical lab, where he works, he said occasionally, when he works late, he cannot get in, because the outside door is locked. It would be convenient.

I don't know who had found him, I was afraid to ask, to find out, whom could I ask? The police? No, Mrs Bowman answered me, "Mr Sims has it all in hand." Then she added, "A good job he is dead, that horrible man."

People approached me, saying they are glad he was dead. I wish they would not talk to me. I go to my office, I always call it that. In my mail are a number of orders. The staff will return on Monday week, so I had better get a move on and prepare the work. As if nothing has happened.

I call at the estate agents, ask about the lease of my premises. It was made out to Sylvia Fleischer. Now I know the reason why I have never seen the lease before. They say, "The next quarter is not due, for a month."

"Can I see a copy?" Yes, it was made out to Miss Sylvia Fleischer, surprise, surprise. The agent said that he would not let the place to that man. Mr Bennet, my former landlord at Linden Garden had given me an excellent reference. "Punctual with payments, clean, very pleasant." He can recommend me, he said.

The estate agent smiles, he has heard he is 'no longer with us'. Strange euphemism.

I take my copy of the lease, say hello to the Pocket brothers, the jewellers, my landlords of the ground floor of 135 Notting Hill Gate, W11.

My staff are tactful. Nothing has ever happened.

I found out: everybody had been interviewed by the police. At my rooms, the Bowmans, also everyone in Notting Hill Gate. Pamela Chamberlain, my employees can't imagine what happened, the business was doing well. My boyfriend, Charles Bradshaw, he was seeing me once or twice a week, and I never told him anything was wrong.

People say that they are glad for me. I wish they wouldn't. They don't know that I am party to a murder. Am I? Could it have been an accident? No, suicide, not him, in three days he was dead. The way the people talk to me, almost as if they are congratulating me! I keep thinking that it's my fault. I don't have the right to condemn someone to die. But I didn't, I only wanted him away, and then the feeling came back, yes, I had felt he would die.

Small businesses are exempt from purchase tax, the turnover is limited. This is for tailors, the bespoke kind, the milliners, the make-do-and-mend shops.

I know I am well above the limit. Hupperts pointed it out to me. I have sold thousands by now. This I find out if I add up the delivery notes of the goods I sold to my customers. I sold several thousands worth. My order book, I very carefully kept all the purchases. I usually paid cash. If it was a large amount they gave me a proforma invoice and then Mr Russell sent a cheque from Sylvia Russell (Kensington). Why did it take so long to get that permission for me to trade?

"This is the past," Mr Sims tells me.

"Am I responsible for the purchase tax to be paid in?"

"Yes, in a way you are. The bank in Hammersmith told me that Mr Russell opened the account with a cheque made out to Sylvia Russell (Kensington). They never knew him, a new account, blocked at present by government." I now use Barclays.

"Can I get into trouble? What can I do? Let the Government have the money in the old account. They can have the lot. I want rid of it. There must be a lot of money left. Give it to charity."

And this was the end of it. Or so I hoped.

I no longer thought about it, the blouses sold well, a lot of money came with prices at 72 shillings and threepence a go.

One day I received a letter from A. Russell, Fife, Scotland. They asked about the estate of Mr John Russell, now deceased. If you steal property, and you died, I am wondering, can your family inherit it? What have you stolen? It was not his money. I ask Mr Sims to deal with it. I don't want to know. It is the past.

Now as everything is in the clear, I feel I would like to expand, open new accounts. I am astonished when the buyers tell me, "We wondered where those beautiful blouses were made. They look handmade, there was no label."

Hupperts claimed my goods were made in their workroom. Hand-finished, the lace trim was sewn on the fabric with a button hole stitch. I had seen this type of work done on my mother's clothes, Haute Couture, from the Wintermeir salon. Handmade buttonholes, seams oversewn, by hand.

I employed three finishers, two were Italian and grumpy Miss Alma Wilmersdorffer was a refugee from Bavaria. She always found something to complain about, mostly the coffee, the instant was no good, or the tea. Coffee and tea were free, no charge. The workroom was too cold, or too hot. I listened patiently, promised to look into it, and then we forgot about it.

I travelled all over England, made a tour to discover the best clothes shop of the town, I let them have my blouses, yes like Haute Couture made, or other separates but at retail production prices.

I enjoyed my travels, stayed the weekends away. Looked at English heritage. Wonderful. I stayed in good hotels, or preferably in inns, pubs. The food was locally sourced and much more 'wholesome'. Hotel food was poor, they had lost their continental trained staff.

When the first floor in 135 Notting Hill Gate became vacant, the Church Embroiderers had left, I took over. Created a sumptuous, so I hoped, showroom, thick carpets, Chinese embroidered panels on the wall in the large room. The smaller room became my stockroom for the finished goods. I had to take on outworkers, mostly foreigners, who had married British soldiers. Those girls had been taught sewing and embroidery by the nuns. So good to keep my standard of work. Harrods put their own labels in my blouses, so did many of their shops, like Dickens and Jones. And when the attic floor was available – it had been empty for many years – I decorated the rooms in cheerful colours and made a staff canteen, free coffee or tea in the smaller room. I still took my coffee in the Linden Café, where I met all the actors and other 'beautiful people'.

Swiss business connection

I had approached the Swiss Embassy Commercial Section in order to be put in touch with manufacturers of Swiss lace and embroideries. Several firms sent their representatives. I was looking for edgings and all-overs for the blouses.

My eyesight, I am very short-sighted like the Japanese, revealed that 'corrections' were needed, the 'brides' were weak, might tear in the laundry. Brides are the connections between the lace. Also, I wanted to avoid the seams needed at the points of the collar.

For theatrical costumes which I produced, I got my inspiration from portraits at the V & A Museum, who were very helpful. I spent many enjoyable hours there. I could produce authentic-looking garments/costumes at a fraction of the price of Beaumonts (one of the leading theatrical costume suppliers). Directors favoured my firm because of the price. Phillip Saville commissioned me to make clothes for his TV programmes and films. A number of actresses were sent to be dressed.

Copies of my lace and embroidery

When too much of my work had been copied, I seriously investigated the lace and embroidery situation.

The Schiffi machines, working on the Jacquard principle, could be adapted. These machines were ten to fifteen meters long and hired for production when required. I had stipulated that designs chosen by me, and/or improved by me, would be exclusive to Sylvia Russell

(Kensington). These machines could be hired by the Swiss Lace manufacturers, mostly situated in St Gall.

This was very costly, and it worked on the principle of every stitch to be duplicated 1000 times. It was said 1000 needles worked in unison. Because of this high cost, the manufacturer's repertoire was very limited, in fact they hoped to receive orders for these established patterns.

My 'improvements' resulted in very good sales for the Swiss, especially in South America. My 'Roses' all-over became a best seller. I had a letter from St Gall, Switzerland, asking me if I would supply some of my garments for an exhibition.

The strengthening of the 'brides' and at the collars for clothing made it more attractive. The memory cards were now used automatically, could copy anything. The very flimsy 'brides' might tear in the laundry, and by catching the iron. Selecting the traditional design, the Points de Venice, and floral pattern, no waste. I arranged that after strengthening, they could be cut, giving the required shape.

That seam of the collar-points deserved a better treatment. With my short-sightedness, like the Japanese I could see what was wrong, what needed attention.

"Strip" lace was common, edging half an inch to three to four inches. For the lace collar on dresses or blouses, the points had to be stitched together, this was looking ugly and amateurish.

In a Swiss Trade article I was called The No. 1 Designer. Well, now, the English making up trade could not copy my work anymore!

Unfortunately the publicity claimed for my designs and my garments was poor; for the shops like Harrods and Hupperts, I was their workroom, they substituted my small label for their own.

The Swiss Chamber of Commerce approached me. Invited me to submit a parcel of my garments, representing the Swiss manufacturers I used, for exhibition of a large fancy show in Grosvenor House, Park Lane, London, W1. Swiss watches, Swiss foods (chocolate), textiles from Basel – and other assortments, etc. etc.

I sent a box of blouses for the exhibition. Almost exactly those of St Gall. The Austrian Trade was to copy a cheaper form of the more high class Swiss St Gall work, situated in Lustenau. I sent a selection, making sure that all my suppliers of the articles were represented.

A great honour to be selected. It showed the name of the lace factory and my name, this on a separate leaflet. A whole room was dedicated to my work, pictures of the Schiffi machines, with photos of the staff working the Jacquard rolls.

Also shown were photos of the famous film stars wearing my blouses and a sixteenth-century portrait of Hans Holbein's gentleman with a lace collar, the lace collar copy also on display.

What publicity!!

Cousin of Pianola embroidered the majority of our blouses – lace trimmed. Antique lace.

Why do I explain this work in detail? Because of the money it brought me, it made me rich.

The Swiss representatives, calling on Sylvia Russell (Kensington), told me that my idea had resulted in large orders. And I still could write orders in German, though with some mistakes – which I corrected with red pencil.

I experimented, using their existing designs, this would cut the cost. Shaped appliqués mainly for dresses were my next project.

I was told that these sold especially well.

Theatrical and retail

I now had two businesses, one the retail trade, and the other theatrical production, including bespoke work for film and TV actresses.

They guarded the secret source of their costumes. Harrods and Hupperts inserted their own labels and claimed the clothes were made in their own workrooms.

For one starlet I made a silver lamé dress with a draped skirt. After filming she sold it to a friend. I said, "Why ever did you do that?" She replied that she couldn't refuse because she was offered such a high price. She usually complained that she had no money.

But the producer needed to re-shoot the scene, so the dress had to be remade because she was the focal point sitting in the front row.

I had originally found the silver lamé in a remnant box. I always looked in those as you never knew what you would find. The nearest match was some silver fabric which looked like it was some Air

Force weather balloon fabric. Unfortunately it was too stiff and wouldn't drape, so I made a copy in shiny cream satin. Not nearly good enough, but it would have to do.

This brought me in contact with the producer who gave me regular TV work as well as dressing actresses, as my charges were a fraction of the cost of Haute Couture companies and the famous theatrical costumiers, Beaumonts.

While I enjoyed designing for theatre and TV, it was seldom lucrative, as I had to travel to hotels or to studios which was time-consuming. I hadn't allowed for that in the bills.

I remembered actresses not by names, but by their measurements. For example Jean Kent had a tiny waist, made to appear even smaller by forty-four inch hips.

I designed a cocktail coat in copper-colour silk which was interlined to give it more body. It was low-necked in order to show off the diamond parure, which had been loaned by a top jeweller. It was delivered by a security guard. If I say so myself, Jean looked stunning. She wanted to buy the coat and they allowed her to do so as it had been custom-made for her.

Another time Phyllis Calvert bought retail one of my lace blouses for the production of *Mandy*. The blouse was trimmed with two rows of Guipure lace roses. It was very beautiful. This caused a bit of an argument with the producer when she put in an inflated invoice to claim the money back; the producer demanded to have the original receipt.

Often there would be rush jobs, I had to pay my staff double wages, taxis home, as well as dinner. I sent out for meals from Mr Levi's pub across the road; he specialised in steaks.

There were many actresses I designed for: Margaret Lockwood, Margaret Rutherford and Diana Dors.

Mr Holzer, the owner of Hupperts, asked me to make a blouse taking inspiration from Diana's dress, which she modelled for a full-page spread in *Vogue*. It had a Broiderie Anglaise frill around the neck. For a production of *Blythe Spirit*, featuring Margaret Rutherford, who was a delight as the eccentric clairvoyant, the director commissioned me to design a green ghostly costume for the character of Elvira. He said it had to be fluid and float like a cloud.

I purchased a length of silk organza and a length of silk chiffon. On the costume, large sections of the fabrics were attached at the shoulders and wrists. I would have liked the actress to be nude underneath, but she refused. Body stockings were available but I didn't know where to purchase them. So I was forced to custom-make a sheer one which I dyed flesh-colour using tea.

I finally managed to solve the problem of the fluidity on stage by sending home for my vacuum cleaner. By reversing the suction to blow I achieved the desired floaty effect. Better than the room fan I had at first used, which was not sufficient.

Margaret Rutherford was delightful as the dotty clairvoyant.

Easter Sunday

It was eight o'clock in the morning. The bell, very loud and insistent, had awoken me. My boyfriend Maurice had come up from Brighton, where he had a lectureship, he was holding a very large bunch of flowers. "I called at Covent Gardens on the way." So large, I needed a bucket. I had promised to visit Mrs Stein, she is not very well. "She can have half of the flowers."

We set off, walking through Holland Park. The Steins lived in Pembroke Gardens, on the other side of Kensington High Street.

When we opened her bedroom door, she called out, "Sylvia, Sylvia, I can see the baby."

Mrs Stein was supposed to be clairvoyant. How could she? It was the first time I had had intercourse in months. I had not missed any periods.

It was a short visit; we did not want to tire her. I thought it was very strange she had said she could see the baby. That would be wonderful, I was thirty-four years old, it was time I had a baby, before I was too old.

Now I had my periods, as usual, but my breasts were sore. Perhaps there is a baby. My very slim waist was expanding, I got a better girdle. But there was a second period. My boyfriend said, "Get an examination from your doctor." Doctor pronounced me definitely not pregnant. Mrs Stein had said she can see the baby, it was only two hours after we had had intercourse.

I was travelling for Sylvia Russell (Kensington) by night train, to an appointment in Edinburgh at 10 o'clock. They were good customers, the best shop in Edinburgh, Forsyth. Mrs Jeffrey, Maurice's analyst had come for tea. He told her that I hoped I was pregnant, but had already had two periods. She explained to us about phantom pregnancies, if the wife wants it. Therefore Sylvia gets the signs.

"I know a good gynaecologist," she continued, "he is also a gland specialist, he will tell you why you are gaining weight. I will make an appointment for you." She phoned him. "Dr Karnicki will see you today, he had a cancellation." I went to Harley Street, oh, a very posh waiting room. The examination took a very long time. "You can get dressed now. You are pregnant, but only just."

"I have to travel tonight, with the sleeper train, to Scotland."

I'd return about 6 o'clock to Kings Cross. Dr. Karnicki said, "Give me a ring from the Kings Cross Station. I shall wait for you in my consultation room. We have to have a discussion."

Dr Karnicki explained to me that he thought I would miscarry. My womb was open. "If you want this child, you have to be very careful. You live on the third floor, go very careful on the steps. Eat only small meals. Avoid travel."

Avoid travel? I do the sales, but I think I will manage. My clever little girl clerk, Miss Barnes, she was a treasure. She said she had never slept in posh hotels before, she was looking forward to it. "They know me," she said, "from the telephone, I always give my name when I talk to customers."

I had my third, then my fourth period. Dr Karnicki said, "Every day is one day more. Your womb is not closed, but you are still pregnant." I saw him every week. I recalled Mrs Stein had seen the baby, on its first day to earth, when it came to us. Mrs Stein is clairvoyant. Yes, she is.

I had been frightened, no men, no lovers, since Keith had stopped loving me. Was I to be married? Maurice was a lecturer at Brighton. He wanted a marriage. Mrs Jeffrey told me it was not good being unmarried, illegitimates were disadvantaged, in spite of 'flower power'.

Mrs Jeffrey was 'pushing' me for a wedding. Maurice saw her every week, her fees, not standard, became very high. When the baby was at four and a half months of life, I gave in, I consented to be married.

For the baby, I prepared the most beautiful layette. The baby basket has Swiss embroidered trimmings. The dark green canopy, to keep the sun out, or the rain, was in French grosgrain. I bought hand-embroidered pillow cases from Fortnum and Mason. I had the second bedroom decorated in peach colour – not knowing if it was a boy or a girl. Cuddly toys, beautifully handmade, artistic ones, a lion and a monkey bought from Harrods were sitting in wait on a shelf.

The baby was due on Christmas Day, nine months from the Easter Sunday prediction.

Amanda's birth

Dr Karnicki had worked it out. We expected the baby on Christmas Day. Everything was prepared. We were all very happy.

I wanted a Christmas tree, a real one, with needles. Shepherd's Bush Market, that's where they were selling them. It was very foggy, I put a scarf over my mouth. Maurice scolded me, "I should not have allowed you, going out in this weather, but you know what Sylvia wants, Sylvia gets."

It was Christmas Eve. On the continent it is considered the most Holy day of the year. Lovely, to have a baby born on the most Holy Day – Heilige Nacht. A baby conceived on Easter Sunday. My baby had other plans, it was more sensible than its would-be mother.

I had developed serious breathing difficulties, Maurice phoned Dr Karnicki, he had said stay in touch. We did not expect a house call on Christmas Day.

He smiled, "The baby is clever, it wants to wait. Keep in touch."

Baby announced herself at 6 a.m. on 3rd January 1957. Mrs Champ packed my suitcase. She has looked after me for five years, as my housekeeper. She comes every morning, does my shopping, talks to Wednesday the cat. Wednesday is a very special cat, she deserves that I write a whole chapter about her, I'll do that later. Mrs Champ does not like Maurice, she puts up with him, so she says.

The nursing home is in Exhibition Road. My room is small. The furniture is shabby, "could do with a bit of paint, with the amount they charge". I agreed with Mrs Champ, but I am not interested in the furniture. I never thought it would hurt so much. I promise to phone her as soon as baby arrives, she has to go home to give her brother his tea, and feed Wednesday.

Where is Doctor Karnicki? He is still in Harley Street.

"You are not ready. He does not want us to give you gas or any other analgesic – not good for the baby. He will come later."

I can't push, I am too exhausted, I am fully dilated. Dr Karnicki gives me an injection. The baby just shot out, she is so small. Cries three times, quite loud. She is perfectly clean. "Don't wash her, just a little oil." She weighs five pounds, less one ounce. She is twenty-one inches long, very skinny. The time is 8.37 a.m. Thursday 3rd January 1957.

I am surprised she looks so pretty, like a little doll. I had been told that newborns looked like dwarves, or little old men, wrinkled. Then the phone rings, 8.40 a.m., Maurice. The nurse tells him, "We're not finished, come in half an hour." She is talking about the afterbirth, I presume. Dr Karnicki said it was very large, surprisingly so. I was told my womb had never closed, perhaps the afterbirth closed it. I don't talk now. I feel euphoric, heavenly, yes. Maurice arrives.

'Amanda' looks like his family. He was waiting impatiently to view his daughter. She is sleeping now. The doctor tells him she is a healthy baby, everything is perfect.

Mrs Champ arrives next morning, to admire the baby. "What are you calling her?"

"Not yet decided."

She tells me Wednesday, my little cat, misses me. Mrs Champ has to show her, by opening my bedroom door. "See, she is not here."

Dr and Mrs Stein visit me on the first day of the baby. Mrs Stein tells me our baby looks exactly like little Helen, the twin her son lost, just a year ago. Helen was still-born. I never knew that there had been twins.

The staff are very kind to us. When Maurice arrives at lunchtime, they bring him a tray with a good dinner. I am upset, I want to feed my baby, but there is no milk. The baby knows where the milk should be, she nuzzles on my breast. No milk comes. I hold the bottle on my breast, she sucks it.

Mrs Jeffrey comes to visit. "You are not feeding the baby?"

"No, I always intended to feed her, I want to be a good mother, I have no milk."

"Sometimes it takes a long time. If you really want to feed her, you must try harder."

I start to cry, I am very, very upset.

Mrs Jeffrey says it is a psychological. Because I am working, want to continue working, the body does not produce milk.

I tell Dr Karnicki, he is annoyed. "That woman again! It is glandular inefficiency. We have produced a perfectly healthy baby, a pretty baby. Are you not satisfied? You should be grateful. There are good milk foods on the market, she won't go short."

I tell him that my great-grandmother had no milk; she had a wet nurse for her children. I also recall that some other members of my father's family had a wet nurse.

My mother had an abundance of milk. My brother Arnold was very small. Mother was only four feet eleven inches. The doctor asked if she would consent to give her surplus to a baby which was dying, for lack of milk (no artificial milk available at that time.) Karl, our coachman waited in front of the house, to bring the milk, wrapped up together with a hot water bottle to bring to the sick child, which survived.

Maurice had bought a little book of names and their meaning, both male and female. Starting at A, the explanation and origin of the name. When he comes to Amanda he loved it, we both call out "That's it!" Amanda – the Loved one.

Amanda Irma, after my late mother, and the name day Saint Genevieve, Saint of Paris.

Returning home, Wednesday is delighted, follows me around. She comes to the cot and purrs, purrs. She recognized the baby belongs to all of us, her as well. Wednesday, my very special cat.

Sylvia Russell (Kensington) is doing well. One of the Italian girls, a former school teacher, manages. Irene Zinircynska, a Polish girl, is the cutter. Miss Barnes comes every day to my flat with the post and gets the instructions.

I am taking a holiday at home for three months, until Amanda is a little bigger. She is a most hungry baby, never sick, never vomits food, and doesn't cry. Only calls, but does not cry.

Mrs Champ says she has nothing to cry about, when everybody loves her, even the cat loves her!

She is a greedy feeder. A shepherd told me, when a little lamb is born underweight it becomes a greedy feeder.

Is Amanda like a little lamb? She weighed twelve pounds at three months, normal weight, at her christening in March.

Wednesday, my little cat

Wednesday my little cat was very curious. I allowed her to stay. Not everyone was welcome to Wednesday. Wednesday knew the difference between workmen and friends, even if friends were dirty or in old clothes. When workmen came, Wednesday hid in a cupboard, or behind the settee. How did she become my little cat? Walking home I had seen this kitten, looking through a garbage can. I said, "You won't find anything in that bin, it's only paper and ashes!"

The kitten jumped down and walked after me, about ten paces back. When I opened my house door, she was in, whoosh, and sat at the front door of my flat, meowing, meowing, meowing.

"You must be hungry." I could only find calves' liver, my dinner, in my fridge, it went quickly, gone. I put down a saucer of milk. The kitten did not touch it; the bowl of water, however, was very welcome. It had started to rain. It's not stopping. "Well you can stay for tonight." I opened the door next morning, she was gone. That was it. Sentimental, I must be, I walked by the rubbish bin again. Why should it be there? I had told her that it was no good, no food there.

At 2 a.m. in the morning, I was awoken by loud meows. Finally it registered in my brain. The kitten! I went down, opened the door, she knew the way, waited at my door. I gave her some food, some water, took her back down. She came back to my door.

"Ok, we'll find out if you belong to anyone." I enquired at the police station next morning; put a note on our garden gate. Later, I put an advert in the local paper.

The policeman said, "When they find out it's a female, they throw them out. If we take her, we can only keep her for two days."

"What happens then?" "Oh, we have her put down." This was before we had the charities dealing with animals. The veterinary services also were primitive, "We have to put her down," he repeats. "It's a shame."

I could not let that happen to her. I called her Wednesday, I know that is not a cat name, but she had found me on a Wednesday, when I took her home with me and allowed her to stay.

Returning home from work, still a block away, I could hear her. She sits on the window sill, meowing. Then is at the door of my flat, greeting me very loud.

My gramophone was of great interest to her, she had various tastes: Her favourites: Brahms, Beethoven; Mozart was best. She sat quietly in front, listening. Do cats appreciate music? Classical? I had never heard of that before.

She likes Mrs Champ. Mrs Champ cooks her lights and liver, fresh from the butcher. She will not eat the tinned cat food, sniffs at it and walks away. My little cat, Wednesday.

Hupperts

Huppert rings me at home. "Why is your stuff selling in the shop next door?"

"They are not, I am sure you are wrong."

"There are several of your blouses in the window, next door to us."

"I don't believe it, why don't you send in one of your girls to buy a blouse, it won't be mine, you can then examine it."

I am annoyed and surprised how much my work gets copied. But selling it next door to Hupperts! Young Mr Holzer rings back. "The same material, yes. But seams are overlocked, machine-made buttonholes, you don't have those machines. What can we do about it?"

I tell him that last week when I bought pyjamas in Shaftesbury Avenue, the owner of the shop approached me. She said, "I better tell you, a girl came in and offered me blouses, she had a boxful. When I looked at them, I recognised them from Huppert's window, I believe you make them. I thought they might be stolen. Of course I refused to buy them from her. Her name was Henny."

Henny had been one of my outworkers. She had an overlocker. My staff told me that Henny manufactured now. Of course it was easy to take off the pattern of my blouses, before machining, from the cut-out pieces. The Berwick Street shop. There was a label on the goods I had bought from Berwick Stationery. Young Mr Holzer said again, "What can we do about it?"

"I won't buy there any more, that's for certain."

The material comes from Switzerland, St Gall, I believe. I will buy direct from Switzerland. I contacted the Swiss Embassy Trade Section. They were very helpful. I asked to be put in touch with the manufacturers, to get samples or find out if they had an agent, possibly in London. They also sent photos of Guipure Laces. These were more suitable for church vestment or curtain trims. Some more Point de Venise, or copies of seventeenth or eighteenth century collars, I had seen on paintings. My father had a lace collection. I remembered these laces very well.

I ordered those I considered suitable, a sample, most needed adapting, therefore I sent them sketches. Yes, I am good at drawing, I always have been. I selected two firms.

It will be difficult for them to copy my designs now! I can stay exclusive. The allover, material by the yard, in thin cotton lawn came from Lustenau, just over the border in Austria. It was cheaper, but I preferred the dearer, better Swiss quality.

I had to 'improve' the lace, the Guipure Edgings. Their 'brides', the links connecting, needed strengthening, so as not to tear in the laundry. I send them sketches, enlarged in detail. I designed floral edgings, rose patterns, daisies, all kinds, also Point de Venise type edgings. My condition was exclusive, it must be exclusive, only to be sold to Sylvia Russell (Kensington), exclusive to England. They told me that my designs sold very well in other countries, particularly in South America. Then there came a stroke of luck for me.

The British Government reduced imports. Only firms who had imported previously could now get a license to bring in the goods. That stopped the others from getting these goods. My silks and damask from Lyons, France, my Swiss embroideries and lace, and also the Swiss fabric, my georgette. Most of the high class stores in England belonged to the Harrods Group. My regular customers. They took sixty per cent of my output. Next came Hupperts – naturally – then some high-class boutiques, or 'the best shop in town'. Grundees of Jersey was a good customer. I took their buyer to Levi's pub across the road for dinner, and if she had time, for an evening theatre show. I was now well established.

Maurice came up from Brighton every week. He took Amanda out for treats. He asks my little clerk, Miss Barnes, to do the typing of his articles and also the books he is working on at present. Miss Barnes refused. "I am busy, this is not my job." Maurice sacked her.

"I am not employed by you." She is right. Maurice made a scene.

Miss Barnes did not turn up for work. There was a letter, she would stay until I could replace her, Mr Hurst had no rights, he did not employ her.I was devastated. We got on so well, the staff loved her. I put up an advert for a clerk in the showcase at Lyons, and also in a newspaper. To my surprise, a nice man came, "I read the advert in the Lyons showcase. Is the job still vacant? I am Captain Lewer. Not Royal Navy, I had a commercial boat, a small one, I did all the clerical work myself."

"The pay is small," I said. "Why do you want the job?"

"I am retired now, bored at home, the hours would suit me."

How lucky I was, he took over, my staff, the foreign girls, the Italians, spoiled him, made him coffee, brought his sandwiches. And in return he spoiled me.

My brother Arnold, on his visit from Canada, said, "It gives your firm a 'standing' to employ a man of this calibre."

Maurice had found a girl who wanted to be his typist. She was a primary school teacher from Todmouth, now working in London. Amanda's Saturday outings became irregular. Amanda fretted."Where's my daddy?"

Amanda said her first words at only ten months old. She soon had a vocabulary; prominent was 'mau', not mama or daddy. 'Mau' meant animal. There was a mau, mau – cat. Mau birdie, mau woof. Trees were important, were studied by Amanda, sitting in her pushchair. She was taken every day to Holland Park, around the corner. Mr Peacock, why is he so beautiful, and Mrs Peacock only brown? One can hear his cry, his talk, a mile off. Horrible. Let's see if the pussies are out, on the little pond, they go fishing for the goldfish. The park keeper put a wire net over the pond, pussies put their paws through the net, were sometimes successful.

Nursy, my cousin Elizabeth, a trained children's nurse, looked after Amanda (Mandy) in the afternoon. Auntie, now called Auntie Betty, my housekeeper, was much loved.

Mandy was almost two years old, she didn't crawl, refused to walk. "Up, up, up. I don't like it." One had to put her back on the settee. The doctor, when I called, said, "Nothing wrong with her legs." She has by now almost a full set of teeth, and what a vocabulary! The doctor says, "We can't be clever in everything. She'll do it in her own time."

Eventually, Mandy got up, ran around, perfectly, without help, at two years of age, in the park. She patted the dogs, even the big ones, without fear. Mandy asked me to give her Panzers Frankfurt sausages, to feed the dogs. Mandy tells me, "There were two big penguins. Big, big, in the park." Two nuns, I find out!!

Wednesday (our cat) liked lights and liver, cooked by Auntie for her. Auntie did not like cats, but Wednesday was different. She never drank milk, only water. She liked to supplement her diet with the Tradescantia, also called spiderwort or wandering sailor, which was kept on the kitchen windowsill. She ate one pot of these per month. Her sand box was kept on the veranda, used by her for urine. The excreta was disposed of in the front garden, neatly. One had to wait for her to finish, at the open door, because she was so afraid to be locked out, and would run back in even before finished. Who had closed the front door on her? Don't close the door.

Every month or so I bought Wednesday her new toy, a little mouse made of real fur. I hid it, anywhere in the flat. She found it, brought it to me, to show. The mouse lasted no more than a month, it was chewed to bits. Wednesday did not play with the ball Mrs Champ had bought for her. However, the ball was of no interest, perhaps it did not smell right. Mrs Champ said, "I don't like cats; that foul tom of my neighbour's stinks. Wednesday is different."

Once we went on holiday for a week. We had put Wednesday in the much recommended 'cat hotel'. Bringing her back to us, they said Wednesday was fretting, she would not eat, "until we put the food into her own dishes, luckily you had given them to us". Wednesday brushed against my trousers, then went around the whole flat, purrs at Mandy, comes back to me, purrs. I tell Wednesday, "I'll never put you out again, anywhere. I promise." Mrs Champ offers to cat-sit in the future. "I can do some ironing, or special cleaning. This poor thing, she missed us."

Christmas Holidays

My staff asked me if it was possible to have a longer holiday over Christmas, telling me there was a problem with school holidays and the nurseries were closed. My order book was full, orders due for delivery by February. "Why not?" I said. We were doing well. Orders were to be delivered after the sales. "We will close for two weeks. You have the Christmas Day, Boxing Day, and your December bonus. I'll pay you half-pay for two weeks. No, don't worry, you will still get your summer holidays."

One of my Italian girls, a former school teacher, was acting as manager and kept the work book. I was lucky with my staff, all good girls, honest, reliable.

On 20th December, we 'locked up'. I gave the keys to Mr Pocket, my landlord. I had wanted to visit Susan and Richard in Philadelphia USA, this would give me the chance.

Amanda

I am very happy to stay at home, looking after my little darling daughter. Mrs Champ helps me to bath her, she is so wriggly, obviously she liked the water. The last feed is at 11 o'clock, she sleeps through the night, wakes up at 8 a.m. She calls quite loudly to let me know she is ready and starving. She does not cry. "What an easy child," people say. "We were up half the night with ours."

I am still sorry I cannot feed her, Dr Karnicki scolds me, I must be grateful. My baby gets nappy rash. Why? I have the nappy service, this should not happen. I use gauze and terry towelling. One is not allowed to have laundry hanging outside, not in Holland Park, a very posh district, it's against one's lease. The Harley Street Baby specialist is sent by Dr Karnicki. "Nothing wrong, sensitive skin, use Morhulin, a very thin application. It takes four days." He is right, the rash does not come back, ever. I recommend this cream, to anyone who needs it – magic!

Laugh or Cry

I am content to do my work, my designing. Again I am travelling all over England. I talk very little, do not take part in the conversations going on. I go into the kitchen, to wash dishes. My husband Maurice calls me stupid. "Yes, I am," I think. When I was young I used to be considered clever. I get easily frightened. Some music, such as march music, really frightens me. It makes me shiver, then I realise it is the music the Nazis used for their meetings, the Hitler Youth for their demonstration walks.

My husband advises me, "You should go to an analyst, go to Mrs Jeffrey, it might eliminate your fears of the past."

On my first interview she makes me talk about my parents, especially the difficult relationship with my mother. I talk about my grandmother, father's side, how nasty she was to my mother. She is six feet tall, the matriarch, my mother a dainty four feet eleven inches. The grandmother always in floor-length black garments, my mother in the latest fashions, purchased twice a year from Haute Couture. I am supposed to be the favourite of the grandmother, it is said I look like her. Suddenly I realise she is the reason I cannot bond with my mother, she prevents it, has prevented it. To know this is a revelation. After all, this Miss Jeffrey knows what she is doing.

Mrs Jeffrey suggests three weekly sessions. I don't like her, why should I tell her my secrets?

I say, "I have not got time for three weekly sessions, I am busy working."

I do not say I don't want to spend this money, this is an enormous cost. This was my only interview with her. If I want to face my past, my inner life, I have decided I will write down, as honestly as I am able.

I begin my book, later called *Laugh or Cry*, from childhood, as this is my honest self-analysis. Surprisingly I can recall the childhood; I can hear everything said, verbatim, I can see it. I write it down, sometimes from five o'clock in the morning. I also see my childhood in my dreams again.

The march music does not disturb me any more. I hate, yes, hate, the grandmother for destroying my relationship with my mother. My parents are dead, I cannot repair the wrongs. I do not type, my writing is long hand, now quite a lot of pages. I must number them.

What is troubling me? Not my early childhood, not my relationship with my parents. How come that ordinary good people are turned into monsters?? The Transition. A report about what has happened in Germany.

In 2006, my first book, *Laugh or Cry* was published. I donated free copies to all secondary schools and colleges in the north-east of England, in the hope that my true and honest account of my childhood in Germany during the rise of Nazism is never forgotten.

Family Gril

The Red Cross answered my letter by return. It was easy to find my family after the war. I had given them Ettiene Gril's name. My late Uncle Arthur, my father's younger brother, had worked together in Parish with the Ettiene, who was a famous writer, who had received the Légion d'honneur. Both their children had grown up together.

Jaques Gril joined the Maquis, and Eva Fleischer also worked in the French Underground, Elle Fait la Route. Preparing the way for our parachutists and other heroes (spies), to enable them to return to England.

Eva had married Jaques, they had two small boys. Eva and I were very close, we felt like loving sisters. I visited them often, the Silver Arrow was running every day, from Victoria to Paris. I preferred to use the air service when tickets were on offer, cheap weekend tickets by British Air. The air station was in Kensington High Street, very convenient for me – just a walk away.

It was wonderful to be with my family. We had a lot in common, our interests were the same, Arts and Crafts, especially pottery. I was a member of the Oriental Ceramic Society. Jaques was a potter, he sculpted mostly animals for a Moslem potter who was not allowed to portray animals because of his religion. I had studied comparative religion, I wanted to know what I felt – had to know what I felt – for several years. Our father had brought us up non-denom, he had told us that (modern) religions were just like different languages, there was one God for all of us, different aspects for different people. Jaques, Eva and I talked about religion for many hours.

Arnold, my eldest brother, was living in Toronto. He was a well-established accountant and business consultant, and had inherited my mother's love for opera. He attended performances and other music delights in different towns, even different countries.

We were meeting in Paris. When I stayed with Eva and Jaques, I had booked Arnold into the Hotel Tholoze, Rue Tholoze, as he had promised to take me to the Moulin Rouge which was nearby. The show was a disappointment to us, I had hoped for a spectacle, a creation, like Toulon L'entre. It was cheap, sexy and fully of smutty jokes – oh-la-la! I presume it was directed for an American clientele. The Paris Opera was not in season, so Arnold decided on Salzburg in Austria. He took me to Les Halles, to taste the French Onion soup, which was served in the early morning hours, for the porters. While we waited, I asked him why he had not married.

"I think I missed the boat," he said. "At my age there are only divorcees and widows. There was once a girl, a medical student. We loved each other. I told her I could not offer marriage until I could afford to keep her, suitably. I had not yet passed my accountancy exams. 'Alas, to marry you is my greatest wish.' She would not wait, she married someone else. What about you?"

"My boyfriend could not get a divorce, although they had not lived together for a long time. She told him she would not let him see his two sons if he divorced her. He said he was not fair to me, I should be married. So he gave me the push." Two sad stories.

Trip to the USA

Cooks Travel Agency in Notting Hill Gate had been very helpful. "Flying, or do you want to go by boat? There is the *Mauretania*, the sister ship to the *Queen Elizabeth*. You would enjoy the experience. Friends persuaded me, *Mauretania* it was. I booked A deck, second class. A special holiday programme for the season.

I had booked my taxi, allowing good time to take the boat train. Unfortunately the Westminster Bridge was closed, owing to roadworks – diversion.

I was frightened – would we arrive on time? "You missed the train," the porters shouted.

"No I did not, there is another in five minutes." I grabbed my cases. "Hold on, hold on."

"We'll try," said a corpulent porter. We both ran. Yes, I caught the train, I managed to get in at the back, into the goods wagon.

I shared my compartment with an Australian girl. She told me she had missed her boat before, and now had to pay extra: "The *Mauretania* costs more, that leaves me quite short."

I said, "I am sure the purser on the ship will contact your family, to arrange some funds . Hopefully," I added.

"Do you really think so?"

"Yes, I am sure," I said, but I was just guessing.

Arriving in Southampton Customs, my papers were correct. "Entry to USA unlimited times."

I was glad I did not have to share my cabin, there were two beds. I studied the folder with the ship's program, lying on my table. First port of call in France, I had not realised this…where??

Meal times, how to call your Steward, Entertainment, in case of fire the exits.

Dinner would be in two hours, I decided to explore. Long passages, I found many. Numbers, so many numbers. Very confusing. There were staircases, locked up, with signs to first class. I returned to my cabin. I rang for tea. The steward told me it was now cocktail hour, but he would be pleased to bring me tea in the cocktail bar. Should he show me the way? "Later, thank you, I'll have to change."

It was common knowledge that one 'dressed up' on boat journeys, especially liners. I put on my jacket, own make, of Lyons Damask with Silver Thread, as supplied to Harrods Stores Evening Dress Departments. I followed other guests walking in the corridor, I presumed they were going to the cocktail party. I was slowly sipping my glass of Rhine wine, when I was approached by a middle-aged man. "Excuse me, are you Sylvia Hurst? I recognised you from the trade papers. I always look at the passenger list when I travel, in case I know someone. I must say, it was not a good photo, you are much prettier. May I introduce myself? I also am a designer, like you. My work rooms are in New York. Here is my card." I did not like the look of him, he was ugly, and so pushy.

"Thank you," I put the card in my handbag.

"Don't go away, I would like to talk to you, let's sit here." I did not want to talk to him, but what could I do? I sat down. He started to quiz me, where did I sell, were they buying individually or through the head office?

Nosy bugger, he is pumping me for information. I tried to get away, saying I had arranged to meet my Australian friend. I had not, but I needed an excuse to get away from this man.

"Nice to have met you," I said. The orchestra was strumming up, next door, the Maître D, standing at the door, gave me a flyer with tonight's performances.

I made my way to the dining room. I was shown to my table, a small table for two. The buffet was beautifully arranged, very artistic. I chose my hors d'oeuvres.

Returning to my table I found a small girl sitting there.

"Excuse me," I said, "this seat is taken for an Australian lady."

She answered, "I was told she joined her Australian buddies, so they gave me this table." She could see I was not happy about this new arrangement.

"I am going home for the holidays, my school is closed. I spent two days in London with an aunt, but she did not want me over Christmas."

I put my plate down. "The buffet is very good."

"I have ordered soup, and the salmon salad, so I don't want the buffet as well."

"Have you any brothers or sisters?" I must make conversation.

"Yes, there is a new baby, and a new mummy. That's why I was sent to England to school."

I said, "I am going to see my sister and my brother, I have not seen them for a long time." We were busy eating, no conversation needed.

The orchestra played the latest tunes, the girl knew them, she hummed, then some classical music, which I knew. The girl had spotted on the next table a knickerbocker glory. "I am going to have this – scrumptious!" I chose apple pie, bad choice, the pastry was raw.

I was tired, "Don't stay up too late." I had been up since 5 a.m. packing. I said, "I am for bed."

There was a knock at my cabin door. "Sorry, Madam, I have to screw the porthole shut." Why is that? I am A deck. "There is a storm brewing. Sometimes the waves are fifty foot high."

I put my bedside lamp on, it was dark outside, noisy. I felt queasy, it is only 6 a.m. Better go back to sleep. No, to the basin, this was the chicken, or the hors d'oeuvre. I am better now, rinse my mouth out. At 8 a.m. I rang for the steward. "May I have some tea?"

"Don't fill your cup more than half full," advised the steward. "They said it would get worse."

"Oh dear, I hope not."

"I have been assigned to look after you, I am your stewardess. You did not go for breakfast."

"Oh no, I could not," I said.

"Well the dining room was almost empty, shame, all that nice food." She brought me tea and toast, I had the tea.

"There were only a few for lunch," she reported. "Do try, just a little, of the toast."

"This is the third day now, you really must try."

"Have you any peppermint tea?"

"What a Christmas! The band has given up, I think they should be used to it by now." The dining room is half closed, because it's empty.

On Boxing Day we got into calmer water, the wind stopped howling. "Good programmes, also a film," said the stewardess.

"Thank you, I'll miss it, but I shall try the dining room." The band played Christmas music. I was told my table companion had been in earlier, gone to the film performance. I ordered chicken soup with rice, hoping I could manage this food. The second performance of the film was for 8 pm. I might as well go, I joined the small queue. The people were leaving. The Designer was amongst them, he had spotted me, he waved. Half-heartedly I waved back. The film was about Father Christmas in New York, I had seen it before. Boring. After a while I got up, went back to my cabin.

I was still 'under the weather' so I crawled back into my bunk. I must have fallen asleep. I woke up, there was someone moving around in my cabin. I fumbled for the light. It was that horrid man, the Designer. I screamed.

"I missed you," he said.

"Are you better now? Oh, you are so beautiful!"

"Get out, get out," I screamed. He came nearer, tried to kiss me, "I'll ring the bell." Yes, I rang it.

"I thought you wanted me to visit you."

I rang the bell again, he saw it. He scuttled out, closing the door behind him. I was shaking. The stewardess came. "May I have some coffee?"

"Don't forget to put your cases out, for collection," she reminded me

Arrival in the USA, in the harbour, I had not expected the Statue of Liberty. She was very large, quite imposing. One was required to leave one's cases outside the cabin door, label and cabin number firmly attached, to be picked up later on terra firma. I waited and waited, surely they would bring my cases. I went to enquire. A search was made. Finally my cases were found. They told me they could not understand why they had been found in a different section of the ship. Who had moved them? Yes, I had certainly followed the instructions I was given.

My passport was stamped. The Customs official seemed interested in the very beautiful doll I had brought for my little niece, Irene. It had real hair which one could style and plait.

I remembered Margot, my mother's Jumeau doll, very precious, who also had real hair, a kid-leather body, and exquisite clothing, all handmade. I had brought with me the bills for all the presents, the doll, two large woollen rugs and the antique miniature domino set, which was made of real ivory and ebony. I knew Arnold would appreciate it on a long journey, it could fit into a coat pocket.

The Customs official was kind to me. He said, "You know there is an important restriction. This doll, you bought it in a sale?" Its cost had been many times over the allowance.

Arnold and Richard were waiting for me. "You are about the last one out, we waited for hours."

I answered, "They could not find my suitcases, they got mislaid."

"Where shall we go to eat? I hope you are nice and hungry," said Richard.

"I don't know, where do you suggest we go?"

"Do you want Jewish food, French food, or perhaps we could go to the seafood place, the one with the giant crabs?"

I was intrigued.

"Fish, lobster, giant crabs, that's all they do."

"Let's go there, I've never seen giant crabs before."

When we arrived we were given a white plastic apron, to tie under the chin. There were hammers on the table, one for each customer. "To open the legs."

These legs were huge, I did not realise crabs came in these giant sizes. I was intrigued, but felt a bit squeamish. "I'll show you how to do it," said Richard. I watched and learned. Bang, bang, the legs cracked open. There was an assortment of chips in small bowls on our table. Arnold and Richard were very efficient in demolishing the legs, not I; the legs looked so ugly, it put me off. The ice cream served was quite delicious. What an experience!

Richard left us, he was driving back to Philadelphia where he lived. I was to follow in two days by train. Arnold had booked both of us into a downtown hotel. We sat in the lounge.

Arnold and I had been very close in our childhood, it felt the same now, for both of us, after so many years. We told each other about our life, our work, our interests. Yes we liked the same American authors, *How to Kill a Mocking Bird*, Jack Kerouac, *On the Road*, Jack London, *White Fang*, the Wolf stories, J D Salinger, *Catcher in the Rye*.

"I have tickets for the opera, tonight 27th December 1954, it is the premiere of the *Saint of Bleeker Street*, by Gian Carlo Manotti. I suppose you have not heard of him?"

"Oh, yes I have, I went to his *Consul* when it came to London, that was in 1951. It was frightening, he got it so right, the anxiety. Everyone waiting for the visa, which never came, and the secret police, just like the Nazis. Some people in the audience cried, they were so moved."

"I did not see *The Consul*," said Arnold. "I don't know if it came to New York after London."

We had front stalls, I was grateful, because I am so short-sighted. My hearing is perfect.

The next day Arnold took me shopping. The department stores were fantastic, similar to our Harrods, but much, much cheaper. I did not want to spend the small allowance the British government had allowed one, however, Arnold was generous. There was Macey's, Grimbels – a fantastic store, and we admired the fantastic jewels in Tiffany's window.

"It was the Grimbels who gave the deposit for Uncle Kuno's and Aunt Clara's release from Nazi prison, direct into Himmler's pocket, in 1938. You ought to visit Aunt Clara. Uncle Kuno has been dead a long time, but the old girl is still alive."

"Perhaps on my return visit."

Arnold put me on the Philadelphia train. I had been most impressed by the wonderful architecture of the railway station. "That's Roosevelt's doing," said Arnold, "to create work in the 1930s."

Richard's wife June was the private secretary of the Dean of the Philadelphia University. Their apartment was ground floor, small, I slept on the settee in the living room.

I gave June the beautiful wool rug. "Our car is heated," she said, "the flat is thermostatically controlled. I suppose one can use this rug when one watches ball games, but Richard and I never go to ball games."

I had brought the wrong present. "Would you like to choose one of my blouses I have brought?" She looked, said, "I would never wear those, no thank you." I looked at the blouse she was wearing, exactly like a school uniform blouse, with a Peter Pan collar. Wrong again! I was to stay with them for a few days. Visit Susan and her family, living a few blocks away.

Orange boy, the cat, was friendly. "He is not ours, he is a stray, he makes the rounds for foods. One can't let him stay for the night, or he thinks you own him, one has to chase him out."

Both Richard and June were working, "I thought the university is closed for the holidays?"

"Yes, but we have extra conferences, and I am the hostess, the Dean is not married."

Richard had all the latest prize-winning novels of American literature, good for him, good for me.

It was bright sunshine, I decided to visit Susan, I am good at maps, but this was easy, streets straight and numbered. I had no cap, no hat, conned by the sunshine, my ears fell off. Irene, Susan's little girl, was delightful. "Thank you for the doll, Auntie Sylvia, but will you read to me my new book?" These were animal stories. I tried to read them in very different tones and making faces, I never knew I had it in me.

Her husband Philip came home for lunch. "I am not on duty," he said. He was a doctor. His specialty was osteopathy in the local famous hospital, but he also had his own practice, downtown. He was very proud of Susan, told me how she had helped to stretch out his GI wartime G allowance to finish his medical studies. "Money was tight, I'll tell you how Susan coped."

Susan interrupted, "You can't believe how wasteful they are at the local supermarket in the butchery department. They still are." She showed me three chicken carcasses in her fridge. "They cut off the legs and the breast, the rest is wasted. I can get three carcasses for twenty cents, enough to make coq-au-vin."

Philip said, "She made all the fancy dishes they serve in the French restaurants, chicken in mushroom in white sauce, and Italian style with red wine."

"I've learnt it, there are good cookery books, our mother never let me help, and you certainly did all the cooking for both of us."

Susan very much liked the blouse I gave to her, she said, "We can't buy anything as good here, you ought to export them."

Philip was very pleased with the beautiful Scottish plaid rug, he said the size was large enough to cover him, when he had a rest on the settee. Philip took me aside, he said, "Don't talk about your family, Susan is very delicate, she gets really upset."

I answered, "I never talk about it, not to anyone, not even to Richard. I am so glad he survived this dreadful holocaust."

Philip said, "She had a nervous breakdown once, she had to go to hospital. This upset her more, so I put her in a private clinic. Better company, nice middle-class ladies, Susan quickly recovered." Philip drove me back to Richard's flat. Susan gave me a helmet with ear flaps.

Our family had exported to the United States since the middle of the nineteenth century. Corsets, yes, then paper novelties. "What about you?" asked Richard.

I looked in my suitcase for my work folder, in which I had kept the very flattering write-ups from the papers and photographs of famous actresses wearing my clothes. I couldn't find it, it was missing out of my cases. Also missing were two blouses. It slowly came to me. Why were my cases lost? I suspected the designer, who had quizzed me about my retail outlets. The telephone numbers of these store buyers had been inside the folder. He must have thought I was watching the film. But I was in bed – I am sure he took the cases for a look-see. I had placed them outside my door, but they had turned up in a different section of the ship. The last one out, that's why I had to wait to retrieve them.

Richard said, "Go to the English Embassy Trade Department when you get back to New York, ask for advice about Export. Show them your work. Sorry about your publicity. What a louse." I first had to change my sailing ticket, I couldn't face another day of the dreadful weather.

"Please can you change my ticket to an air fare? I was ill almost the whole time on the *Mauretania*. I couldn't face another trip. Cooks can arrange my ticket to be changed. I had now three spare days in New York.

I made an appointment at the Trade Section of the British Embassy. I took with me the three blouses I still had left from the six I had taken with me – two stolen, one to sister Susan. The lady explained it was difficult: import restrictions, duty, complicated forms, in my case more so because of country of origin, as the material was not

British. She said, "I have seen your work before." She fetched an export magazine. Yes, there is my blouse. Exactly, a full page, by a Swiss firm. My stipulation to the manufacturer for my designs had been not to sell in England. I had meant the lace, the embroidery, not the exact copy of the finished article. French designs were copied often – usually without permission. Why not Kensington – London designers? Yes I have given permission to sell the lace, not the article. I had been very doubtful about exporting before as I did not have the clerical staff to deal with it. I decided there and then it was no-no.

Arnold said, "Visit the old Aunt Clara, Uncle Kuno's widow." She was still nice-looking, complimented me on my fashionable suit, handwoven tweed, grey with pink flecks. I gave her one of my blouses, let her choose. "Visit Hilde." Her daughter and her children lived on the outskirts of New York. Aunt Clara wrote up for me the detailed instruction on how to get there. Three different trains, the elevator. No she did not have a timetable, but they were frequent. No she did not have a road map either.

I was frightened to use public transport. The trains seemed to race through those cavernous holes. Coming into a station someone blared out, quite incomprehensible, where the train was going to, no indicators, no large maps on the wall. People were pushing to get in and out of trains. I gave up. I did not have the telephone number to apologise for my absence.

I had some spare time now. Museums. Yes I still was the museum hound! One could buy catalogues in full colour, excellent reproductions. One of Arnold's friends took me to a Russian restaurant. Blini with caviar. I don't appreciate caviar, it's not much different from the orange roe fish one can buy – which I don't like either.

On my return, Customs waved me though. The plane was air-conditioned. I'd stated seven hours in flying time, but arriving a day later – time difference. "We will soon be arriving in England." I awoke to the announcement. Looking out of the window, England – beautiful!! It looked exactly like the print on the map. The tide, the waves were enormous. I was glad I had cancelled my trip on the boat.

Arnold visited us in 1957 to look at his little niece, Mandy (Amanda), born in January 1957. She sat in her cot and raised both arms in greeting, smiling at him. "What a friendly child," he said.

Every time she saw him, she made him welcome. The sales lady in the Toronto department store advised him what articles of clothing to send, which at that time were not available in England, like all-in-one furry suits, which zipped up, heavy-weight knitted tights in primary colours. Headgear with ear-flaps. Arnold loved the opera, he was knowledgeable, a gift inherited from our mother. He wrote to me, that in Salzburg he had met a charming girl called Elfriede. Would I look after her, on her three-day stay in London? Her ship was sailing from London. All visitors like to go on a sight-seeing tour. There were special buses, but they looped around so quickly, and mostly at a distance away. I decided to hire a taxi, collected her from her hotel and we went slowly around London, I gave her a good commentary, as I was very familiar with the sights. She had heard of Harrods and the Roof Garden of Derry and Toms, we took our refreshment in both places. For entertainment, I had booked us into *West Side Story*. It was a wonderful performance, both in sound and backgrounds. Arnold had asked me to buy twelve red roses to bring to the ship. I bought a large box of chocolates. My taxi took me to London Harbour. "Where is the ship?"

"No idea, lady, that's as far as I go, I have another booking."

I never realised how large the harbour was, I struggled with the long-stem roses and my outsize box of chocolate. I wish I had brought a plastic bag. Thank goodness I had allowed plenty of time; it took me about two hours to walk, the large ship was at 'the other end'. Thank goodness I made it in time, hoping that the steward would deliver my gifts to the correct person.

I had found Elfriede a charming girl, very quiet. She spoke some English, she told me she loved opera and also Mozart. I hoped Arnold would marry her, but she only referred to him as 'my friend'. Arnold offered to reimburse my expenses, but I told him I was delighted to meet her, no thank you, it was my privilege.

Hospital stay

When I was taken ill, through doctors' neglect and stupidity, I did not get better, had a lot of pains. "Take Alka-Selzer, don't eat all those raw vegetables, those salads." I could not go to work, my secretary came every morning to my flat for instructions. Friends suggested I should visit their wonderful doctor, an Indian called Sharma. I tried to get an appointment, but was unable to book earlier than three weeks' time. He was very popular with the arts crowd. He was fashionable. I told his secretary it was urgent, please book me in, she answered, "Everyone says that it is urgent." I had difficulties getting down from the flat – living on the third floor, step by step, sitting on my behind.

Dr Sharma's consulting rooms were very luxurious. The waiting room was not papered, but had woven silk panels on the wall. I had to be helped onto the examination couch. He scolded me, "Why did you not come earlier?"

"Because she would not give me an appointment."

"You are very ill," he said, "I want a colleague to have a look at you a Mr Kurtz, he is a surgeon."

Mr Kurtz and Dr Sharma decided that an immediate operation was needed, they made arrangements for the hospital. He gave me the phone, "Tell them to bring you some night clothes, and to look after your daughter." I asked my housekeeper, 'Auntie' to take Mandy home with her.

It was all very quick, I was prepared for the operation by the sister. That's the last I knew. I woke up the next day. The sister said, "You are a lucky girl, we caught you in time. We had three specialists working on you. Be grateful that you had the top man."

It took several weeks to get my strength back. The disgusting details included several attacks of appendicitis, scars showing, cysts on both ovaries, severe peritonitis. I don't think I want to state more about these details. I didn't run a temperature when I arrived. I was so ill that Arnold sent money to me, he thought my personal expenses would be even higher.

I offered to return the money to Arnold that he had so kindly sent to me. I had been worried, asked him to look after Mandy if I died. He promised, glad to have such a lovely child. He wrote that the money was a gift.

Near Oxford Street Circus were the premises of an antique dealer, he specialised in prints, and lithographs, from as early as the Italian Renaissance. He let me look through his folders, I was made welcome. I had told him my grandmother had given to me on my fifth birthday, the complete works of Raphael, a large book in red linen and gold-tooling. He also sold 'modern stuff', if you like that sort of thing! Yes, I liked that sort of thing. My late father had introduced me to the work of Fauves in Paris and to his artist friends in Munich. The Nazis now had his collection, I presumed.

There was *Dejeuner sur de Herbes* this had been done by several artists in Paris. Green background, black and white fully dressed gentlemen, lovely ladies. I bought this, it was in good condition, the signature was PICASSO. His early period I thought, I liked the pink and blue period. That horrible picture of the woman with front and side face I considered a 'nightmare'. Father had given me the Picasso book when I was thirteen years old. I had taken it to school. Miss Tranthagen, our Arts Mistress, showed the female horror to the class – the rose and blue period works. She said, "This is typically what we call 'Intartete kunst'. Now you know why our Fuhrer is so against it, this Jewish art."

I put my Picasso treasure – another dealer had authenticated it for me, he was not an expert – in a cardboard roll, together with a popular print, free in the Sunday papers. The customs in Canada let it through, no charge. Arnold had it framed, liking it in his bedroom. I knew he would like it. Another time I sent him a Chinese embroidery of a dragon, about six feet in length. The fantastic gold embroidery was mounted on scarlet silk, amongst multi-coloured flowers, a work of art. It was antique, bought by me at the Dolls House, an important antique dealer in Kensington Church Street. Arnold did not have to pay duty.

My father, before his marriage in 1919, had frequented Paris. He met the 'Fauves'. At that time they had difficulties selling their work. Father said Picasso made paper-rubbish. His early work, the blue and rose period, was totally different. Father was also very friendly with the Munich Art Set. The greater part of his and my mother's honeymoon was spent in Munich. I called Picasso's 'abstracts' his nightmares! People paid for this?

Arnold wrote that Elfriede was now a receptionist in a hotel, no other information. So there was no intended marriage. I did not dare to ask.

Several years later he visited us in England. Mandy was four years old, he asked her where she would like to go?

"To the Museum."

"Which museum?"

"I want to show you the dinosaurs," she said. "Tricoceratops is my favourite. He does not kill anyone, he has a collar of horns." Mandy was good at words, even strange ones. Arnold tried to order for her the *Geographic* magazine, but it was not available in England. He sent her books on dinosaurs, and also nice Canadian articles of clothing.

Richard wrote that Arnold had got married, to Lili, with a teenage son. I had received a printed card, but no details. Was she a widow? Divorced? Jewish? Then a letter arrived, written by Lili, to say that Arnold was no longer a Father Christmas.

Trust

I was so surprised when people trusted me, an unknown girl.

On Kensington Church Street, was a small shop selling carpets. Looking and admiring the carpets on display in the window, the man (the owner?) invited me in to have a better look. I was most fascinated by the one called Shah Nadirshah on the peacock throne. I know a little of Moghul History, their colourful artwork. I had read the Persians took the peacock throne home to Persia and it became the Royal Coronation Throne. The man was delighted with my knowledge, he supplemented it by explaining the weaves, the handiwork, number of counts per inch, vegetable dyes.

I could not take my eyes off the Shah Nadirshah. "Would you like to buy it? I'll make you a very good price, as you have the knowledge."

"Yes, please."

"Ninety pounds."

"I don't have much money on me, about £20, could I pay in instalments?"

"Most certainly." He rolled up the carpet and tied it with string for easy carriage. "Goodbye."

Halfway home I realized that he had never asked me for my name, address, or any identification.

The following week I returned to pay £10: "You did not know me," I said. "How did you know I would come back?"

"I knew I could trust you, young lady. The carpet is one of our prize possessions. I have seen copies of it, one on the cover of a carpet trade magazine. Our carpet is most beautiful with an animal border and showing that only Allah is perfect. They made a cow with two heads, a very obvious mistake."

Near Kensington High Street was the jewellery shop of Sybil Dunlop. If I needed to give someone a present, I look there first, to see if there is something appropriate at a price I can afford. A very small man with glasses is usually in the shop.

Mr. and Mrs. Stein had given me a large Buddha for Christmas. I had given to her a necklace made of netsuke beads, the smallest I had ever seen, beautifully carved. Mrs Stein felt some extra length would be desirable, because of the weight. We went to Sybil Dunlop's. The man suggested each netsuke should be interspaced with a round gold bead, solid, in fourteen carat. Mrs Stein was delighted when she tried it on. Perfect, the long length looked wonderful on her cashmere jumper. The price was £50. Mrs Stein was haggling about the price, I was most embarrassed. There was a lot of gold, also for the fastening at the back. The man was very firm, and did not reduce the price: "We only have fixed prices." I was getting more embarrassed. I apologized. I was sorry I had brought her.

I sincerely hoped he would not hold it against me. On my next visit I bought a small moonstone pin set in a mount of silver. I always lingered near the showcase on the wall showing the most beautiful dressing table set I had ever seen. The peacocks were all of different sizes, in bright green. "This is Sybil's masterpiece," explained the man. "Only this morning some Americans came in, money no object, but the work which had gone into the garniture did not interest them. 'What is the value of this? Of that? What would it fetch on the open market?'" The man said he was rude to them, was glad they left without purchase. "They should take their cheque and pin it on their rears. They must be nouveau riche."

"That would explain it," says I. I told him that I had never seen such beautiful work before.

"The shop will be closing in a couple of years," he said.

"I'll miss you," I reply. "What will happen to the stock?"

"I have connections."

"What about the peacocks?"

"Would you like them? I would be happy to see them in a good home."

"Could I really have them?" The price was far less than I had expected for a masterpiece. He put it in a box, gave it to me.

"I have not much money on me."

"That's all right. Enjoy it."

"I will, thank you." So far I had not paid a penny. He never asked me. I never haggled; my mother had taught me that it was common. Either you can afford, it, or forget about it.

I realized that arts shops, craft shops, quoted me less than marked on the tickets. How come I was treated so well?

Saturday was my weekly shopping day. I lived in Strathmore Gardens, a cul-de-sac, near Kensington Church Street. Kensington High Street had the gigantic Barkers store, with a wonderful food department, offering even deliveries if wanted. Derry and Toms, with Biba, with the roof garden, nice for a tea break, and Pontings for a variety of pre-war fabrics, I wondered where these came from.

Kensington Church Street is one antique shop after another, every single house was converted. A very pleasant shopping trip, very relaxing.

In the open gangway was a painting of a lady. Why she was there I could not fathom out, it was an antique bookshop. I studied the lady, so beautiful and so sad. No frame around the picture, there seemed to be a hole as well.

I went on and did my shopping. Barkers had wood pigeons, under the counter, for account customers only. The shooting crowd brought their surplus in. I found this additional 'meat' helpful with our miniature meal portion – rationing was still in force long after the war had ended.

Next week the beautiful lady still stood in the passage of the shop. No harm in trying, how much? £15 – that was three weeks wages of an average man, a shop girl often only earned £2-3.

"Who is she?"

"It says in my book she is a Mrs Woolf. Sorry I have no details." I paid for it. "I'll come back later, in about an hour, to collect her. "Righty ho," said the man. My husband said, "She looks like Virginia Woolf – that's the Bloomsbury set."

I had never heard of them. "I'll bring you a book about them."

The Bloomsbury set, I was shocked, really shocked. My mother's instruction to me had been “never let a man touch you nearer than the elbow”. Nice girls are virgins before marriage. This was the true, I thought. Free love was all right, if you loved each other, real love is okay.

But such going on, homosexuality, scantily dressed girls, with bare breasts, displaying themselves. No thank you!

I hang the picture in the spare room, but she was so beautiful!

It was her marriage to Leonard Woolf that quietened her down, so it seemed. Her sister was also wild, she was an artist, but I did not like her work at all. Modern art. Virginia was a writer, seemed to be popular, did I not enjoy her life of self-inspection, of harping on about women’s rights, possible because in the clothing industry men and women work practically together, excepting the sweat shops in the East End I had been told about.

Marriage problems

Maurice is at home for the summer holidays, from the university. He finds the flat crowded. "Too many women," he mumbles, going out. He had said, "Listen, I want you home for 7 o'clock, surely that is not asking too much?" I try to be home, so that our evening meal can be served punctually at 7.30 p.m.

The buyer from Binns, Middlesbrough, arrives at 5 p.m. "You are my last port of call." Most fashion houses are near Oxford Circus.

"May I get you something?"

"Yes, please, I am famished; I've had nothing since breakfast, leaving with the 7 o'clock train."

"Would you like roast beef or smoked salmon sandwiches?"

"Roast beef, rare."

Miss Barnes orders these from Mr Levy, in the pub across the road. A waiter will bring them, well covered with a serviette, on a tray. Seeing the very generous portion, she asks, "Are you joining me?"

"No, no, I have an evening meal; I am used to continental meal times."

By the time we have finished, her order was quite large, I call a taxi for her, to drop me on the way at home first.

Maurice says, "What time do you call this? It's almost 8."

"No, it's 7.32 p.m. Dinner won't be long." I am apologetic, anything to avoid a row. I always give in.

Mrs Jeffrey, Maurice's analyst, is away on holiday. Where is he now? He's been away almost all week. I soon found out, I am shocked. My goodness, what next? He is phoning me from a mental hospital. He has booked himself in, as a voluntary patient. I know he has had three sessions a week with Mrs Jeffrey, she is away on holiday. Does he think they will continue his 'treatment'? He is angry, on the phone. "No way, I've not even seen a psychiatrist! They only took my particulars, said I was not sent by my GP or anyone. Please get me out of here, I cannot discharge myself, you have to come and get me."

I travel to Surrey, sign the papers, he is very quiet. I take him for a meal. "First thing, tell me why?" I never did get to the bottom of it, other than Mrs Jeffrey was on holiday.

The girl from Todmorden, Valerie, offers to type his manuscript. She seems to be a sensible girl. She is on school holidays. They spend much time together, where? I don't want to know. Mrs Jeffrey has returned. Sessions are three times a week. She is costing me a fortune. I work it out; Maurice has given me £5 per week. He has to have some money given back to him. £5 per week is what an ordinary workman earns. Maurice is only an assistant lecturer. I cannot ask him these delicate questions about money.

We see several films. The theatres are closed. We go to Ramsgate for a few days, the air there does wonders for me, helps my breathing which has been bothering me lately.

I tried to remember what my late father would have advised. He did the Eastern Breathing exercises. Perhaps these might help. I had been reading books on Yoga. Also books by Ramana Maharshi.

In Hampstead was a Yoga Centre. I telephoned, found out when there were lessons for the general public.

I went, and to my surprise I was introduced to Shri Nandi, the man in charge. They called him a saint. He said to me, "You are not for the class, I will teach you myself."

At my first lesson he made me sit opposite him, on a mat.

He then explained to me about the very chapter I had been reading at home. How did he know? That was it. My breathing improved.

Maurice is friendly with a lot of ladies from the Art circle. I am very hurt and annoyed when I find out that the invitations to parties or dinner which we receive, sent to both of us, he has taken these other women, saying Sylvia is too busy. Sylvia would never have been too busy to go, no. And I have to apologise, why I could not come to the dinner, which I would have liked to attend.

I have my darling Mandy, which makes up for any hurt. Maurice has words with Nursy, he says she interferes, so he sacks her. Mandy cries, she loves Nursy. I advertise for an au pair, mornings free, to study. Her English classes are in Kensington High Street, School for Foreigners. Mrs Champ does the housework and the shopping, as before. The au pair is to go the park with Mandy, Holland Park or Kensington Gardens, bring her for tea with me at 135 Notting Hill Gate, in the canteen on the third floor. Or play with her at home if it rains. To get her ready for bed, waiting until Mummy comes home. Mummy tells her stories, look together at picture books, also grown-up ones, Vikings or Romans and Greeks. They are beautifully illustrated. There is now a tale, the one which Mrs Rabbit tells Mummy, about her little rabbit boy called Cherioko. Why this name? Because he always says 'cheerio'.

I really don't mind if Maurice stays away, in fact I welcome it – if it were not for the Saturdays, when Mandy expects him to take her out. She gets quite upset, sits near the window; she cannot understand that he has not telephoned if he cannot come. I found out that he is staying with a girl called Katie. She is Irish, a dancer, but not now, she has grown too tall.

When I see him in the Linden, with Savile and Jane, I tell him that Mandy is upset, she was waiting for him. He replies, "You are using Mandy to get me to come back to you." My goodness, I think, this conceited man, I wish I could get rid up him. It's only for my darling Mandy that I put up with him.

He tells me Katie had said, "What do you want to bother with Mandy for? You can have other children."

Maurice said Katie is going home to Ireland for a couple of weeks; Mandy could come and stay with him. What is Katie's place like? Is there a separate bed? I went to see, and had never before seen such a filthy place. Maurice, who was so fastidious, how can he live like this?

"I would like to tidy up a little, send some bedding, before I can send Mandy."

"If you like," he gives me the key. "I can stay with Philip and Jane."

I am ashamed for him, I ask Mrs Champ to help me with the clean up. Then I fill the cupboards with tins and what they call 'dry goods', such as spaghetti, rice, biscuits and bacon, and anything else that will keep. She can sleep on the settee. Mandy is delighted. I tell her she is a big girl now; she has to take her father out, to give him treats, outings. I give her some money, also some change for the phone, "in case you need me".

There was the zoo, the planetarium, and a Disney film. Mandy had a good time. "When can I come back, Daddy?"

He brings Mandy back and there is a row. "I don't owe you anything, I never loved you," he says. "Don't you ever tell Mandy she can come any time."

It has been four weeks, I cannot phone him, her phone is not working, the bill most probably unpaid. Mandy is upset. This is no life for either of us, her upset is my upset. We should both get away, disappear. He would never find us. I have visions, I could change, I have read adverts in the paper. Furnished cottage supplied on Estate. References. I am a good cook. Can I apply? Who would give me a reference? How could I walk out on Sylvia Russell (Kensington)? What about the staff? Give redundancy money, give holiday money, and give a good bonus. So many thoughts going round in my head, I needed to think of my darling Amanda.

PART TWO

Hollings College

Job Interview

Do I really want a change? I walk past the newspaper kiosk in Notting Hill Gate Underground Station. I buy the magazine called *Prediction*. Why have I bought this magazine? Nursy buys it, it is rubbish.

At home I look at it. Perhaps it will tell me if I really want to change.

Gypsies – "Touch my hand with silver." The magazine is called *Prediction*. I might as well look at it, now I have bought it, I think. If there is someone local I might as well find out. Yes, right in the next street, a Mrs Ireland. I say to myself, silver? I am not paying more than £2. I am not going unless it is right away. I am not going unless she speaks proper English. She qualifies on all accounts. She can see me at once. She lives in Ladbroke Road, two streets away, has a cultured voice.

"Give me something to hold, for better contact." I give her my watch. "I can see two leases, for premises, why two? But they are all right now."

That is quite correct, they have come through, the lease for my flat, and the lease for my business premises. They both are renewed now. I think this information is to give me confidence in her. It is most unusual to know about two leases.

"Are you seeking a change?"

"Yes, I am, I don't know, perhaps I am."

"If you are willing to uproot yourself, you have to prepare some publicity. I know, you never pay for publicity, it has always been free, but this is different. You need current photographs, you need letters of recommendation."

I am completely 'flabbergasted'. She gives me detailed instructions on how to get the new job. "Don't volunteer information, only answer questions, when asked. Speak clearly, there are a number of people at the interview."

That's all she said. "Please give me £2. Strangely, I always charge £5. Why am I charging you only £2? Very strange, but now I have said £2, £2 it is."

My God, someone 'up there' wants me to get this job. This clairvoyant woman is there to help me. She is a white witch. I get my letters of recommendations together, have duplicates made. Harrods, Hupperts, TV, *Vogue Magazine*. I have photos done, well-known actresses in my clothes, made by me, my designs.

Lecturer II, Salary £1720 per annum, to start in September.

I am told by friends that this is a good salary, a good grading, Lecturer II. I didn't think so, I've been earning much more.

Interview at Hollings College, Wilmslow Road, Manchester, 10 a.m.

I need a sleeper train, it takes four and a half hours, London to Manchester.

I am nervous What do I wear? Traditional or designer garb? My fly-away hair can't be helped. There are several candidates, one man tells me he is a bespoke tailor. What is he doing here? Is he applying for the designer's job? I doubt it. Two young ladies, about twenty-five to thirty years old. One elderly lady, about fifty, I should guess. I am the last one to be interviewed. They were pretty quick, quarter of an hour only for each.

I realise I have forgotten my most important item, the list of customers of Sylvia Russell (Kensington).

"This job was advertised for over a year," the committee tells me. "We had no intention to employ a designer without industrial experience," they explained. I realized they meant designer/cutter. The committee handed around my testimonials. In my brief application I had mentioned sixteen years in the industry. I called my premises work rooms. This seemed to worry them. Do I know manufacturing?

"I do not cut by industrial machines. We cut by hand, never more than two or three layers, because we use very expensive fabrics. This makes it very economical in the cut, no waste." My turnover surprised them, £28,000, before purchase tax (this would nowadays be at least ten times that). "Very impressive." I was asked to leave the room. I thought I had muffed it.

"Would you come back in please? Congratulations. We will send you more details in a few days, about the job."

I was refunded my fare money.

I telephoned Mrs Ireland, to thank her, "I've got the job." She said that it wouldn't be easy – politics, jealousy. "Good luck, you deserve it."

The Warden of Ashbourne Hall, Residence, was an anthroposophist. Mrs Stein had written a letter to introduce me.

Because of the summer holiday, Ashbourne Hall, the residence for female students, could offer me a room. The Hall was straight across from Hollings College. I was told this strange-looking building was generally known as the toast rack.

Miss Churm, the Head of the Clothing Department, took me to the staff room to introduce me over a cup of coffee. I recognised two ladies, they had been at the interview. Both were part of my design section, to work under me.

"How do we address you? Mrs Hurst or Sylvia?"

"I prefer Mrs Hurst, I am of the older generation."

"Please excuse us." They left.

There was a rumbling noise. "Whatever is that?"

"We don't take any notice of that, that's from the toilets next door. They cut out the sound-proofing as part of an economic measure, builders' suggestion."

Miss Churm said, "Mrs Hurst, here is your syllabus and a temporary timetable. You are in charge of the B group, we have two full-time classes, A and B starting next week."

"Do the students sit an entrance exam?"

"No. Group A is from Grammar Schools, Group B from Secondary Modern."

"How do you select them? Do they show their art folder, or other work?"

"No, I interview them. We'll talk later, see me at 11 o'clock, at my office." We did have an entrance exam.

A grey-haired lady approached me. "I am Margaret. My class does not start for another hour, I am on prep. I teach sewing. Would you like me to show you around?"

She seemed friendly enough. Margaret said, "You need resources first, that is stationery, and to get your trolley. There is a drawer for you here, we all have a drawer. Refectory is on the first floor, two sittings for lunch. All clothing is on the ground floor."

It was a vast building, many sections. It was first called the Domestic and Trades College; they changed it to Holling a few years ago. They made a lot of changes. "We have many part-time classes in our Department, such as Millinery or soft furnishing. I did an upholstered stool in an evening class. They stopped some of the classes, like lacemaking, you know, macramé, and torchon and cloppel, as that teacher left. We do the City and Guilds, different ones. The tailoring department is across the yard on the other side. They don't belong to Miss Churm, but they share the facilities. Catering is the biggest here, all kinds."

I found this interesting. "Margaret, I have to see Miss Churm at eleven. Thank you, I'll see you later."

Miss Churm's office adjoined the one of the principal, which had a waiting area with soft leather easy chairs outside.

Punctually I knocked at her door. "Come in, Mrs Hurst. If you have any questions, this is the time."

"Oh, I have many questions. Firstly, how many students are in my B class?"

"We aim for sixteen, of course there is wastage, for both of the full-time courses. For our part-time, day-release industrial courses we take as many as apply. We are aiming for the Clothing Institute exams, just starting up. It was the committee that engaged your services; I'll have you know, I was against it. I would have preferred one of the two ladies you met, they both have ATD."

I remembered only too well, at the interview they told me that the position was for someone with good, relevant industrial experience and that the position of Lecturer in Charge of Design had been advertised over a year ago, nationally and in trade papers. I had sixteen and a half years in industry, my own workrooms. I was a known designer. It was my turnover which had impressed the Committee – £28,000 in 1960, nowadays perhaps multiplied by ten.

The interview proceeded, far from friendly. Who was leading? I needed information. City and Guilds had sent to me various publications, with syllabus, by return, offered more if I needed it in the future.

Miss Churm had given to me the syllabus for the main fashion course. I was surprised, very surprised, not to find pattern drafting, which I considered one of the main, if not THE main work of the industrial designers. She said, "We use the Vogue patterns or Butterick. Yes, we find these are very good, we adapt them."

I said, "I would like to include pattern drafting, quarter-scale and full-scale." Of course the students would need the approved quarter scale measures and set squares. "Please may I include pattern drafting? I think I absolutely need to do this. I'll bring you my basics. May I show it to you? I'll bring it to you at your convenience, I know how busy you are." Was it a yes or a no? I continued, "What fashion magazines do you use here, any of the Continental ones?" At this time Paris was the leading fashion centre.

Miss Churm answered, "We have *Vogue*, *Tailor* and *Cutter*, *Elle, Textile News* and the *Export Trader.* With the continental ones there is the difficulty of language."

"May I suggest *L'Officiel,* it covers the Haute Couture shows in Paris. It comes out four times a year, very expensive, £2 four times a year plus postage."

"I suppose it is in French?"

"Yes, of course, I could translate. I am not perfect, and there may be new words which I don't know. I have been taking *L'Officiel* for years, I can get it in London from the Titchfield Street Shop. They stock all the mags. Worldwide. They also stock the *Petra*, the German magazine, the one which includes three patterns inside, included free, very good patterns, good fitting. Perhaps for your 233 or 234 (City and Guilds) classes."

This conversation was not going well. It was one-sided. I could feel

Miss Churm was annoyed with me. I repeated, "Three good patterns, it would save quite a lot of money. I could translate that too, I meant the fashion side, not the recipe for baking and hints for the home and shopping."

"Put all this in writing, with the addresses," said Miss Churm.

"Where is my office? I was not shown it."

"You don't have an office, you use a table in the staff room. There is a drawer there for you."

"Yes, I was shown that. Thank you."

"You keep your prep work on a trolley which is more convenient." I was dismissed.

I found this most unsatisfactory. Where would I put my books, my fashion magazines, particularly the ones which had photos of my work? I had kept all my *L'Officiels*, they gave 'profiles' of the couturiers, reports of the fashion shows in Paris. There were folders with newspaper cuttings, photos of my work for the lace and embroidery industry in Switzerland.

I felt I must look for a quiet place, there must be some space for me somewhere. I walked around the building, with my trolley, opened doors without knocking, "Excuse me, wrong room." Until I came to a narrow store room, used mainly for cleaning materials which were stacked on the shelves. Most of the shelves were half empty. This will do. It is now mine. I need a table. Resources promised to find one. There were chairs standing around everywhere. Mrs Hurst had now an office, not officially of course. I moved my 'gear' in. A large piece of cardboard divided off my area. I studied my timetable, was surprised that it covered thirty-four hours instead of the usual thirty, also that I had three evening classes.

Contact with the day release classes would bring me together with the local clothing industry. I decided I would tailor my syllabus after a discussion with them, I then would know better what was needed.

I was looking forward to the costume history class, having worked with the V & A for research and practical work with television.

In my timetable was marked one and a half hours for design of ladies tailoring.

When I called I was made most welcome. I explained that twenty years ago I had worked at Suits and Mantles.

"We are bespoke tailors, all of us from industry, mostly retail."

"What magazines do you have?"

"Only the *Tailor and Cutter*," I said. "The Italians are best for knitwear and menswear, so I am told. The Paris Couture always shows outer wear. I have asked Miss Churm to order *L'Officiel*. Balenciaga and Ungaro usually are good for outer wear. show interesting feminine outfits, latest designs for outer wear. I can help you with the paper pattern, that's my forte. There is a shop totally devoted to mags in Titchfield Street, near Oxford Street in London. They have all the magazines published the world over, you might find it interesting."

They thanked me, "See you next week."

New textile machinery is for export only

The converters bought the grey clothes for about ten pence per meter. The cloth was woven in India or in the Far East. Imported to England to be printed. The average price was now £3.50 -£4.00. The middle man made a tremendous profit. Every week I read about one or two of the Lancashire factories producing cloths, closing down. The new up-to-date machinery, which was able to run three x eight hours shifts, was for export only! To be shipped abroad. My cousin in Paris explained to me that the newspapers in France gave it much publicity.

Textiles were the number one industry in France. Agriculture was number two. Small holdings and small firms producing speciality food, often quite famous.

The French farmers laughed at the Common Market Regulations, new rules for safety, sterilising etc. Eva laughed, she said, "England invents rules, France ignores them!"

Jacques and Eva, my cousins in France, said that the newspapers, including *Figaro* Paris, gave the closing down of the textiles/weaving industries great publicity.

They claimed this was the reason France objected to England joining the Common Market. "They have wrecked their own industry, we don't want our economy wrecked!!"

Example, our cheeses, mostly they are products of the small farms, have been produced for hundreds of years to secret recipes. These rules and regulations would finish the industry. Big co-ops took over in France – La Vache que Rit.

Our industries had closed down, forced by the competition abroad, who could work three shifts, twenty-four hours. Our old machines were not up to it.

The new textile machinery produced in England was for export only.

Lunchtime

I found the food in the canteen not very inviting, who had cooked it? The catering students. They start at 10 a.m., then it is kept hot in vast-looking containers. I sat at a table. My staff entered. I knew they had seen me, but they chose a different table. No chance of conversation.

I was surprised that other staff from clothing came over to my table and introduced themselves, were friendly.

Miss Churm's syllabus had priority. I interpreted the Colour Circle, Figure drawing, sizes in relation use, I knew about eight-head theory, I would adapt that for fashion drawing, possibly on large cards for the wall with corresponding small copies for handouts. I remember 'handouts' from the Bendit Fashion course in Berlin. They had claimed a "résumé of your lesson and the visual handout is most important'.

My classroom for my Class B held no information. A blackboard. The store cupboards were bare. I held a meeting with my staff. I told them of my background, my work. I asked them about their industrial experience, and was not surprised that both of the ladies had none, both were art School trained. It seemed they kept avoiding me. I was settling in.

I stayed several weeks at Ashbourne Hall eating at the high table. A local agent found me a flat in Barlow Moor Court, Didsbury, two-year lease. Later I found out that he had omitted to tell me that children under sixteen years were not allowed, except at holiday time. He offered me very suitable accommodation, a small estate was being built, suitable for academics, near the university. There was a primary school right next to Hollings College. I paid my deposit. This house was very conveniently located, to have Mandy's school right next to my work.

If there was to be a general staff meeting, I was only informed by chance; I would have missed it, had Margaret not told me.

I prepared large cards of pattern drafting, with corresponding A4 handouts. This was my priority, I did my work in my new office, and was glad to be left alone.

My students, fourteen girls and two boys arrived in good time on Monday morning. They were aged sixteen to seventeen as I had been told. I introduced myself, gave them my working background, promised to show them photos. "I would like to know what made you choose Hollings College? Do you see your future career in the industry, or do you want to become a designer? Please write it down, we have one and a half hours left. This is important for me, to get to know you."

Next lessons were fully occupied by looking at my *Vogue*, *L'Officiel* and others. I pointed out my work contained inside and showed them the original drawing of the garment, with samples of fabric and trimming attached to it. Unfortunately the name of my firm, Sylvia Russell (Kensington) was not mentioned, only the name of the actress wearing it on the photo, her name was important. The kids all knew Diana Dors, Christine Norton, Jean Kent, all well-known from films. Films were important, they mostly went to the performances. I could feel I had gone up in their estimation.

I started with the Colour Circle and the eight-head theory. The handout of the skeleton did not produce a figure, far from it, impossible to translate it into a fashionable lady. Ladies' average height was five-foot-three-inches at that time. "Miss, I cannot draw."

"Don't worry, you will, when I am finished with you."

They laughed. "That will be the day."

"Most of you will have catalogues, bring those in, those figures are the ones the industry is used to, they looked six to seven foot tall, caused by elongated legs. I started with pattern drafting, using my Berlin-Bendit Atelier acquired knowledge. I encouraged their 'scribbles' helping to improve their ideas, their design. "Yes, that's what I wanted to draw," they said. "Thank you, now it looks right."

Paris was ruling. Paris decreed what colours would be 'in' next season. British clothing manufacturers would send their staff to Paris, paid entrance fee to their selected couturiers, to purchase the toile (cloth pattern) of the selected garment to be copied, entrance money to be deduced, and hopefully remembering many other designs, 'in their heads' not paid for. Also to be copied – near enough – later sold for the high street. Copies to be made at home, I had experienced this, copying of my designs, but I was flattered and just produced more designs, used different fabrics.

My students could make patterns of their designs. I corrected them, the best one to be chosen to be made up in their sewing class. I was happy, I had a good relationship with my B-class students.

I had written to our top fabric producers, announcing I was in charge of fashion design. I asked for swatches of their latest new designs. I received them by return, usually with a nice letter. They remembered me as Miss Russell, of Sylvia Russell (Kensington), because I had been written up, several times in the trade papers.

I explained to my class that these swatches are in the shop fashions by next year or the year after. Only a few of the important firms like Tootal or Treforest print their own. The grey cloth (undyed) is woven mainly in the East or India, much cheaper, before it goes to the converter for dying.

My relationship with my staff was non-existent, felt hostile.

When I received offers of chosen designs, free lengths of fabric, usually six to ten yards, Miss Churm decided that these belonged to the college and locked them away in her store room. What could I do? I asked the firms to send them to my home address.

Liverpool was the centre of workwear, aprons, overalls, also rainwear, jeans. They put up a competition for new designs, or aprons etc. Hollings College accepted the challenge, as did many other colleges, for the Aprons and Overalls, only some of my B students were interested. However, I had a pleasant surprise. Several of their designs I found were excellent, amusing, a new look. Their products, their own design. Had to be made in secret. Margaret, the sewing teacher was sworn to secrecy. Class A also took part in the competition, as there were three prizes to be awarded.

I had my favourites, my first choice was a very large over-shirt, like a man's, in dark, striped shirt material, of heavy weight – to encourage the 'husband' to help at home. What a good idea! The sleeves were long and wide, elasticated, to protect their suit sleeves. I also liked the apron with the outsize pocket, which featured an embroidered smiley on it. A copy of a Paris coat with high waistline, it was so elegant it could be worn outdoors, no one would know it was an overall. I was on friendly terms with the embroidery teacher. One of her ladies did a nice appliqué of the smiley. I had shown my B students the swatches of the new avant-garde psychedelic fabrics, called Nantucket geometrics, or interlocking circles, in very bright colours. The apron design was fairly standardised, bound in contrasting red bias-binding. A very 'with it' garment. These were my favourites, of the eight to be posted to Liverpool. Miss Churm rejected the men's shirt overall as completely unsuitable; she said, "Impossible, we cannot send this." This had been my first choice. We decided, my Class B and I, that it should enter the competition, entrance date only two days away.

I telephoned the Workwears Headquarters to find out if there was a possibility to have a parcel taken in in the evening, was there a night watchman? I took the Liverpool train, leaving Manchester at 5.30, it takes one hour. I engaged a taxi, for the return journey to Overall Headquarters. I got a receipt for my parcel, returned to the station, back in Manchester by 10 o'clock.

I felt it was not up to Miss Churm to allow or disallow competition entries.

Surprise, surprise, Hollings won first prize for the men's shirt, second prize for the smiley, and third prize for the psychedelic. My class B was jubilant. Miss Churm was furious. "How did you get this garment there?"

"By train," I said.

A few days later the principal passed me on the stairs. "A good show, Hollings won all three prizes," he said.

"Yes," I answered, "my B Class."

"You must have good students in B class." He asked to see my timetable. "This is not correct." He cut my contact hours from thirty-four to thirty, the norm, and my evenings from three to two.

"Mrs Green has been absent for three weeks. Miss Churm told me I must look after both classes." This occurred sometimes in my time with my B Class. I was running around like a headless chicken!

"We have to arrange this differently," he said.

I felt these difficulties had been designed to make me realise that this position in Hollings was not for me. My accountant had warned me, "You'll be back, don't give up the lease of your premises, don't sell your machines."

I talked to my B Class about Fashion Centres in Europe and also where fabric was produced; these often became leaders in colour and design. Italy was represented by the Count Emilio Pucci who entertained buyers in his Palazzo in Florence, showing them his creations of colourful silk fabrics in swirling designs. Feragamo had ladies' shoes, handbags, belts in finest Italian leather.

In the Provence of France, a heavyweight cloth had been produced since the Middle Ages, strong enough for working in the mines – De Mines – known as denim, our workwear favourite.

For the wholesale market, Sidney Smith, London embroiderers produced fine work, reasonable. I had used this firm in the past myself.

Because of Nazi persecution, the Jewish fashion trade had transferred from Berlin to London and to Manchester. The fur trade had also transferred from Leipzig, East Germany, to London.

Our factory in Goeppingen, which had been the cradle of the Corset Industry in Europe, closed, almost closed, production, except for the remedial garments, designed by my father for crippled figures, or ladies who had lost their bust, or one of them. They sent photographs in several position and measurements. It had frightened and upset me when I saw the photos.

I had received a swatch of denim from the producer. Already at age fifteen I had wanted to make for myself some hard-wearing leisure wear. When I chose some denim at Mr May's fabric shop (he was a distant cousin of my grandfather) in Camberg, where my grandparents lived, he would not sell it to me, saying it was only for workmen's trousers.

I showed the denim swatch to my class. They agreed it would make good, hardwearing outfits. They assured me they would like to wear them, particularly the one in a purple and orange colour. I admired the design of the male student, he used white bias binding and fastened his 'bomber' jacket with the outsize press-studs, size 000, one and a half inches across. They looked like silver filigree buttons.

By sending my report, including the preliminary sketches of the leisure wear, I received an enormous parcel of denim from the manufacturer. It had been addressed to me, but all my mail went into

Miss Churm's office. My mail was college mail. I agreed. Miss Churm said denim was not suitable for leisure wear. She locked it in her private store room. That's the last we knew of it. 'Denim is not suitable!' Ha! Ha! My class called her Miss Churm, the worm!! Schissht.

My day-release class co-operated with me, I had no interference to my syllabus from Miss Churm. I thought she most probably did not understand our work.

For day release; the most important lesson was pattern drafting, grading and pattern engineering. Eight-head theory and fashion drawing. How to make reports for the record book of the firm. Introduction to the colour – the circle. Colour mixing for designs, inspired by Emilio Pucci, the famous Italian designer. The class copied him. I was delighted, I was told one of the designs of our class went into production at the converter.

Measurement and sizes, those officially given in books were not correct, especially for children, teens and outsizes.

The day-release class told me that their bosses took a great interest in their work done in my class. Sylvia felt useful.

One day I found my office had been 'invaded'. All my fashion magazines, *Vogue* and other leading magazines, collected over many years, had disappeared. As they contained photos of my past work, I was very annoyed.

I insisted that my staff lecturers, Miss Davis and Mrs Green, who had never worked either for or with me, had to return them forthwith! "You can keep the *L'Officiel*," I said. They said they wanted to cut up everything for teaching aids.

These two ladies never talked to me, certainly did not accept that I was to be in charge of the Design Department. The other members of the Clothing Department were nicer to me, almost respectful, accepting my authority, my work background when I was in London.

The tailoring classes had much improved, they were now up to date in work and design. Their head of department had travelled to London to inspect the Titchfield Street magazine store. He told me it was a godsend. "Thank you, Sylvia."

I am pleased to find that the magazine *Petra* had been delivered and is available to C & G 234. I translate the relevant parts and have them duplicated. The students of 234 are mostly private dressmakers, housewives who want to better their income by becoming teachers. The patterns are for basic clothing designs, very useful and of course free.

I have a dress dummy in size 16, this seemed to be the most popular size. I show them how to take a model pattern of this dummy, having previously cut a basic shape, using pins, to thread mark. This is called modelling or draping, the method most used in France by the many small dress establishments.

Remedial work. There are several adjustments needed, for different figures and sizes. Older ladies seem to have a shorter neck, therefore shirt collars do not fit at the back. Curve the back part of the collar, that remedies it. Large bosoms, the measurement shows two to four extra sizes. Extra inches must be added in uneven proportion, perhaps three/fifths front, one in back. An extra seam in front is required to make the armhole smaller.

Curvature of the spine. A saddle (yoke), in a halfmoon curve, with gathered extra material will look like a fashion item, and cover up the 'hunch-back'.

We follow the City and Guilds syllabus. I find most items familiar and well-known to the ladies. They use the commercial patterns of Vogue and Butterick, which their customers bring in together with their chosen fabric.

For the Costume History for my full time B class, I have decided that this will give me the opportunity to further their general education. There is Costume and there is History. I explain about Fashion Cycles. Looks can alter very quickly due to economic and social pressures. I have prepared supplementary sheets and cutting sheets for patterns which would enable them to make costumes. Many I made from the art postcards collected during my travels – two shoeboxes full.

I am starting with Egypt. The handsome pharaoh wears a gold knife-pleated skirt. Cooked by the sun on hot stones. Knife pleating became very fashionable in 1950, commercial cleaners would re-pleat to regain the knife-edged look. My drawing of the handsome Pharaoh was on a thirty by twenty-inch card, which I had duplicated into (8-4) foolscap size, as a handout, to be coloured, in gold paint.

My supplementary sheets showed the young Tutankhamen,

Nefertiti, Akhnaton. I told them about these well-known personalities, showed them my books.

Next was the Greco/Roman period, here pictures, including Minoan. The latter wore tiered skirts, often bare-bosomed, three to four layers – all on my thirty by twenty-inch sheet. The Victorian ladies also wore these skirts 1860-1880. Greek ladies' garments had no style. Sometimes the two pieces of cloth had been fastened with several buttons on the arms.

Madame Vionnet, the Alsatian Couturier, at the beginning of the twentieth century, used plain-cloth draperies, her clients did not know which was the front or back of the dress.

I tried to choose interesting personalities, to give the background of the time.

Example: The career of the Empress Theodora, dressed in coloured gems and strings of pearls are like a 1920 Flapper. She was daughter of the Baer-feeder, became a bare-back rider, then the official girlfriend of a general, advising on how to win battles; he married her when he became Emperor. She converted to Christianity, and was declared a Saint, Saint Theodora of the Catholic Church.

Every period had a representative drawing, with the social and/or economic background given.

Knights in armour, ladies with wimples, cavaliers in lace-trimmed garments, the Reformation, the Quakers, the class found it fascinating. "Better than Mills and Boon!" they said. And to every period was some item which was used in another time – the fashion cycle.

The class said, "Miss, we hated history lessons at school, it was all dates, wars, battles, what a bore!"

The class spend their pocket money on the cheap paperbacks on History, 50p Penguins or others.

I had promised my students to show a photo of a costume we had made, it was for Queen Elizabeth I. Abrahams, the fabulous costumiers, charged fabulous prices. This was the reason I had been contacted by film and TV producers. The producers were responsible for keeping the cost of production down. This was before Hollywood spent millions.

My costume of Elizabeth I had been photographed on a dummy. It had been worn by different actresses, when they played Elizabeth

I. I had studied the photo of her paintings. The Venetian Velvet, same, was used by upholstery firms for wing chairs, was produced in Belgium at £40-£50 per meter; three meters covers two armchairs – not in our price range.

How did we keep the cost down? The Venetian velvet for the main fabric. We took the damask curtain fabric of same design, and mounted it on heavy woollen coating. From a distance there was no difference in looks. The many brooches which fastened the front. Woolworth had imitation brooches in diamante and coloured glass, imported from Czechoslovakia, no difference. The fancy lace collars, we had been able to get these from St Gall, Switzerland. I showed them samples of the fabric, one of the brooches, a piece of the collar lace.

I had to starch these heavily to make them stand up stiff around the neck. No difference. Pearls and beads came from Trimfit, London W1, an importer of fancy goods.

There had been a disaster, a telephone call from the TV company told me that the collar had melted, flopped under the strong Arc and other lighting. I reinforced them with floral wire.

The TV company had a clothing wardrobe. Very large, from one end of the wall to the next wall. The costumes, when not in use, had a label fastened, to show when used production, date, actor, producer, not to be used immediately lest the public remember it. Sometimes they were rented out to theatrical companies, amateur ones.

The costumes ranged from those for royalty, through to middle classes, and costumes of the Workers Guild. There were clothes for the working classes, included the beggars. They were kept in large chests, only the century was given. Working classes wore the same clothes for several centuries. They employed ex-art school students to make this on the premises. Pinafores were worn by females, smocks, shirts and just pieces of cloth for Romans and suchlike. Art schools also taught costumes. They sometimes produced costumes for amateur theatres. I was told in order to get the fancy Venetian Velvet or medieval look, stencils were cut, for the gold paint to be brushed though. The only drawback was the gold sometimes fell apart, "rained" through onto the stage, if the actor moved. There was also a story of using milk- bottle tops for costumes. I did not believe this story.

For the Queen's Coronation many people purchased a television set; that was quite a rarity before that date. It was very expensive and in black and white.

For entertainment people had relied on the theatres, which many towns had. The touring theatrical companies stayed a week, having a repertoire of several plays. If they were successful, many seats sold – they advertised in *The Stage* – the theatrical magazine. Sometimes the tour lasted several months or more. This was a much sought after occupation for teenagers and upwards. It included a wardrobe mistress, usually an art school student, to repair, iron, or even copy the clothes if they wore out. The students seems to be fascinated with anything to do with the theatre or films. They were always busy with the ironing board. If it was a musical, they had a musical director travelling with them as well. Seaside towns were popular, the audience was not critical. Shakespeare and classical pieces were usually demanded in larger towns. If the show flopped, no one got paid, not even the landladies of the theatrical digs. Sometimes the money situation was so serious that parents had to send railway tickets for the return home.

Simple costumes were home made. Elaborate ones were hired. The TV companies hired them out – sometimes.

Theatres were converted to film palaces. There were always queues for the evening performances. Less and less jobs for the stage-struck youngsters. Children collected cigarette cards of the stars, performances of their favourite actors. There was a brisk trade in exchange.

Continental actors and actresses had come to England, Nazi-persecuted. Conrad Veidt and Peter Lorre played the villains, Anton Walbrook was a very good-looking hero. There was the beautiful Hedy Lamar and Elisabeth Berguer. The Swedish actresses Greta Garbo and Ingrid Bergman went to Hollywood. Elstree and Denham Studios were busy and produced excellent films with our English actors.

The TV Company had told me they were sorry I was leaving London. Perhaps they could arrange for me to continue. They did not want to lose my work for them, neither did I.

I had to two (or three) evening classes at Hollings, this should have given me four hours, a half-day a week compensation. Could I arrange to come on Friday afternoons for discussion of the designs? They would arrange the fittings on Saturday mornings. I put this proposal to Miss Churm. After all, the connection with the art world would be valuable for students. All those famous people. Miss Churm made sure I always had Friday classes. She was not interested.

At that time, off-the-shoulder garments became popular for evening and wedding wear. These had to be boned, just like the late 1790 garment. These bare necks were allowed, by decree of the French King: "only the nipple, no more can be showing".

In the evening separates section of Sylvia Russell (Kensington), I had offered boned bodices, shoulders free. I had worked together with a corset manufacturer, doing long-line bra (bodices, no cups) to cover them for me in black velvet. They fitted well, were safe – worn with a circular black skirt or coloured Dirndl. I trimmed the bodices with elaborate Guipure flowers; these were designed by me and made up in St Gall, Switzerland. I showed photographs of my past work, write-ups from Shop-hound of *Vogue*, *Elle* magazine also enthusiastic about my designs. The debutantes were invited, very prestigious, for the Queen Alexandra Ball at the Grosvenor House, London. This was an annual affair, much sought after.

My friend Pamela Chamberlain had been invited; she wore her specially made off-the-shoulder, white satin dress. It was boned in the current fashion. Disaster, her partner stepped on the hem and her two breasts popped out! Embarrassed, he covered her with his jacket. It was a long way to the door.

It was a hot summer, I had worn my boned velvet bodice often. It was safe. It fitted me snuggly.

Now back to Hollings College.

For the yearly fashion show, Miss Churm and her second-in-command friend, Miss Comley, plus Fashion Design, selected the garments. All students were represented.

Mrs Hurst was not included in the staff choices for selection. Never mind, as long as the B students had a showing. Schoolchildren had been invited to the dress rehearsal in the afternoon. Miss Comley was the compére. These were mixed classes. Some rude remarks were made from male pupils if a girl had plump legs – "tree trunks". Chest flat – like a board. It went well, no mishaps, no trip-ups on the temporary stage. At the end was the announcement, “We won three prizes for the Liverpool competition of overalls and aprons.” For the fashion show copies of the apron had been made as the winning aprons had been retained in Liverpool. The competition was of overalls and aprons, the winning garments had been retained in Liverpool for their fashion show.

Miss Comley announced: “In reverse order. Third prize: the fashionable housewife wears an apron made of Nantucket psychedelic print. Second prize: a loving smile would make work a pleasure, embroidery courtesy of Sidney Smith, London. First prize: it won international acclaim, a large shirt, made in heavyweight fabric, this will induce any male to be happy with housework.”

Waiting in the wings to contribute were the staff of the design section, and a little girl struggling with a very large bouquet for Miss Churm.

Miss Comley continued: “May I present Miss Davis ATI. May I present Mrs Green ATI.” And then, very loud, “Here is Mrs Hurst, the Lecturer in Charge, and again, Mrs Hurst – Alles Raus, Alles Raus.”

I turned around, walked down the steps, along the front row, out of the hall.

I knew they wanted me to leave, now they had made it public. What hatred!

Did they know that Alles Raus was the roll call of the concentration camps? I doubted it, most probably it was their personal hatred of me, their fear, their insecurity in their positions. Teachers now could be dismissed or transferred if found lacking, or not up to their duties. Should I leave Hollings? No, I am doing a good job. I am useful.

“Alles Raus” – tonight when the committee and the manufacturers attend the show, most of them are Jewish, they know about “Alles Raus”, having relatives lost in the Holocaust. They would be offended.

I must talk to the Principal. “May I see the Principal?”

“Have you an appointment?” asked his secretary.

“No, but it important, very important.”

“Please wait.”

I sat on the leather chair outside his office. Then I entered. “What is so important that it cannot wait?”

I related “Alles Raus”. I could see it meant nothing to him. I explained. "It is the roll call of the concentration camp. My parents died in the Holocaust. I am sure your Jewish guests tonight will be, yes would be, offended, they know what 'Alles Raus' means. Possibly they have relatives who died in the concentration camps. Hollings might lose their support."

The Principal was worried. "I did not know. But of course we can't have that. I'll stop it." He did.

"We did not know about the Holocaust," said Mrs Green and Miss Davis. They did not apologise.

I said, "One should not use language one does not understand. Perhaps you thought it meant 'get lost'. We can't all be tri-lingual, like me," I said. The Nazi roll call at the concentration camps, where had they read this phrase?

My friend Alison, called the Miss Manchester, of the *Evening News*, introduced me to an interesting set of people. My social life improved.

There was a large envelope marked 'Clothing Institute London' delivered for me. I was most surprised to read the content: They regretted that I had been unable to attend the official ceremony in London. For my services to the Clothing Industry I was awarded the Degree of ACFI. They are thanking me for my valued contribution to the industry. I had never received the invitation to attend the ceremony in London. Perhaps it got lost in the post, or lost somehow. How? Where? I was told the decree is like a Doctorate.

The Manchester newspaper has asked me to judge a competition of women's clothing, made by clubs, Women's Institutes. I have not received yet any of the details. I could do this in my prep hours, but I need Miss Churm to give me leave of absence. She says she is busy, she will deal with it later. My friend, Alison McKechnie (the Miss Manchester) phones me next evening. Her editor had received a letter from Hollings College Principal, suggesting that Miss Churm would be a more suitable judge than Mrs Hurst. His reply was short: it was not up to a headmistress to tell a newspaper whom to appoint as a judge. I declined to be involved in this affair, it might cause more unpleasantness for me. "Get someone else!!"

I had an early morning dental appointment, Miss Churm had allowed me two hours off. The tooth extraction must have been difficult, there was bleeding, the dentist told me to go home, cancel my classes.

The bleeding did not stop, there was a whole bowl full of blood. I phoned the dentist. He told me to go to the hospital; Withrington Hospital was just around the corner from my flat. The taxi collected a chair, wheeled me in. The young doctor was laughing at me, for the fuss I had made, using a chair. He stitched me up. "You must sit up," he said. I felt I couldn't sit up, I slid to the floor. The nurse screamed, "Cardiac arrest, no pulse." I could hear her, looked down from above, it was interesting.

There are several nurses, two doctors, I was watching them, looking down, they do things to me. Then they put me on a trolley. "We caught her in time," said a doctor. I had to stay three days in hospital. My good friend Alison, Miss Manchester, brought me home.

I was very upset by the call, Alles Raus, Alles Raus.

The clique, headed by Miss Churm, included Miss Comley, and the two ATI ladies, Mrs Green and Miss Davis. They were the established Clothing Department. None of these ladies had industrial experience. I tried to comfort myself by saying to myself that everyone else, the other ladies of the Clothing Department, were friendly and made me welcome, also the tailoring section. My students are getting on well with their work, that is my main object.

I pray for guidance, how can I handle this situation? Why do those ladies seem to hate me? Perhaps they are afraid; they lost, could not get rid of me. I am the only person in clothing with relevant industrial experience. I can't forget it.

I buy Christmas presents for my family, to send off first week in November, that's what it said on the post office poster. Christmas is getting earlier and earlier, I resent that the Christmas offers start in October.

I think a lot about religion. The Nativity. Surely the official version is wrong? There were no inns in Palestine at that time. Cattle were kept in the house, in a separate room, which usually was tiled and hosed down daily – cleanliness would prevent the milk going off. The tiled floors have been found. What about Joseph, depicted as an old man, leaning on a stick? (Catholic version.) Could he have taken Mary and baby to Egypt, 300 miles away – a very long walk, even for a strong young man, or a man in his prime. The three wise men are sometimes called kings, it is said it was by astronomy (the Star), they predicted the birth of Jesus. I consoled myself by drawing on large sheets thirty x twenty inches, the Christmas Story.

- A domestic scene for the holy family, in the stable, tiled floor.
- The shepherds with their flock, listening, with wonder.
- The Three Kings, one elderly, from the Middle East, one younger, from India, and a handsome black prince from Africa, all bringing presents.

My gigantic Christmas Card? This is my answer to Alles Raus. I offer it to Mr Jones, our principal. I say, "Here is my Christmas card to the College."

He is delighted: "We could put it at the entrance, on display boards, if that's all right with you?"

"Must be anonymous!!" I said. He replied, "As you like."

I purchase some gold-coloured satin, a sale item, very cheap. Resources staple it onto the display boards. Secrecy, please.

The Clothing Department closes December 13th for holidays, but the Catering Department open their restaurant, it is their main season.

Good will to all men!

Trips to London

Only occasionally I travelled to London. To sometimes call at Trimfits, Berwick Street, for their fancy Czechoslovakian imports, which were almost identical with the real thing: pearls, jewels, fancy buttons, brooches, for costumes for our Drama 'A' Level plays.

I usually left Manchester with the early morning train. My lunch was missed out in order to complete my shopping.

Mandy attended Target School.

Auntie Betty (Mrs Champ) and her brother, Dukonkeli, had sold their house. They moved to Hounslow. Mandy stayed with them. Mrs Champs' daughter had recently married, she was glad to have a 'little daughter' living with her now. Mandy attended the Target School.

I ask Mandy, "How was school?"

"I did not like the restaurant. We do *Janet and John*, they are boring. I got a splinter in my hand from the desk. I had to see the nurse."

"Did it hurt?"

" No, the dentist gives one a sweet, and says, 'brave girl'. The nurse does not give sweets."

The new house had been scheduled to be ready in three months. I paid my deposit, they wanted one third of the cost. The agent wrote, the house builders have found there is ground water, a great deal; there was a little brook there and the houses were built over it. Our new estate will not be ready for some time. The deposit was not refundable, not yet. Mandy had to continue in Target School. I wrote to her every week, sent little presents. She answered back. Every third week Mandy came by British Air, care of hostess, to spend the weekend with me. I paid Auntie a generous £5 per week, I did not want any economic measures, on the contrary.

Auntie took her, by taxi, as no bus went near the airport, and collected her Sunday evening.

I collected Mandy from Manchester Airport. Not an ideal situation, but we were happy, we were together. Mandy and I visited our house. Yes, they were building it, somehow the foundation stood in water, all the other houses in the little estate stood in water too. Little progress!

Father Christmas

Mandy spent the first Christmas holiday with me in the Barlow Moor flat, the foundations of the Beckford Houses were still standing in water. I was told it was a very big job, they had found the trouble, an underground brook.

We went shopping to town. Paulden's Department Store had advertised invitations to see Father Christmas. He was standing in the toy section, with a big table, Mandy was fascinated. She studied the table for a long time, "Mummy, can I ask him for the toy railway on the table? That is what I want."

Father Christmas came near. He had been watching us. He looked at me, I shook my head. He said, "Little girl, I don't think you have put your order in, we have none left, you should have sent it in some time ago. This is a big job, the elves are busy, perhaps next time. You are the little girl who does not want to go to bed?"

I nodded my head.

I found the price list for various sizes of railways. The big one on show was terribly expensive. But I could manage the second size for next year. I was spent up – with the air fares. Mandy came every three weeks to Manchester, care of the air hostess, and the taxi from the airport was dear as well. I was going to save up for the railway. What Mandy wants, Mandy gets!!

For the next Christmas I had ordered the railway, a large one, the second size, not as big as the one in the shop. It depended on the size of one's table.

It worked perfectly, it was quite easy to control. I had not bought the accessories, such as trees and people and sheds, all standing around on the outside of the track. We did not need these. When Mandy went back to London, I packed the railway in a suitcase, her favourite toy, to take back with her to London. This is not the end of the story.

Mandy's room in the next house will be decorated in lilac, including lilac curtains. Her carpet and bedcover will be mauve, her favourite colours.

The Telegram

There was a telegram. An appointment had been made for Mrs Hurst to attend Tavistock Clinic in London to discuss Amanda Hurst, for 10 o'clock, next morning.

I rang Tavistock, I told them I had been ill, could I postpone the meeting? "No, it is too late for that. See you in the morning."

I could not get a sleeper, but the attendant said, "Unless we get too full I will let you have the compartment by yourself. This midnight train will wait in London, on a siding, you can stay until 8 o'clock."

I arrived at Tavistock House, I had no idea, what was wrong? Mrs Champ was also puzzled when I had phoned her.

It looked like a Tribunal, three women sitting at a large table, studying a folder. "An application has been made for Amanda to become a Ward of the Court."

"I don't understand, what is this application?"

"It is against the law to foster children without permission of the court."

"Fostering children?"

"You have given Amanda to be fostered without permission, do you know anything about these people in Hounslow? How long has Amanda lived there?"

"About these people," I reply, "I have you know she is staying with Auntie Champ. And Auntie Champ has been with her from birth, she was my housekeeper."

"Why is Amanda staying with her?"

"Because the house is not ready, they have found ground water, it should have been ready months ago. It is serious ground water, but now they have channelled it away. They are just putting the roof on."

"You mean to tell me you are waiting for your house to be completed? Then you will take Amanda?"

"Of course, of course. I see my Mandy every three weeks, she comes up by British Air, care of a hostess. I can't afford the travel costs more often than every three weeks."

"Well, that puts a different perspective on things."

"Who made the application?" I ask. "Several people, a Mrs Jeffrey who works here." I promised I would let them know when my house in Beckford Row was ready and Mandy would be with me in Manchester.

Mrs Jeffrey. She has it in for me. Last month two men came to Hollings College, said they could not find me at my home address. They were a collection agency. They said I owed several thousand pounds for medical fees.

"There must be a mistake," I said. "I don't owe anything, to anybody."

The men showed me papers. "You can have a copy. For Maurice Hurst to Mrs Jeffrey, owing this large amount."

"My divorce is coming through, final. Why should I pay this? He has not lived with me for years."

"You have always paid it, we were told."

"Let the woman he lives with now, let her pay it," I said.

"I don't think we can enforce this. We apologise." They left, "Goodbye, Madam."

Mrs Jeffrey, my husband's analyst, will not get my money, that was for sure. But to try and take my darling Mandy away from me, that she thought she could do that! I was certain she knew that Mrs Champ had been my housekeeper. Maurice complained about too many women in the flat often enough.

When the new house was finally ready, and I could have my darling back, Aunty Champ made difficulties in sending her back. Somehow she had thought Mandy was her little girl, because I would have no one to look after her. Nursy also said I would be too busy.

Mrs Champ, Auntie, refused to bring Mandy to the airport. I had to ask Maurice to take her, they both went by train. I collected them from the station.

"Oh the house is lovely," said Mandy, "and my room is all mauve and purple (her favourite colours), you remembered, Mummy!"

"Maurice, where are her clothes?" I asked.

"There is just this little hold-all. There were difficulties. I'll go back and ask for her things to be sent."

After a while I was informed there was a big consignment. A bed, a wardrobe, a folding table and a number of boxes. Maurice had asked for Mandy's things. I had wanted only her clothes, her toys, her books – that is all!

A misunderstanding, he must have asked for her things.

I had written several times to Auntie to thank her, but she never answered my letters. Why did she send the furniture? I did not want it, I did not need it. She never answered any letters. She was cross, hurt, annoyed. Mandy did not ask after her. I wondered why? What did she say to her?

I unpacked the clothes and toys, put the unwanted furniture in my empty garage – I did not drive.

"Where is your railway? It's not in any of the boxes."

"Auntie gave it to the Plescher's boy, next door."

"Why did she do that?"

"Because her table was not big enough, and she said railways are not for girls."

I can remember we had arguments about what is 'suitable for girls' when I had bought a little cement mixer which Mandy had admired. "What a thing to buy for a girl," said Auntie. Mandy did not play with dolls, not ever; only animals, the furry, cuddly animals.

Out shopping I found that Paulden's sold small railways all the year around. Really, it was very small, I bought it though, better than nothing. I told Mandy these little railways must be left over from Christmas trade, not from Father Christmas. I was told one can add rails and wagons etc., separately, any time. There was a catalogue.

Gradually our little railway increased in size. When I went into town, I bought some items, which were on display at the store, some were even reduced in price. Suitable or not suitable for girls, I could never understand this.

The railway is used by both sexes. Mandy's railway was given to our cousins in Montpelier, France many years later – they love it.

I have given Mandy my writing desk, which is an architect's writing table, so that she can draw her large pictures, of fish and other animals. Mandy is good at 'fish drawing'. I have bought her many books, the large ones called coffee table books are beautifully illustrated.

When I had phoned Auntie saying, "I am going to keep Mandy," she seemed surprised, saying she thought Mandy was going to stay with her permanently, hoping I would send her back.

"How can you look after her when you are at work all the time?"

"I am her mother."

The headmaster of the primary school next to Holling College interviews me. I tell him Mandy cannot read or write.

"Several of the children in her class cannot read or write," he says. It does not seem to disturb him. Mandy does not like the new school. She is frightened of the assembly.

"If you have been naughty, you get the cane."

Mandy's class teacher, Miss Collier, is a very nice young woman. We discuss Mandy's difficulty. "She is very bright," says Miss Collier. "Perhaps I can help." Each child was asked to tell a story. Mandy tells her of the Queen of France who had said, "Let them have brioche if there is no bread." Mandy explains to the class what brioche is. "We have brioche for breakfast, when I visit my cousin in Paris. I have been many times. Sometimes I go alone, care of the air hostess, when my mummy needs a babysitter."

Miss Collier asks me to explain Mandy's story. I tell her that we have no family in England. When we lived in London it was easy, and cheap to fly to France. I was often away, on business. Then Auntie Champ looked after her. Sometimes Auntie was away with her family in Ireland. Then I sent Mandy to spend weekends with Eva and Jaques, my cousins, and their three sons. A lovely time for Mandy. Miss Collier offers to teach Mandy privately. Reading first, and I let her draw loops. Mandy is good at drawing: loops and fish. Success!

Within six months Mandy can read. Mandy is still frightened at school when the headmaster is around, she gets all quiet. The headmaster says, "She is abused at home, that's why she is so quiet."

Miss Collier says, "You should hear her at home, so lively." He does not believe Miss Collier. Mandy tells me she is frightened because of the assembly hitting. She has never been hit.

Miss Collier got married, left the school. I talk to my friend Dorothy. I have known her a long time, she is an anthroposophist, a fellow at Manchester University in charge of Dyslexia and related difficulties. Dorothy comes twice a week to our house to teach Mandy writing. She is very successful. Within the year, Mandy can read the newspapers, at normal speed, and also her books. Miss Collier visits her. She is delighted with Mandy's progress. But Mandy's writing is not nice, in fact, whilst legible, pretty ugly. I don't mind as long as it is readable.

I have a lot to be grateful for. A loving daughter. She is a good companion. We have an interesting time together. She likes my friends, who are mostly working at the university. Her great friend is Uncle Don. He is a metallurgist , a professor in charge of his department. Mandy has a scientific streak, she wants to know why: "Uncle Don, tell me about rust. What is rust?"

He shows her the electron microscope.

"Strange you should ask, I have just asked two students to work on this same question." Mandy visits him sometimes, they have discussions. He shows her the wind channel. Mandy is interested in biochemistry. This is above my head. I am an 'art bod'.

PART THREE

Ashtons

An acquaintance – we met on a holiday in Ibiza – told me of her life in Israel. She was with the Alija, a refugee from Germany, a Jewish girl, good-looking, red-haired. A Sergeant of the British occupation forces met her, they fell in love and married.

They returned to England together. She could not have children, she said, "Really, we tried," but was overjoyed then to be offered a boy and a girl – the parents having died in a car crash. Could she take them immediately? Her husband had been demobbed by that time, was now an accountant. She was a teacher in junior school. The Adoption Society said, 'You'll like this, both children are red-haired, exactly like your husband and you."

The little girl was Mandy's age, they sometimes played together. Whilst she was looking for part-time work in the Educational Supplement of *The Times*, for just a few hours per week or supply teaching, she came across an advert she thought might interest me. I had told her about my 'Alles Raus' story, which she had found shocking.

Ashton Technical College of Further Education was looking for a Lecturer in Charge for manufacturing and retail fashion, to cover Clothing Institution and City and Guilds courses. Yes, I agreed, I found that very interesting, it would give me further scope and I would be free from the politics rife in Hollings.

I wrote to Ashton for details, which I received from the Lancashire Education Committee, saying that the position was to cover the needs of their local clothing industry.

I phoned and asked to be allowed to look at the premises, which was granted. I was told a whole floor would be allocated to the Department. It looked to me like a fresh start.

One room had three table model electric sewing machines, another three industrial tailoring ones. That was all the equipment I could see. No large cutting tables or other machines. The college had now 6,000 students, over many different departments.

I lived in Rusholme, Manchester 13, it would mean at least one hour travelling by bus, should I apply? I knew I had to give three months' notice to Hollings, no time to lose. I discussed with Mandy the need of a daily baby-sitter, as I would be home much later. The Clynch family, neighbours, offered their sixteen-year-old daughter, should the need arrive.

I applied for the position; I received an invitation to attend the interview. I did not think the other applicants could offer my experience or my background, including the lady in an electric chair. My credentials were: sixteen years in the industry in London, in my own firm Sylvia Russell (Kensington). I showed my impressive customer list, England's best stores. My family had manufactured clothing since 1849, internationally. At present I was the Head of Design in Holling College. I was holding ACFI from the Clothing Institute. I was told that the existing Fashion Section in Ashton College was part of the Art School. The tailoring part was closed now.

"We are awaiting several more persons from the Lancashire Education Committee. Could you return after lunch?"

I lunched at the local pub. The other applicants had left.

"If you consider accepting the position, what are your proposals?"

"To create an industrial course, there is a great deal needed."

"Three years ago, all the equipment, everything, was newly purchased," they said.

"For dressmaking," I replied. "Not manufacturing. You only have three electric table models, no other machines, except those tailoring ones, no tables large enough for cutting clothes or making patterns. We will have to start from scratch, in fact we need everything please." I had made a large list out, on my previous visit.

"Can you tell me, would I be in charge – administration, finances?"

The committee members agreed to this. "I can assure you if it is to be my department, if I am engaged, I will take all my efforts, all my strength, to get ready for courses by the end of September. The first thing I need is a plan, of the building, the floor plan, including the electrical outlets. I can work from that.

"We will send your engagement by post immediately."

"Thank you," I said.

After my letter of employment had arrived, I gave written notice to Hollings College. This resulted in an interview with the principal, immediately.

He said, "Mrs Hurst, I realise it was wrong to engage a new member of staff for design, without your presence. This omission…"

I interrupted him, "It doesn't matter now, I am leaving."

"Would you reconsider?"

"No, I have accepted a different position now, from next term, as Head of Clothing in Ashton-under-Lyme College of Further Education." I showed him the advert from Ashton College.

"I was not aware that they offered the Clothing Institute courses."

"They don't, not yet, but they will," I said. "Our loss, their gain," he replied. I got the permission from the Clothing Institute. I was ACFI!!

How much time did I have to get my department ready? Easter and Spring Bank Holidays, the long summer holidays. All my spare time.

I received a letter from Manchester Education Committee thanking me for my valued contribution to Education.

Ashton-under-Lyme College was open on Saturdays, I familiarised myself with the lay-out, including existing power points. I had received the floor plan I had asked for. It was duplicated for use of the building department to carry out my improvements. They called my new course, 'Designer Technician for Industry'.

Setting up my Department

I submitted my suggestions, my demands to the principal for approval. He passed these on to Mr Smedley, the head of the Art School, who became the liaison between me and the varying parts of the building department.

There was little actual building work, only two stoothing walls.

One was to divide a large room to create my sewing-machine room, the other to give me a small office and one telephone.

To Building Department
2 stoothing walls
The twelve (2 x 6) very large wardrobes were put end to end to make the two walls needed – so no building work was involved.
To Joinery Department
3 long wall-to-wall tables
The wood was available, I was told.
To Electrical Department
A great number of sockets, see plan.
To Plumbing Department
2 toilets, 1 male,1 female with washbasins
1 washbasin in large workroom.

I gave copy plans to all concerned.

Equipment and furniture
There were 12 large wardrobes, standing around empty. Shelves for students' work in progress and for storage were to be put in. 10 of these.
Additional lockers to be added in the corridor, for the increased numbers of students. The Lancashire Education supply had these in stock.
4 chest of drawers, 2 cupboards, there were spare ones in the college, also chairs and stools.
Machinery
The sewing room was to be equipped with 18 electric sewing machines, for the 16 students expected, plus 2 in case of breakage.

Mr Smedley told me that for all equipment demands have to be submitted to Lancashire Education yearly in advance, some take two years, and they must have detailed estimates. What could I do?

Second-hand machines could be bought often very cheap, half

price or less, there was a supply firm – for the out-of-date models, but they were still good. How much would that cost?

I approached the Principal, I suggested we should have a meeting of the manufacturers, asking them if they had spare old models to help us. The meeting was a success, I got seven sewing machines, 'turfed' out because of low speed, and two overlockers, plus one buttonhole machine. All free gifts! Students do not need fast machines!!

I had submitted the following details:

> In the industry, the clothing designer works hand-in-hand with the sample machinist in order to make his design a production number. It must be easy and quick to produce, often needing a slight alteration of design to facilitate this.
>
> In our, the student designer's case, the sewing teacher would be consulted. Each student must have his/her own machine.

The Lancashire Education Committee gave Mrs Hurst permission to order her requirements. Naturally I bought everything second-hand and asked for discounts.

Lancashire Committee reminded the college that they had granted much equipment three years ago. Mrs Hurst answered – for Non-Voc, not suitable for the industry.

What had been bought was consumables – this is the term used for fabrics, sewing materials, paper on rolls and for drawing, etc.

Mrs Fryer, the dress teacher, had used all the allocation granted already for this year, Mr Smedley informed me. He had no money left this year.

I asked to be shown the Requisition Book. Sew-and-Sews, the local shop, supplied fabric, zips, buttons, etc. All at retail prices! What an expense! What a stupid waste going retail! The Principal granted me an extra £100. That was a drop in the ocean.

Sylvia Hurst was not worried. She had a good plan, as follows:

I contacted the fabric manufacturers, Tootal, Treforest, etc., informing them of my new appointment as Head of Clothing, asking for the swatches as before. Success, I also received sample lengths.

Mrs Fryer had craft-bought paper, brown, rolls. The same strong quality I had used when sending my blouse parcels to customers. My brother Arnold – living in Canada – had told me how he had advised a hard-on-heel client to collect the free leftover paper rolls from news print, which could damage if not removed from the printing machines in time. I applied this knowledge to my needs. No longer expensive paper for patterns was bought, the only cost was the transport from the newspaper offices to Ashton, and even sometimes this was free, when they delivered it.

Zips – wholesale for samples, one penny per inch. Buttons, bought in a 500-gram box, everything bought wholesale, sometimes it is a gift.

My Hollings B class was upset that I was leaving. Their B course was a three-year course. A great surprise, they told me they had decided to transfer to Ashton College, to complete their course work with me. I said I doubted that was practical, Ashton was a good distance from Manchester Central.

"Oh, I've thought of that, we can arrange two coaches, at pick-up points. Some of our lads are in transport."

"You'll be over eighteen, your various authorities have to pay fees."

"We've already consulted them, they said they understand that we wanted to stay with our teacher, it made no difference to which college they paid the fees."

Still, I doubted if this would be possible, what would Hollings do with the empty student hours? A B class student delegation went to see the Ashton Principal. "I'll let you know, I doubt it, we've never done this before," he said. I knew it was impossible, but I was deeply touched by their loyalty.

I spent all of my summer holidays to get my department ready. Mr Smedley had been at first so co-operative but he became more difficult. He resented that I did not need his advice, he became niggly. I no longer could write my own letters, he 'censored' them, having them re-typed. I cannot type, always having employed a secretary in the past. It especially annoyed him that my department's finances were controlled by me – after all, he did not understand what was needed – how could he advise me? To my letter, asking Tootals for their new swatches of fabrics, Smedley added a requisition form, the usual form for purchases. By return he received a short letter, that Tootal does not supply colleges or schools – that was the end of my free supply.

Luckily the layout of my department did not disturb him. Mrs Fryer and Mrs Stewart, the embroidery and craft teachers had their own rooms, sharing a stockroom. These two rooms adjoined my own rooms. I had admired Mrs Stewart's art work. The students had made pictures, using pulses, bean, nuts, for portraits, landscapes, old-fashioned motor cars. Delightful! These pictures were pinned up on all the walls. I had never seen this type of art before. And I never will again. On my return from holiday, the mice had had a good feed, most were half-eaten! She should have protected them with plastic, sprayed with anti-mice poisonous stuff!!

Mandy and I

We had intended to spend our summer holiday with a prolonged trip to Italy, Rome, Florence; we had studied my art books, all those treasures!

Mandy was very understanding.

"We have to postpone our trip, darling, I'm sorry."

"Yes, Mummy, I realise, the new job is more important."

"Auntie Eva and Uncle Jaques in Paris have invited you," I told her. "The boys love you." I sent Mandy care of the air hostess for a four-week holiday. They had a good program – of course it was not Rome or Florence. Auntie Champ, in Hounslow, offered a two week stay – very nice. Nursy was also happy to see her, she often took her out for treats, the zoo, film shows, museum.

My Ashton timetable had been approved. I needed a sewing teacher, industrial. In my Hollings class, 234, Advanced City and Guilds, I had an exceptional student, a Mrs Slater, who for many years had worked as a sample machinist. Her written English was good. I had been surprised of the low standard of written English of the part-time and day-release students.

My friend Alison, the 'Miss Manchester' helped me to write a prospectus for our Manufacturing and Retail Fashion courses. Our designer/technician courses would lead to middle management in the industry. Our Retail Fashion was accepted by the large stores for training for Assistant Buyers. The elocution and modelling would be useful, they said, for the Geordie accent.

Our courses would contain two 'A' levels, Drama, and one of choice, offered in evening class at our college. If a student did not have 'O' Level English, they could retake it. Ashton evening classes re-sits. If 'O' level English was not passed, then they could re-sit in June. Without 'O' level they would have to leave the course. They all passed.

An invitation to the Fashion Show was included with the prospectus, refreshments were provided.

The Principal gave permission for the Parks Department to make the floral display – for the Fashion Show – they did us proud. Mrs Fryer, the elegant fashion (non voc) teacher was the compère. Alison, Miss Manchester attended the Fashion Show with me. Some of the clothes made from Vogue patterns were quite nice.

Alison said, "If you write a review of the Fashion Show I will place it in the local papers, this might help you with your recruitment of students for the coming year."

Our prospectus had been successful. I offered interviews in early evenings: "Come with parents, and a work folder, if possible." I was allowed to use the committee room to select my own students. Mark you, my appointment, did not start officially until September! I accepted the usual sixteen students per class, a few more in case they changed their mind.

The Principal called me over: "Mrs Hurst, have you seen our good review, have you read it?"

"Yes, sir, I have, I wrote it."

Sylvia was speaking to a manufacturer on the phone, Bellman and Herz. His voice sounded so familiar. I suddenly said to him, "Who was Herzele?"

"This was my late wife, who are you?"

"I am Sylvia Fleischer, the daughter of Julius Fleischer, from Goeppingen." I had asked the manufacturers for help.

Mr Herz let us have all the remainder of the cloth of the lays (the fabric). Some were as long as six meters. All the latest fabrics. Bellman and Herz was a fashionable firm. All free gifts.

Bellman and Herz became our patron, and benefactor. "Please write, that the proceeds of gifts are solely for the use and administration of Mrs Hurst." Other firms gave me the same assurance. I remember Miss Churm locking my fabrics away in her private store room.

Mrs Otto Hertz had sent me a nice letter, together with a large parcel of a length of remainder fabric. He writes he would like to meet me, perhaps one evening in Manchester.

"Could I bring my daughter with me?"

"Delighted," he says on the phone. Mandy's table manners are perfect. She was very entertaining. She gives us a resumé of her school, the High School of Art, in Strangeways. Yes, right next to the prison. They are not allowed out, it's safe.

"My full name is Amanda Irma, after my late grandmother, Genevieve, that is Saint Genevieve of Paris. My name day 3rd January." Otto Herz noted the date in his diary. Mandy continues, "I like Paris, that's where Aunt Eva and Uncle Jaques live. I visit them sometimes, I travel with the air hostess, when Mummy is busy. I have no relatives in England, I wish I did."

Mr Herz says, "Mandy, I never had any children, I also wish I did. My brother loves being a grandfather."

"I wish I had a grandfather, my mates in school tell me they take them out, and they give them treats and presents."

"Yes, it's nice to be a grandfather," says Mr Herz.

"Mr Herz, would you be my grandfather? Am I not cheeky when I ask you?"

"Yes, Mandy, please be my little granddaughter. That's settled."

They both hugged, and kissed, all in the posh restaurant. Every month we are invited, to exhibitions, to stately homes, such as Knutsford – they have a special display of old carriages. Always somewhere new.

I tell Mandy that we had, in Goeppingen, a barn for the carriages, the landau, the closed ones for bad weather, the large sleigh, which

† Thread marking: a cotton 'walks' from pin to pin before they are removed.' Chalkmark spoils the fabric, its stains.

seated four to six people – counting children. Karl, our coachman allowed me sometimes to go with him on the back and hold the reins. We played hide and seek in the barn. The visit to Jodrell Bank was the best. Mandy had a very long conversation with the guide. Mandy is a science bod, she tries to explain to me. I don't understand. I am an art bod. But Grandfather is interested. She tells us what she has seen on the Electron Microscope. Uncle Don Lees, the new husband of Auntie Barbara Wainwright, is a professor at the Manchester University. He is a great friend of Mandy, invites her to visit him.

Weekends are reserved for outings, the Pennines are near, the heather covers miles, what a wonderful sight. My free time, weekends, Mr Smedley thinks otherwise, Sylvia is part of the art staff. When I taught at Hollings College, the Manchester Authority asked for introductory classes to be given to schoolchildren, aged about nine to eleven years old. Another job for Mrs Hurst: "You'll think of something," says Miss Churm. "Craft classes."

It is near Christmas. I had bought a mobile made in Sweden, four little angels flying over lighted candles, made of thin metal cut-outs. I am wondering, would they fly over strong card as well? Yes, they do. Two sylko cotton reels, cut in half anchor the candles, which are fixed with a single screw on a small piece of wood, a little paint – red, silver, or gold.

Victorian ladies in underwear have to be dressed in Victorian costumes. Strong card for the cut-outs to be attached. The children research the library, another success. What next? I ask Mandy for advice, what interests kids? She had designed a teddy bear, made from two pieces of cloth, quite simple to make, not like the complicated one she was given on her birthday. It's made from scrap material, two pieces only: "Anyone can do it, even if your sewing is lousy." For the stuffing I ask a manufacturer of duvets for his waste, he has sacks full, to be discarded. It must be washable, safe for babies. The stuffing for toys, sold by craft shops, is grey wadding.

In education circles, the word had got around about these craft classes for schoolchildren. Because I am no longer in Hollings, Miss Churm directs enquiries to Ashton College.

Mr Smedley decides, quite rightly, it would be better to offer this service to the teachers, to give them the details, the know-how. The

Art School invite classes for the Instruction of Teachers:

Lancashire	On Saturdays
Cheshire	Once a month 10 a.m. – 12 noon
Derbyshire	Materials will be provided.

This is my free time, I don't get extra pay for my extra work, the preparation. I have to approach the manufacturers for remnants, the cuttings, the waste between the lays, large enough for the animals. The stuffing. Mandy designs a whole series, a cat, a lion, a rabbit, a frog. Success. The schools sell them at their Christmas stalls.

The teachers' classes were popular. Mr Smedley puts on repeats.

I complain, when the cost of the paper, the card, my taxi-fares to collect the stuff, is charged to my Clothing Department. I have to ask the Principal to tell Mr Smedley it is a college expense.

Mrs Slater

Mr Smedley had interviewed Mrs Slater, and given her a full-time position, as Assistant Lecturer B. The gradings were: Assistant Lecturer A, Assistant Lecturer B, Lecturer, Lecturer I, Lecturer II (that was me). I really should have had the higher grading of Senior Lecturer, with less teaching hours (contact with students) but I could not fill the contract hours for the classes, so I said nothing.

I suggested part-time staff, people I knew from industry. The pay was poor for them, but they did not care about the money, were proud to help. They were allowed mileage, but what about travelling time?

Prospectus. It went off well, my beginning at the new job. Students seemed to love the college.

The former dressmaking students of Mrs Fryer's class decided to stay loyal to her. They joined my program only in some of my classes. Next year I would have a full intake, of another sixteen students.

I had five male students, one tall good-looking Chinese from Hong Kong, married to an English girl, one black Caribbean, who had told me at the interview he hoped to manufacture clothes back home. He was very well spoken, he already worked part-time at BBC Radio

Jamaica. Two gorgeous lads, friends, very artistic. They had worked for Rent-a-Man, a company who supplied staff by the hour. And another boy, I thought he was bi-sexual but don't talk about this, or notice anything. He liked to try on the clothes of the other students' work. Yes, the boys seemed better designers than the girls. The Rent-a-Man boys liked the fitting they gave the girls so they told me! I had a good time.

The new, latest fabrics from Bellman and Herz were very stimulating for the students. Three of the wardrobes had been filled with the new fabrics.

Our boutique, with three separate display areas 'belonged' to my retail students. They had lessons in display, given by the part-timer, who was an assistant display manager at Lewis's store. Spotlighting was important. Our electric department obliged.

For Drama A Level I managed to get the old films. We had chosen the *Importance of Being Ernest* by Oscar Wilde. One of my rooms had been fitted out with a large screen, good for demonstration purposes, good for lectures. The Principal had allowed me this screen, I explained that it was for all the college to use. I was pleased to say I was right, the room was in almost constant use. The row of special chairs which had 'trays' attached, useful for writing up lectures, which were sometimes enhanced by the use of an epidiascope.

Miss Moynaham, the head of the refectory, was a wonder. Two sittings, at 12 and 1 o'clock. Fresh food of a very good quality and very cheap. Yes, the refectory served excellent food. At Christmas, the festive dinners were served at no extra charge.

The college gave a party with Father Christmas giving present to the staff's children. There were hundreds. It was well organised, by year, suitable presents, no kissing or sitting on Father Christmas' knees!

We were working now for first-year interim exams. Every week we discussed topical questions written on the blackboard, to be answered in writing. Later on, I discovered that this had helped the students to overcome their fear and anxiety of exams. Students who had difficulties were encouraged to seek help from the teachers. Mrs Slater was kind and patient. She explained, encouraged, helped with personal problems, all in her prep time.

All full-time students had a two-hour session in the General Studies

Department. One of their first lessons was always to write about the difference between school and college.

The Principal called me to show me the result of one essay: "In college the teachers care for you, you are an individual, you get help if you don't understand, they are patient and kind and will repeat difficult questions." The Principal said, "You and your staff can be proud – carry on."

The mock exams in February helped to show us any weakness in teaching.

Students' best designs were made up, kept for our fashion show in June. If students wanted to purchase the clothes they had made, they could do this, at a cost of near-to-nothing. Even so my college fund – from our gifts, was adding up quite nicely. Manufacturers sometimes sent donations to me, if they were pleased with the progress and/or knowledge gained of the day-release students they had sent. Our money, which belonged to the Clothing Department, for our sole use, caused jealousies in college.

I was called into the Principal's office; he said there had been serious complaints, as follows:

I was giving unnecessary fittings, twice sometimes, I made students strip, I told students they could not model their own garments at the Fashion Show.

"I don't understand, can I have more details? Who complained?"

"Mrs Fryer's class." Oh yes, I remembered Mrs Fryer fitted the clothes over their dresses, even over winter woollies. I said I could not do that, this was not correct, you cannot fit clothes on top of other clothes. They did not want to take their clothes off, they were cold. I said let's stand near the radiator, let's warm them up. The leisure wear, the bikinis or the bum-frills – the extra short skirts – why were they not allowed to model their own garments? I said I remembered from the Hollings Fashion Show, that in the mixed classes of co-edit boys and girls, the boys called out 'Tree-trunks' when a girl had very plump thighs or a 'double pair' or 'meat for two'. I explained this to the Principal, it made him laugh. They had said I had lesbian tendencies, wanted to touch up their bodies. I was shocked. Two fittings, yes I repeated, was needed, they had pulled all the pins out, neither had chalk marked or cotton marked the fitting.

"Did you notice anything was wrong?"

"No, it did not occur to me, I am not peculiar."

"This is serious," said the Principal.

"I agree, I am not a paedophile or a lesbian." I was not prepared for this. Was this the same? Was it like Holling's College, Alles Raus! Alles Raus! The students who complained were from Mrs Fryer's class, talking about me. She sometimes referred to me as the Jewess.

When I had phoned my White Witch to tell her about my change of college, she said, "You'll find politics are also rife in that college, much envy. Your work is important, valuable, carry on."

I called on a solicitor, a friend. He said, "If there are developments, call me, otherwise do nothing. It might be a good idea to ask a male friend to give you a lift home, to wait outside the college for you, next to his car for people to see him."

Next morning Mrs Slater called both classes for a talk.

"I am surprised. You want to work in the Clothing Industry, I have news for you, everyone strips off. You should not enter the fashion industry if the correct fitting of garments are not important to you. Where I worked before, several girls, of same size approximately size 36 (12) were asked to try on the new sample garments, to find out if it was comfortable, easy fitting, before putting it into production for the mail order, perhaps for 2,000 garments. Why did you pull out the pins?"

"To get the garment off."

It had not been chalk-marked or thread-marked, it had to be done again.

"Tell me, are you showing your designs or your bodies at the Fashion Show? In Hollings, at the shows for co-ed schools, the boys, bored, made rude remarks if a girl had plump legs: 'tree trunks', or 'double portion of meat', or small chested: 'flat like a board'. Did you want that? I am ashamed of you."

"We were told to complain," they said.

Mrs Slater confirmed, "I have to be present at the fitting to protect Mrs Hurst from your stupid talk. You ought to apologise."

She was present at the fittings, until I had taught students to thread-mark – not Mrs Fryer's sewing class. When she passed me, she smirked, "So the students will model for you, after all." Talking about me, she says, 'the Jewess'. There was no need to consult my solicitor.

Now I told students about the money side of the industry. I asked them, "What is the first thing in production of a garment?"

They all agreed, "The design."

"Wrong – it's the selling price, what will the garment bring? This is a clothing phrase. There are many people who have to earn their living. If the garment sells for £5, there is the cloth, how much per yard, the sample machinist, the machinists on piece work , the cutters, the overheads with the office staff, all have to make a living. And then you clever people have to design a garment, hopefully attractive, to pay enough for everyone to get their share, their wages. The designer/cutter is in charge, she or he is the only one who is well paid."

The large wall-to-wall tables enable the students to make their full-size patterns of their own designs. There they laid out the fabric of their choice, cut them out for making up. In the second year they learned Lay Making. The industry usually placed three or so patterns together, in the most economical way with little space between, after several tries. Even if only ten centimetres or more is achieved this can result in a large saving as often 2,000 garments are out of one design. Mail orders are the mainstay of the industry. The economy achieved by correct lay making, perhaps only four inches per dress can make the cost saved for the 2,000 dresses for mail order colossal. Hundreds, even thousands of pounds can be saved. Students were proud to save these large amounts, they worked out 'how much today have I saved?'

I contacted the maker-uppers (name given to the making-up manufacturers). "What are you doing with the cotton ends of sewing threads?"

"We throw them away; if not removed on time they might damage the sewing machines."

There is usually 100-200 metres left. Not anymore, "I'll send you a sturdy sack to put these left-over sewing silks in. It will save us a great deal." Ashton never bought sewing silks again.

Correct sizes, study the body, where is the extra weight? The bosom is in front, the arms do not grow longer. Necks grow shorter, collar shapes, pattern grading for larger sizes need adapting, pattern engineering, redesigning seams for economy without losing the design.

All of this knowledge is taught to full-time and day-release students.

For the all-important Ashton Fashion Show, potential employers are invited. We find we achieved a 100 per cent figure of employment. Even Mr Smedley is impressed. He dislikes that he had lost the power of administration of my department.

Anna Pisockyi

For the final exam it is a requirement to get the parents' signature.

Anna Pisockyi has not handed in her paper. Her father is Ukrainian, he does not speak English. Anna is often late to college in the morning. She apologises, explains she has to walk, it is almost three miles. There had been no money left for her for her fares. Only if the distance from home is over three miles is a bus pass available.

I also have noticed she does not take the school dinner, has only a plate of chips, if that. She looks so pale.

What is going on? I am concerned. She is one of my best students, very intelligent, she was the head girl of her former school. I try to have a little chat with her. She always replies, "I am fine, thank you. "Once she volunteered: "At home they don't like me, because I am not a boy." She is the eldest of several children. Her mother had told her: because of you I had to marry your father. Was the pregnancy Anna's fault?

I say to Mrs Slater, "She must take her finals, I had better speak to the Principal."

He calls her to his office. She talks to him. "Her parents don't want her to go to university, they want her to start work or leave home."

The Principal sent a letter to her parents. There is no reply. What can one do for her?

If we make her 'independent' she does not need her parents' permission for the exam. She could get some grants, some allowances. It is not much, because she is under eighteen years old. Not enough to live on.

I still live in Rusholme. I have a spare room, I use it for my library at present. It has a bed, and a table. She could live with me free, the allowances could cover her expenses. I put this to her, see what she says. "They will be glad to get shot of me! Oh, Mrs Hurst, thank you, I would love to come."

So that's settled. She moves in.

Anna did well in the exams, as expected.

Mandy was very happy. "I have a sister."

"Honorary sister," she said.

Mandy wrote down, 'One and rary sister'. Mandy's spelling of strange words were delightful. We always used this term, we thought it was a perfect fit. Oneandrary!

For the summer vacation we decided to go to the Lake District. Walking, bus, lakes, sightseeing.

Anna had studied the tourist brochure. When we arrived in Kendal she wanted to see Levens Hall. It had a famous fancy ceiling and all the box plants in the garden cut into fancy shapes. "The Hall is five miles on the south road." I tell her that we are going to Windermere – in the opposite direction!

Anna said, "It's only five miles."

I consulted my bus timetable. "Nothing for another two hours on the south road, and nothing coming back until evening. I am afraid we will have to do it another time, Anna."

"I could walk it, I was looking forward to the fancy ceiling."

"Anna, we are booked in at the Salutation Hotel, in Windermere, that's the opposite direction, we have to book in before 7 p.m."

"Well all right then, you win," she said.

Arriving at the hotel, there was trouble. I had booked two rooms, the reception clerk had us down for two beds, a twin room. "My mistake," said the clerk. "Unfortunately we are fully booked, so are the other hotels. I could try a B & B for you, I know a good one, it is quite near."

"Please book a single room, no breakfast. We will all have our breakfast here."

I gave Anna the paper with the directions. She said she wanted to stay with Mandy, here at the hotel. "No, Anna. I have to stay with Mandy, because of her insulin injection, we have to monitor those, because of extra walking, her dose has to be different."

This fell on a deaf ear. "I want to stay in the hotel, Mrs Hurst. You go to the B & B."

"Anna, be sensible." Anna pulled a face. We had a splendid dinner, the Salutation was famous for it.

After breakfast we took a nice ride on Lake Windermere. The holiday came up to my expectations, except that the restaurant and cafes charged tourist prices.

Anna had obtained a place at Bath University. "Congratulations, Bath is a lovely town, Mandy and I have been there. The church has a fan-vaulted ceiling. It is a lovely old town."

Anna is looking for a short-term summer job. Holiday relief jobs were easy to get, for ten to twelve weeks. 9-6 p.m. nearby.

Both girls left a mess in my sitting room. The have their own rooms, why don't they use them? It made me niggledy. On my dining table were a number of magazines and 'other rubbish'. There were some pages from a letter, was it Mandy's or Anna's? I did not recognise the writing. I read the first few lines: 'at least I don't have to put with her domineering manner and her dreadful German accent'. She wrote she worked now as a dressmaker, on her own. I look at the signature, one of my ex-students.

So that is how they discuss me, not very flattering. So I read the whole letter, I have always been nosy. Of interest was her final sentence. "I'll visit you, when the old bird is out, I don't want her stupid questions. Mid-week is best. I'll phone."

I was hurt. Is that how they talk about me?

Anna had been saving her money, her allowance and grant and her wages at the job. Of course I did not accept her money. I was glad for her, to have something to get on when in Bath.

Now I felt mean. Let her find a furnished room, until she leaves in October for Bath.

I told her to go, to find this room. She found it quickly, the university was on holiday closure. Many rooms are vacant.

Mandy and I are visiting Eva and Jaques in Paris. The house would be empty. Coming back to college there was a lot of work waiting for me. Part of my holiday job there. I ponder about this dreadful letter. To be fair, Anna did not write it. I thought we had a loving relationship. Perhaps it was a love-hate relationship, I have been told most teenagers are angry about something or other. I know people resent it when they feel they owe something to someone, make them feel inferior. I never tried to encroach on her private life, I never asked about her parents. I did not know if she had not visited them. Did they know she had been accepted at Bath? Mandy and Anna are wonderful together, sharing, laughing, going out to cinemas together. Sisters one and rary!

The London Trip

This was to coincide with the London Fashion Week in January.

The college allowed a minimal sum per student. This covered the rail fare (one free in ten) and two nights stay in the youth hostel in Holland Park (Kensington). Sylvia Hurst was a life member, therefore she could book her students in, without them being members themselves. Two dormitories and one room for the boys.

Details of travel:

Assembly Manchester Piccadilly 7.40 for train at 7.55

Train arrives King Cross 12 noon.

Sandwich lunch on the train for each student.

Maps given by London Transport Underground and buses for central London.

Maps given by Mrs Hurst, duplicated and enlarged A-Z

Knightsbridge Area

Oxford Circus Area

Kensington High Street Area

Day One Travel arrangements

Please note the London Transport keeps changing the location of bus stops.

Cross over street outside Kings Cross.

Bus no. 73 to Oxford Circus – frequent.

Bus fares in Central London are £1, have change ready, no change given.

Day Three – Return to Manchester. Assembly Kings Cross 5.15 no later, read notice board for train platform.

Train leaves 5.30

We have a reserved compartment because this train is crowded.

Train arrives Manchester 9.45.

Have your parents or friends collect you because of the late hour.

Mrs Hurst lived for many years in London, had her workrooms in Notting Hill Gate, W11.

To make the trip a success it is important that we discuss the venue and what we hope to see and learn.

It is London Fashion Week. Because I was well-known as a designer, I have obtained, with the help of a former colleague, the entrance to the major fashion shows. These are not open to colleges or schools, therefore groups of three to four persons are suggested – separately seated.

Day Two – 11 o'clock International Show of wool secretariat. Dorchester.

Day Three – 3 p.m., the London Show, Grosvenor House.

Front seats are reserved for VIPs and for buyers, always. If you arrive early, you may get a seat in the third row.

No sketching allowed, not even on the programmes, just a tick.

Things in London may have changed – it is several years since I have left London.

These are my suggestions:

Oxford Circus:

Dickens and Jones

Fabrics Ground floor. Many foreign imports from Italy and France. Baby Wear, beautifully made.

Liberty's

Windows, displays. Fabrics first floor. Foreign imports of art.

Carnaby Street: more talk than do. The press has exaggerated the attraction of this street.

The London Palladium is in the back street – photos of famous stars outside.

Walk down Regent Street to Piccadilly Circus – shops on right side of street.

Oxford Street, miss out. Shops, mainly multiples, exception is Selfridges.

Piccadilly Circus, you can see foreigners from all over the world. Some are wearing their nation's clothes.

Cheap cafes: you may need this for rest and refreshments.

Piccadilly – the main street. Hupperts, blouses, knitwear, Simpsons, mainly men's sports. Fortnum and Mason, food hall. High class, expensive, fashionable clothes including children's wear.

Passing The Ritz – for millionaires.

Do we have the time? To walk from Hyde Park Corner. Buckingham Palace is on the right hand side from Hyde Park Corner into Grosvenor Place into Buckingham Gate. This is quite a long walk.

Walk from Hyde Park Corner, continue, many small shops – good Knightsbridge window display. Continue in Knightsbridge – Harvey Nichols, good window displays.

Bus to Kensington High Street Holland Park – Youth Hostel. Assembly at park gates – there are, or were, benches or cafes for six o'clock assembly.

Mrs Hurst will book you in. There are public rooms and a kitchen for self-cookers. There used to be dinner to be purchased, I don't know if this is still available.

Day Two – Breakfast from 7 a.m. – cheap.

A taxi shared by four persons is cheap.

Day Two

Kensington High Street – bus?

Derry and Toms is now BIBA.

Barkers is a general store for the housewife.

Pontings for cheap fabric, cheap clothes.

Hyde Park Corner, Park Lane, walk to Grosvenor House.

11 a.m. International Wool Secretariat. Haute Couture from Paris, Milan, London, Loden from Germany, Austria, other European countries. Come early, small groups. Seats possible, third row, in separate groups.

Bus or taxi to Knightsbridge. 1 p.m. assembly at Spaghetti House, Street north of Harrods. Reserved seating. Food is good and reasonable.

Harrods – you have all afternoon. Food Hall, many departments, including a zoo. Not to visit the made-to-measure department. In the back of Harrods are many small boutiques. Find your way back to Hostel. Hostel closes 10 p.m.

Day 3

Breakfast at leisure.

Visit BIBA (Derry and Toms). The Roof Garden is a world wonder, with exotic birds walking about.

Grosvenor House for the London Couture Show.

Hartnell, Molyneux, all the well-known couturiers etc. No sketching, just ticks. Young newcomers to the fashion scene are very interesting.

Show lasts one hour. Bus or taxi to Kings Cross. Rush hour. Time for refreshment. Cheap stall for presents and sandwiches for the train.

5.15 for 5.30 Assembly (look on the board for number of platform).

We have reserved seats.

9.45 arrival Manchester.

I have asked for you to be collected because of late hour.

My daughter Amanda was to stay with Joan Van Hove, a former neighbour, still living in Beckfoot Row, Rusholme, MC13.

Joan recently had opened a shop in Ashton-Under-Lyne, for arts and crafts and household fabrics, like curtains.

I said, "Mandy, I've put your sandwiches in the fridge, Joan may be vegetarian, sometimes she is."

Mandy said, "I think I have a cold coming on."

I say, "I am leaving at 6.15 in the morning, you'll be asleep. Take an aspirin and have a hot water bottle. You go to Joan's new shop, no hurry. Have a nice time, help her a bit. When I return from London, I'll pick you up in Beckfoot Row at about 10.30, earlier if possible."

This was the plan for Mandy.

On my arrival back in Manchester, a policewoman waited for me. She said, "The college told me the time when you would be coming back, they gave me the train time. Your daughter is in hospital, Ashton Hospital. I'll drive you there."

I asked, "What happened? Not an accident?"

"Oh, no, your daughter is ill. We had a call from a nurse, to come to the general shop, the grocery one, near the bus station. The cashier knew the nurse, who was in the shop at the time.

Someone pushed into the girl, she dropped her change at the check-out. People helped to pick the change up, pinched some. The girl was not worried about that, saying she had not finished shopping, she could not find everything which was on the list, she had gone to several shops, but it was so windy, so cold, she did not have her big coat on. She must continue the shopping, repeating this over and over.

The nurse said the girl was running a temperature. It was madness to go shopping in this wind. "Can your family collect you? Where do you live?"

"I am staying with Joan, I have not finished shopping. It was so cold."

"Where is your mother?"

"She is in London with the students. I must finish the shopping."

"Where is this Joan?"

"Around the corner, in the new shop."

"What is it called? Is she on the phone?"

"I don't know, I don't think she got the phone, not yet."

The nurse said, "She has got a temperature, I will take her to the hospital, she's burning up."

The shop had contacted the police station, asking them to send an officer. The girl kept repeating herself about shopping. "She told us her mother was in London with the students, she was with Joan."

The nurse said, "She is ill, she has a temperature, I have to take her to the hospital. I don't know who this Joan is, we have to sort this out later. We can't leave her here, in the shop. So we took her in the police car to the hospital. They put her into a small room, because she became so noisy. She has been there now for three days, she is delirious, keeps on about the shopping. She is also worried about her insulin. They checked her for that, it seems to be all right."

"We found Joan in her new shop, we gave the two shopping bags. Why did she send her out in this weather?"

The staff nurse took me to Mandy. She was asleep. They had given her a sedative, also her insulin, she knew about that, the right dose.

"Better not wake her, come back in the morning," said the nurse.

I returned at 7.30 a.m. with her organic porridge and the cream, and also all her insulin things and pyjamas.

Mandy was so sleepy, she could not keep awake. I told Mandy I have to go to college, but I am back at lunchtime.

I had taken a taxi from the college, it was not far, at lunchtime, my dinner hour. The nurse said, "Mandy had the porridge, we have a microwave, but she would not eat the lunch. She had said it was garbage and threw it on the floor."

"I'll bring something at teatime," I told the nurse. When I left Mandy was already asleep again. They told me she had been rambling about Joan, and saying she wants to go home.

I told the nurse as well that I would return. I don't think Mandy heard me, she kept on saying, Mummy, Mummy, Mummy, and fell asleep again. I thought it must be the sedative, still in her system. The nurse said they had tried to contact Joan. Mandy had said, "she is just around the corner, the new shop." But she was glad her mother had come now.

They transferred her to the mental section of the hospital. There was a nice male charge nurse, he put Mandy in a side ward, a small one.

She is diabetic, she must have regular food. I made little parcels of food, like chicken mayonnaise, sandwiches, and other things she liked.

Twice she went to the loo while I was there and already now she wants to go again. I was wondering if she had a urinary infection? I asked the nurse about it. The nurse answers, but not my question, she asks, "Would you sign this? I need your approval." It was for electric treatment. "We give it to all patients here."

I replied, quite forcibly, "I don't know enough about this, I am not signing this, that is for certain, not until I know more about it. Meanwhile, can she see the doctor, to see if she has a bladder infection?"

"It is the weekend now, I'll see if I can get someone to see her, on Monday."

I was really worried about this electrical treatment. I rang Dorothy Jeffree, my friend from the university, at her home address. She was quite shocked. She said she knows it is in general use now, "They give this treatment, but don't let her have it. We better take her home!"

We took Mandy home, both of us. She gave no trouble, went quietly.

Mandy settled down, but she went continually to the loo.

I rang Mrs Slater, I had her home telephone number. She promised she would cover my classes on Monday, to tell Mr Smedley I would not be in. On Monday, Mr Smedley rang me and told me to get a nursing service to look after Mandy. I tried this (no social services at that time). Their conditions were exorbitant. “If there is no separate bedroom, you need a night nurse, no catering is included, you have to arrange this, etc., etc., a high hourly charge.”

I consulted Dorothy Jeffree, my friend, she told me she thought teachers were allowed time off for a sick child.

I thought Mr Smedley would make difficulties, I felt he liked to give me trouble, if he could get away with it.

When I took Mandy to Outpatients on Monday, the arrangement made by the kind staff nurse, this doctor, he said he was a locum, retired, wondered if it was a urinary condition with mental side effects. He had her urine tested, it was infected. He gave medications. Take three times a day. “Come back in four days, you have my number if you need us.”

We thanked him, I was very relieved, took a taxi home. She was quietly hugging me, “Mummy, Mummy,” in a whisper.

I had contacted the college office on Monday, they confirmed that I was entitled to look after my daughter, if no other arrangement could be made.

At home I cooked Mandy’s favourite food. There was a small grocer’s less than five minutes away for supplies. They stocked a great variety of goods including vegetables and fruit.

A knock at the door, Mandy opened it. “Oh, Anna, Mummy, my honorary sister is here, she’s come to visit because I’ve been ill.”

Anna said, “Mrs Hurst, can you put me up? My family won’t have me. I am on holiday.”

“You are most welcome. Mandy is over the moon! I know it is difficult for you at home.”

Anna said, “I thought I’d try again, but they are just like before. They blamed me for not getting my brother into the grammar school. I did not coach him, they said.”

“Well you are most welcome here. Where is your luggage?”

“I only took this holdall.”

“Have you had any lunch? There is some – I will heat it for you.”

What a coincidence her coming to us, just when I needed help. God be thanked.

Mandy recovered. At first she made difficulties about taking her medicine, saying she had not had the tablets. I found a quantity of thank-you notes and envelopes in my drawer, just the right small size.

I wrote:

Wednesday	breakfast –	take 2
	lunch –	take 2
	dinner –	take 2

I put the tablets inside. I told Anna, "Keep the envelope, when finished, put it on the mantelpiece, she can check it, to see she has had the tablets."

Thursday – next envelope

Thursday	breakfast –	take 2
	lunch –	take 2
	dinner –	take 2

I made out envelopes for the week.

Her insulin record book had always been kept by Mandy herself, except when she was in hospital.

Anna and Mandy had a nice time together. They found good programmes on TV, played card games. Anna looked after her very well, lovingly. My students sent a large get-well card and a bunch of flowers.

Ashton Fashion Show

The Park's Department is most generous. I have not seen any better displays before anywhere. Mr Smedley says, "It's getting out of hand, we have to put on extra shows for schools, and then we can't take all."

Our fashion show had been a great success, the college had to put on two extra performances, not to turn the schools away.

Miss Meynell, a retired famous model, had rehearsed the girls, giving them exercises to improve their posture and shape, teaching them discreet make-up.

Mrs Handworth worked on their diction, elocution and presentation. She had formerly trained actresses, some now famous. What about your Geordie accent? Speak clearly, don't mumble, we are interested to hear your story.

Both ladies worked together with the drama teacher for our show. The visiting judge, who was given the job of allocating the A-level marks in Drama, was most impressed with the standard of the costumes shown to her.

We improved the next year's fashion classes by adding an act from their A-level Drama , Oscar Wilde is most popular, *The Importance of Being Ernest*. For the student to make their costumes, the drama teacher puts up a notice to ask for curtains (washed), that are no longer wanted. Many of these are suitable. I ask for obsolete patterns of furniture fabric from manufacturers , explaining it is for costumes. The result is surprising, we receive many damask, cotton satin and printed fabrics. I give the pattern, after all I have made costumes for TV and films. The result is astonishing, professional. The students love drama and costume. Unfortunately I no longer teach Costume History – I don't have the time. My friend, Mrs Van Hove, RA, Textiles College of London, teaches our Textiles, takes over the Costume History. I give her all my handouts, drawings, notes.

The choice this year was *The Rivals* by Richard Brinley Sheridan, the famous playwright of the eighteenth century.

When I worked for TV in London I was never asked to do male costumes. Now only the naval costume presented me with difficulties. Gold braid was expensive. Trimfit of London sold real gold braid and also cheaper gold ribbons for packing parcels at Christmas. I ordered these. We received free gifts, samples. Furnishing fabrics in eighteenth-century designs were often samples or off-cuts used by the furniture trades. Large samples of the costly fancy woven fabric had been withdrawn from sale. Formerly it was used by upholsters for re-covering wing chairs or settees. There was little demand now. The repeat patterns were eighteen to thirty inches. These disused samples were given to Ashton's. Drama section – I must not call it Department. Mr Smedley would object. The pieces were sufficiently large to make the front section of waistcoats. Messrs Trimfit (London) imported from Czechoslovakia fancy metal and gilt buttons, costing next to nothing. They looked so real, it gave the final touch.

One of our students was 'in love' with her outfit, she wore it to college every day. When she was approached or laughed at, she replied, "You are only jealous." She was right. Fancy waistcoats for evening wear was the latest mode for gentlemen, sold at a price!

Girls could wear the coats, providing they were not too generously endowed. Mrs Malaprop, the young rich widow, had to have a very elaborate costume, to show she was very rich. Satin in lime green and purple, coffee-coloured lace, highly rouged cheeks and a charming smile. The side hoops worn under her skirt, quite correct, made her dress stand out, she had to move sideways to get through the doors. Our fashion show as well reported in the newspapers, the Drama Section got a special mention.

Our principal received a phone call from the organiser of the forthcoming trade show in Manchester.

He was told it would be the greatest show the North had ever seen, bigger than Olympia in London. All the new inventions would be shown, the whole Trade put its best foot forward. Our fashion shows had been seen, much admired. They wondered if they could include it in the show, it would be a great attraction, a treat for the ladies when the husbands examined the bolts and nuts, the new machinery at the exhibition. If possible, could the costumes of the eighteenth century of what was it called, *The Rivals,* of the Sheridan fellow, be displayed at the entrance? Credit would of course be given to the College of Further Education. The models were the students, they did so well at the show, quite professional. Adele Rostein could supply the fashion dummies. For *The Rivals* three male costumes and three female ones would be nice for the display, if you agree.

At the main entrance was a notice in a gold frame holding a sign with outsize letters:

ASHTON-UNDER-LYNE COLLEGE OF
FURTHER EDUCATION has the honour to present
their FASHION AND DRAMA DEPARTMENT.
THE CLOTHES and COSTUMES have been made by
2nd and 3rd year students.
THE WIGS WERE MADE BY THE
HAIRDRESSING DEPARTMENT.
FASHION SHOWS are the following hours,
11 a.m. 2 p.m. 5 p.m.
Tickets available. FREE.
SEE the NYMPHS and the NEW GIANT JACUZZI.

Mr Smedley complained. I was severely told off by Mr Smedley because the School of Art had not been mentioned. I told him the display notice had been out of my hands. He must complain to the management of the trade show.

It did not involve the college at any extra cost, transport and display were laid on.

The display and the show would be a great attraction.

The Principal had agreed, subject to the approval of the Head of the Art School. How could he disapprove after the Principal had said yes?

Second- and third-year fashion students were involved. There had been the men's tri-corn hats made in the millinery lessons. There were the wigs made by the hairdressing section, nylon hair – not real, but looking as good as.

There would be the very new jacuzzi if the students would like to swim, they were welcome. Here are some tickets for it.

Adele Rotstein, famous maker of showroom display of dummies had supplied life-size dummies. They were a most important firm for window displays. They had a full show inside the Trade Exhibition, of male and female dummies.

After two days the fashion shows were only performed outside of college time – in the students' own time, at 5 p.m., not to interfere with their college work.

Our 'hardworking' models received free refreshment, at the café or at the restaurant of the trade show.

Jacuzzis were the latest thing for the bathroom.

The huge jacuzzi was only for the show and the exhibition, it could accommodate ten-plus people, splashing, but the normal size one for bathrooms stood next to it.

Bikinis were in, the skimpier the better. The 'nymphs' wearing flesh colour boob tubes and garlands of artificial flower, attracted a great deal of attraction, they were admired by the male population, even more than the female one.

Ashtons College, the Building Department, had sent a bus load of students several times to see the latest inventions, mechanical and otherwise. The bakery found the continental goodies, different shapes and sizes, a welcome inspiration. They also offered lifts to our first year fashion students who had felt left out.

The trade show was important. The college put on buses. The show was on for a full week. "Whatever next?" said Mr Smedley. He seemed annoyed.

The three male dummies portrayed at the entrance:
One Ensign Absolute (in navy costume)
Sir Lucius Trigger (Irish Baronet)
Bob Acres (male friend)
Three female dummies portrayed
Mrs Malaprop (Delia) wealthy widow
Julia Languish her niece
Lucy – a maid servant.

The costumes looked very professional, also the hats and wigs. The students were very enthusiastic when making them. They all passed their A-Level exam in Drama with high marks.

There had been a generous cheque, sent to the Principal, saying the public had much appreciated the display.

I asked the principal to give the cheque to Mr Smedley.

I was told our very favourable reports in the evening papers upset Hollings College.

My daughter Mandy's GP suggested she has a tonsillectomy. The hospital is dirty, she contracts an infection, becomes diabetic. Ten babies died at the same time in that dirty Manchester Hospital, which was then closed. We both study how to live with this disease. Strict food intake. She sees to her own injections, but she is weak. We have to learn to live with it. She is constantly tired. We move house to the Pennines, for better air, to the outskirts of Slaleybridge. She gradually improves, passes three 'O' levels in spite of her dyslexia.

College life is now peaceful for me. Mrs Fryer has left, aged sixty.

The Unions achieve their proposals, part-time lecturers, over eight hours, and also others, are to be given pensions and paid holidays, like full-time staff. This has a disastrous effect. Wholesale sacking of very good experts in my department. I lose eight good teachers, I can have two new full-timers instead.

I am friendly with the Head of the Bakery Department. He suggests that Mandy can join his classes. If she falls asleep, she can go to the rest room, care of the college nurse. She can come later in the mornings, or at other times, if she is not well. The principal allows this generous offer. Mandy enjoys baking, messing around with the dough.

Fresh air is very beneficial to Mandy, we walk every weekend, weather permitting, in the Pennines, sometimes we stay over, at weekends, in hotels.

PART FOUR

Looking for a restaurant

We have been walking every weekend if the weather is clement, the countryside on the foot of the Pennines is beautiful. In the summer the hills are covered with heather, a really wonderful sight. Our walks seem beneficial for Mandy's diabetes.

There are a number of inns in the area offering home-cooked food. We liked the one in Mottram-in-Longdendale best. It is less than two miles from our house, their food is delicious, no wonder they are always full in their restaurant. "Something like that would suit us," says Mandy. But nothing suitable comes up for sale. Perhaps we must look further afield.

Mandy was working part-time, unpaid, in the Ashton's college lab. She lost her job when an additional full-time lecturer is engaged and takes over.

There is a national offer of early retirement available. I am fifty-four years old, I was interested.

"I always loved your cooking," said Mandy. "We should open a restaurant." So I am looking in the trade and local papers. There are no restaurants for sale, except at ridiculous prices. There is a pub in County Durham, due to death of the owner, Oak Tree Inn, in a village situation. I like the name.

The building is late medieval, the walls are two to three foot thick, even the internal walls. The price is very low, why? I am told the turnover is only £3,000 per annum – almost nothing. Should I buy it? Can I renovate it? On the plus side: the building is large, stands in its own grounds, on a hill. There is a small building in the garden, possibly a coach house, could be the owner's residence, with garage.

I think it may be a Free House. This was the plus. Now the minus.

Car park, there is no place anywhere, for the terrain is too steep. The lady with the key tells me this is the reason the premises have not sold. Also, no fire escape, if the first floor is used. The garden has been like the village rubbish dump. Just about everything has been deposited there, including a rusty bedstead. The rest of the garden is brambles and nettles. I ask my bank to contact their Durham branch, to get me a surveyor's report.

They write: 'We do not send you a report. The pub is owned by a brewery The price of £16,000 is very low. The building is in the main street. Tantobie is an ex-mining village. The walls seem good, also the roof. The garden is very neglected. We have not inspected the property."

The building is just a shell, but of attractive proportions. One has to start from scratch. This would suit me, I hate the plastic pubs with their money and gaming machines – re-furbished they call it. I would like an old-fashioned pub, a Victorian pub, I would make a handsome restaurant. I would give wonderful food, and Mandy would have a job. She'll run the restaurant, be in charge.

I buy the Oak Tree Inn

Perhaps I was hasty, but restaurants or pubs don't often come onto the market (this is 1977), certainly not at a cheap price. I had applied for early retirement. It is granted. No suitable replacement for me can be found at the college, with my experience. It is a large department, with almost 200 students, including the Non-Vocs, there are forty full-time students on the design and retail courses. The early retirement offer is withdrawn, cancelled. Now I have a public house and a college job.

I have to rely on my solicitor, in Stanley, for more help, as I am away all week. The sale had gone through very quickly because I had paid cash. There are rules and regulations, red tape. The Building Department is in Consett, also the Licensing Authorities. I draw up plans, I am a designer, measurements are my forte.

I approach a Durham Bank, regarding an overdraft. They agree, after all, my house in Staleybridge and the inn are both without mortgage. I had been told because I had no experience in the trade, and because I was a woman, aged fifty-four, a mortgage might be difficult to obtain. There is a little outside work to do. There is no car park, I have the solution. Oak Tree Inn has been built on a steep hill. The front entrance faced the village street. The back entrance to the cellar is about five meters lower, into the garden. A slope. I discuss my plan with the builder: we fill the sloping side in, level it, tarmac it. We build a strong retaining wall – but leave about three meters to the boundary fence, to the back street. I think the drop would be too great, this will give me a little vegetable garden for my kitchen herbs, and it would be safer.

On the other side, once the ground is clean, after the rubbish has been cleared, and it is free of nettles, brambles, and potholes, we terrace it – alternating grass and rose bushes. The coach house, or whatever it was, is to be left in abeyance. The outside toilet is to be demolished.

If I am using the first floor, I need an outside staircase. My prospective customers who have recommended the Drovers Forge are very good. I approach them. "No problem, missus, when you are ready."

My solicitor sent my plans to Consett Building Department, saying they are preliminary plans, the interior ones will follow.

I travel every Friday lunchtime from Stalybridge to Durham or Newcastle, not all trains stop in Durham. My job: the garden must be cleared again, brambles regrow quickly, I should have worn scratch-proof clothing! It took three lorry loads to clear the rubbish, and another lorry for the garden refuse. There must be a lawn, where would one hang out the laundry? Local teenagers help to clear up, to earn a little money.

The windows at the front are all higgledy-piggledy, different levels and sizes, this is for the ground floor. I order two very large windows to be made.

We have the clean-up inside, under the wallpaper the plaster is soft and broken. All must come off. The fireplace is working. I order a back boiler, it will heat the bedroom above. The rest of the building will get central heating, the boiler is to be put in the cellar. The kitchen had a stone sink, a wooden draining board, an electric two-burner plate and a yellow fold-up table. There was a pantry, if we remove the stoothing wall, it makes the kitchen larger, the ceiling is okay. Walls and floor will be tiled. There are steps leading into the garden from the back kitchen door.

A new door has to be cut out to the small room at the side, otherwise the kitchen is difficult to reach. There was once an internal stone wall leading to a music room. All walls have layer upon layer of broken plaster, we are now living in a dust storm.

The entrance gets stone flags to the floor, in the traditional manner. When will the dust settle down? Perhaps by next weekend, hopefully.

The local population is interested. What is this woman up to? They knock at the back door, I am in the kitchen. I offer them a beer, my prospective customers, McEwans in a bottle, I say, "It will take time, there is a great deal of work to be done."

They tell me about the sailor who had owned the inn. "He wanted his own boozer, he did not care if he sold anything, as long as he had the company of his friends."

"Oh, that was the reason he had no turnover." I had wondered about it. I had received a demand of £3,000 from a lady who said it was owing to her, she seemed to have lived at the Oak Tree Inn. I approached the brewery for information.

"If you pay her, you still will have to pay us, again, that's outstanding money for beer." I paid the Brewery.

The owner of the local betting shop, his premises were almost next door, he is a mine of information, he knows most people. I offer him a McEwans beer. "No thanks, I will have a coffee."

We had an interesting chat. "Thank you for cleaning up that eyesore, the dump," he said.

"It took three lorries, I had to get a landscape garden firm in."

"There used to be thirty-nine mines working here, locally, all now closed, and now they talk about closing Consett Steelworks as well."

"That will be a disaster with so many of the Tantobie people out of work, already on the dole."

I had read that they were now importing the coal from Poland, because it was cheaper. Who had arranged that? Private Enterprise or the Government? The bookie did not know. I said I cannot understand why the local Durham Members of Parliament had not prevented this, could they have prevented it?

The bookie continued, "You know, you have to be careful whom you employ, all these unemployed miners claim to be builders of some sort. Of course there are just a few genuine ones."

"I need a good carpenter, joiner. The firm of builders I have do the big work, so far I've found them all right."

"I can give you a good joiner, he is really good, he has done work only for me, but he likes a drink. He is called John Ripley."

I had hoped to buy a second-hand bank counter, they are usually made of mahogany, I couldn't find one for sale. Mr Ripley tells me he will work only in old, secondhand wood, the new stuff warps and cracks. He will work for half days only.

The counter in the bar, the old one, is rubbish. Mr Ripely builds a nice new one, panelled. I bring beautiful Italian tiles, blue and gold, in Victorian patterns, bought in the speciality tiles shop in Ashton-under-Lyme. They make a splendid top counter. The back bar is usable, it's made of oak, the shelves are in good order, we can put them back.

For the bar I need a double sink, also a double one for the kitchen. The plumber's merchants don't know what I am talking about. "Double sink? Never heard of it."

"Yes," I said, "contact your London wholesaler."

"You were right, they even have them in stock."

The internal stone wall had to be repaired. We left a large half-moon doorway to get into the former music room.

Whilst cleaning up the stone wall we found a beautiful Eye Stone, it was a real beauty. We set it back in a prominent position. It must have been hundreds of years old. Thank you, thank you, thank you. It will protect me from thieves and felons. I hope it will always stay there. There is a curse: evil doers will be severely punished.

The Eye Stone

I had the Eye Stone incorporated back into the new wall. After a series of disastrous events that happened to various previous employees it became the topic of discussion amongst my customers. Was it just superstition or rubbish? Yes or No?

John Cordell's pub came to grief when the bedroom where he slept burned down. He claimed that he had fallen asleep with a lit ciggy in his hand.

One of the regulars chimed in with "Rubbish I don't believe that! He made me move away from the bar because he was a non-smoker." It occurred to us that it must have been an insurance scam.

Since he has had a heart attack and died, that made three of them. He is the third manager to have copped it. "And, also there was the Dryborough delivery man? He had a fall and received a double fracture."

And then Mrs Textor the cleaner, after the cellar key reappeared back in the bedroom dresser drawer after denying she had seen it, and a great amount of food had disappeared from the kitchen. She ended up in hospital having a double mastectomy and never returned to work.

Gwen, who had taken over from Mrs Textor , shouted down to me in the kitchen one day as I was preparing dinner. "There is a fellow from the newspaper, He wants to write about the incidents related to the Eye Stone."

I approached the fellow from the journal. "It's all nonsense, pure superstition. Don't you dare write about it!"

He replied, "It makes a good story."

"No, don't write about it," I say. "Sebastian's wife told me he has had a dicky heart, for years, angina."

"Yes, his wife told me the same. I've just been to visit her in the Consett pub."

So then, "I tell you now – that it would be very insensitive when the lady has a funeral to arrange, to write about this. Tell your editor I said so."

I had naively thought the Eye Stone would have given me protection. I hadn't taken into account Free Will. Did the Eye Stone punish where it thought fit? Did it?

Subsequently, customers bought souvenirs from Benidorm or the like, pendants or cheap bracelets which had cheap glass versions of the evil eye. It got me wondering if there really was something to it, punishment for evil deeds.

The death of the two managers had nothing to do with me as they were stealing off the brewery. Though Sebastian did steal from me. He had a long-standing heart condition.

It transpired that John Cordell was already under notice from the pub in Cullercoats, when he came to me for a job. He told me that his estranged wife had not only emptied out the pub but also their joint account and had disappeared along with her boyfriend and most of his possessions. So he was in need of a job. When finally it came to light that he had been convicted of stealing from the brewery and that now he had a conviction he was no longer able to hold a license at the Oak Tree. So that was why we parted company. More about this to follow.

Gifts from the locals

A man brings a Victorian till. It is very ornate, of brass. He says, "I don't think it works."

"Perhaps I can have it repaired, would you mind, though, if I can't, if I offer it to Beamish Museum, may I then give your name?"

Another gift was a wagon wheel. "Thank you very much, I'll have it converted into the central light fitting for our main lounge." The man is very pleased about this.

What I don't like are the frequent offers of goods which have 'fallen off the back of a wagon'. A tray of Maxwell House coffee in jars, "very cheap". "No thank you, I don't use that," I say.

"I know where there is one…" is the usual phrase. No, I will not accept stolen goods. I have to invent excuses, not to hurt their feelings.

My builders see to the plumbing. The boiler installations in the cellar are done by the Gas Board.

One morning, early Saturday, I get a visit from the Building Department. They say, "Mrs Hurst, you did not apply for permission for this work."

I answered, "My solicitor did."

"That's the first we've heard about it."

"Yes, I have a letter from my solicitor, but I don't have it with me."

"You are doing an excellent job, so it's neither here nor there. I hear you are a designer. Where did you study architecture?"

"I am a designer of fashion, in charge of a clothing department in a college in Ashton-under-Lyme."

"Fancy that, that's amazing. It does not matter now, the work is very good, if we can be of any help, let us know." They went.

My overdraft is mounting up. At present the bank interest rate is eighteen to nineteen per cent. I am wondering if it would be cheaper to have a mortgage. I had been told it could be difficult. No experience in the wet trade, and a woman, aged fifty-four.

The work is progressing slowly, I am not there all week, to supervise, and some men do not work on Saturdays. I find some of the work is so bad, it has to be redone Well, I was warned by the bookie. The so-called electrician put the light fittings up. They did not work. Finally we found the reason, there were no wires behind them. He said, "I could not get through the stone." He won't repay me the money he had charged. Yes, every miner is now a builder, a plumber, an electrician. No one was ever apprenticed.

Now to decorating; the ceiling is in gold colour, Victorian fashion. The walls are white. I white-wash the cellar myself, repair the holes in the stone wall with extra plaster.

The furniture is no problem, the existing plastic yellow table tops in the bar are removed, replaced with solid oak, from the sale furniture purchased in the Crawcrook sale, held every fourteen days. I advertised for a manager in the local and trade papers. There are a number of replies, most have no experience as having worked as a manager, but are willing to learn. One, though, has twenty years' experience in his own pub. We arrange the meeting in Newcastle, he looks respectable. "Why are you looking for the position?"

He replies, "I have been utterly stupid," seems reluctant to talk, "I had better tell you. I sold my pub, when I came home, after finishing up, our flat had been cleared out, all the furniture gone. It was a great shock, the wife had gone. It was the weekend. On Monday morning I found out that our joint bank account was emptied. How could I have been so stupid? I never knew she had another fellow. I should not have told you all my private affairs, but I really do need a job now." He mentioned a hotel in Newcastle for a reference. "We worked there together, my wife and I, but they did not like her."

"Where do you live now?"

"I am still in my flat, I got some more furniture from the charity shop, for free. I could start right away. I have no children or dependants. God knows where she went to."

"The pub will be a Free House," I said. "Whatever the locals drink. The bar side would be your department, the restaurant is mine."

"I have all the connections with the trade, I would clean the lines myself. I could arrange everything."

This sounded reassuring: "What salary do you expect?"

"Not much, we have to get going first."

"I have been thinking to give half of the bar profit, half share. There is another applicant I have to see, I'll let you know within a few days."

I tried to make contact for his references, unfortunately the owner of the hotel was away on holiday. The receptionist said she had only been there a short while, she couldn't help me.

So I took the risk and I sent him a letter of employment. "Should I bring my furniture?" It was a black vinyl three-piece suite and a single bed and wardrobe. He said he did not have any transport money So I paid him £300 for his furniture and transport.

The solicitor had arranged the license and had a wooden sign made to go over the door with the name 'John Cordell' on it.

I painted a large sign, next to the door: 'Open from 6 p.m. Saturday next. All are invited,' plus another sign on the other side. The locals were standing outside punctually.

We welcomed them. There were crisps and nuts on the bar, also a few sandwiches which our cleaner had made. She also offered to cook the manager's 'tea'. The bar was full. The locals complimented me on the clean look, no more rubbish dump, etc. etc. "Tomorrow we will be open properly, we will charge you then, prices are up on the board." I said, "Pay for the going rate."

A surprise for me, when I arrived the next week, there was a pool table, a music machine, a dartboard, all installed already. Obviously the man was experienced, knew what was wanted.

I found my till had no paper roll in. This rather disturbed me. I quickly went to Stanley, to the stationers, they did not stock them, also the other stationer did not. I had put a £50 float in. "Please keep all receipts of what you spend, pay for."

"Of course." When I tried the stationers in Ashton-under-Lyme, they did not stock till rolls either, I had to ring around Manchester, this proved difficult because the shops closed at 5.30 p.m. – I did not finish work until about 4.15 p.m.

I also bought bedlinen for the manager's bed. A cardigan and checked heavyweight shirts for him from Marks and Spencer, because I did not think he was suitably dressed.

My house in Beckfoot Row had been sold, the money had paid for the Inn, so I arranged for my furniture to be brought to the Inn. Now I could sleep there, no more B & B for me. The manager proved to be popular with the village population. The men told me that the beer is good. I found out that meant it was not watered, apparently most public houses watered their beer.

In the past I had never frequented pubs, unless it was for a meal or a snack. I would take half a pint of lager with my meal or perhaps mineral water or cider. A publican who does not drink! This was hilarious: "Go on, missus, have a pint." "No thank you, I'll have a half of a half with you." I filled my little glass with lager. I was glad that they did not expect me to drink more than quarter of a pint.

I had tidied up the small room next to the passage, furnished it with small easy chairs and little tables. People called it the Snug. Each pub had to have a snug, for privacy, or if ladies came in for coffee or tea. The wall and the chairs were green, green velour. Nice and cosy, and quiet. There were green plants and fresh flowers.

On the other side, the larger room became a multi-purpose room. Firstly, it was my sitting room, somewhere I could do the paperwork of the pub. Secondly, it was my breakfast room, also where people could have a snack or a meal. Thirdly, where I could receive callers, suppliers, and my accountant. There were five tables, now covered with the beautiful Italian tiles from Ashton, this time, green and gold fancy pattern. It contained a filing cabinet and two wing chairs in gold leather, for comfort and rest.

John, the manager, approached me. "I would like to have some pigeons, would you mind if I used the coach house?" "Go ahead, it's empty." "There is someone from the Club, he is very experienced, he will go in with me, be partners." I did not realise that they intended to rip out the internal walls.

There had been no staircase, just a ladder, this was usual in coach houses, where the groom slept upstairs in the hay. The Village Club was nearby, just past the Village Green. Members only.

Champion Drinkers in County Durham

Have you seen the paper?" I was greeted on my arrival by a customer. "Here, have a look." The tabloid had a full-page article: "Champion Drinkers in County Durham. George had told the journalist that he drinks ten pints per night, Willy can only manage seven pints." Horace said his gerbil does not like beer, he opened his shirt and pulled out his pet. "He goes everywhere with me." The gerbil climbed up on his shoulder: "No you don't, go back," said Horace. He buttoned the animal in, so that he could have his drink in peace. "I only ever have three pints," he said apologetically. The newspaperman took it all down. The paper showed the three lads, and the little gerbil. A nice clear photograph.

I knew the manager John kept strict licensing hours. There had been no drunkenness, as far as I knew. The three lads called me over, "What a laugh, that newspaper fellow believed everything. I couldn't afford ten pints," George laughed. But there was a more serious side, another picture of a boy scout leaving the Inn. I contacted the newspaper and asked about our write-up – in which edition was our story? Only in the local one, thank goodness, I did not think any of my colleagues at the college would get a copy. The boy scout wore full uniform, he was carrying something. What was it? John said, "He bought jelly babies." John had a stock of children's sweets, different kinds. I had challenged him before, I told him I did not consider selling sweets to children in a pub was at all suitable. He explained, "The little Co-op shop across the road won't let the children in, only with a parent, and then only one at a time The children have asked if they could buy them here. They have pocket money, that mostly goes on sweets."

I said, "This must stop, look at this picture with the boy scout coming out of the Inn." I sent the sweets to the kindergarten. The lady running the small Co-op shop opposite told me that the kids had been a nuisance, they pinch, one had to watch them.

I had decided to wait until my summer holidays to equip the

kitchen, when I realised that this would cause a problem. I wanted a six-burner cooker, not the huge ranges on offer. I was not in a mass-catering. I wanted stainless steel surfaces, these to be made following the contour of the curved wall – they had to be specially made to my design.

The large, tall freezer had to be narrow width to fit in the space available. I visited showrooms and suppliers in Newcastle, with no success. I wrote to trade magazines which were supposed to give you advice, with no success. I called on the Northumbria Tourist Board, they knew nothing about kitchen ranges. They were kind, saying I might qualify for a grant. Would I be willing to offer afternoon teas? There had been a complaint by people visiting Beamish Museum, saying nothing was available. I paid to be included in a brochure. I promised to write to them when my dining room was ready. But no information about six-burner cookers.

In the end I had to buy a large monster commercial one, plus a four-burner cooker with eye-level grill, the type I was used to. The stainless steel shelving – to my design – finally was fixed. The tall, narrow freezer arrived.

For my dining room, on the first floor, I found a Victorian carved fireplace, with brass fender and the newly available gas fire which looked like a coal hearth. I also found an elaborately carved side board. Tables and chairs came from Crawcrook auction. I needed table linen, the service offered to hotels. I found the local companies said there was no one else in the area, it would not pay them to supply me, not worth the petrol. This was a blessing in disguise. I approached the Nottingham factory who made beautiful lace tablecloths of different designs. I had been considered a lace expert in the past. I chose the different sizes to fit my five tables in the restaurant, put over a base of wine-coloured linen and with two or three silver candlesticks. It gave the right atmosphere, French-Victorian.

The benefit of the lace cloth was that no ironing was required after laundering, just hang these lace cloths up to dry, matching their pattern. I could do that myself, no problem. The carpets were wine red, also for the staircase – very co-ordinated.

Ready for action. First, a restricted menu: steaks, veal escalopes, ham. Sunday lunches with roast would come later, once I knew I had the custom for it.

Definitely no fish and chips, there was a local chippy in Tantobie. Chips would lead to fast food. I was offering French cuisine in Tantobie, very soon my menu grew bigger and bigger, as my reputation grew bigger and better. Booking required, cooking to order, arrive at 7.30 to eat at 8 p.m.

I had sectioned off the cellar, part as a wine cellar. Remembering my father, an acclaimed wine expert, and remembering even the names of the wines, the areas in France where they grew, my wine cellar was impressive. I added Alsace and German wines.

I had also bought one of the terraced houses in the main street, to arrange as bedrooms. By now I had acquired knowledge of reliable tradesmen. It was quickly refurbished by them. The house had been a shell only, the electricity was strung on wires over cup hooks on the ceiling! The walls were good. Never mind, it was all put right, with a bathroom on each floor.

John had to use the very primitive, large bathroom in the Inn, with a geyser supplying the hot water. He did not mind, he had never been used to better plumbing. His bedroom was small.

After the summer holidays, the dining room was only open again at weekends only. The locals bring me welcome, and not so welcome, information. I am told the next door Presbyterian Church has been empty for some time. The contents are for sale. I buy some pews, oak. Two of these together will make nice seating when upholstered, suitable for the bar. Also I buy some ornamental iron work. All is very reasonably priced.

The not so welcome information, very disturbing. I am told John buys expensive pigeons. He takes money out of the till without putting a receipt in: "Wads of notes." Yes, I am told, "one cannot steal from oneself". His story to everyone is that he sold his pub in Cullercoats to buy the Oak Tree Inn. He is half owner. He refers to 'my pub'.

I refer to my college as 'my college'. This is usual. Still I am worried about the money side. The weekly takings from the bar are only barely sufficient to pay the beer bills. Why no profit? I keep my building and food expenses strictly separate. The accountant had warned me that the 'Wet Trade' is reputedly dishonest.

I like to familiarise myself with the district. Previously I had visited Newcastle, as I had two outlets for my blouses there, Fenwicks and

Binns. Sylvia, the museum hound, had also found the local museum. I am told there is another good museum in South Shields, also a pleasure garden with rare roses and a kiddies' railway. The Tynemouth old priory is not much, just stones! All well worth a visit.

My kitchen is not yet fully operative, so midweek I can have time for myself. Transport to the coast is frequent, the Metro. Yes, it was a good visit. I could stay at the Grand Hotel at the coast, it would be interesting to find out what the competition is charging. They are fully booked, a wedding. The receptionist is helpful. Sorry the restaurant is full, the wedding. She recommends a B & B in Cullercoats, but does not think they do meals. There is a chippy nearby. I book into the B & B, it is opposite a pub. I ask the landlady if she knew the former owner. She said, "Former owner? Yes, the one in South Shields. He came with his children. To swim, when it is not windy. We have terrible winds here."

"I mean the pub across the road."

"He has been there for years." Strange that – I must find out. I enter the pub across the road. I am the only lady present. I order orange juice.

"It's early in the season, we get busy later," the man says. "Are you on holiday?"

I say, "No, just a short visit. I was told this is a lovely part of the country by someone. Do you know John Cordell?"

"Do I know John Cordell?? I had to sack the lousy bastard, he was robbing me blind, with his pigeons."

"How long have you been here?"

"Well, I don't know, it must be five or six years."

"Can I have another orange juice please? Those babies are so small." John's claims of "I sold my pub". It is all lies, I thought. I am a stupid fool, too trusting. The bar is getting popular, but the profit has disappeared.

We have a mixed darts team; a Leek Club; the Yellow Brick Road raffle (I brought that in); and now a mixed clientele because of the Real Ale.

I had written to my good white witch, Mrs Ireland, for advice, giving my home address only. She was living at that time in Guernsey. She was a wonderful clairvoyant, her advice was always accurate. I was particularly concerned about Mandy's state of health, but I did not give any details.

When I explained to Mrs Ireland that Mandy was Diabetic 1, she said she jumped to the wrong conclusion, she had 'seen' her inject herself, and sleeping it off in bed. She was sincerely apologetic about this mistake, which had been Mandy injecting herself with her insulin.

She writes back:

"I cannot understand it, I see you as an Oak Tree – I don't know what this means. There is a clinging vine. I certainly don't like the man. I see beautiful patterns." I had not given her the Oak Tree address. The clinging vine must be Mandy. And the man!!!! The beautiful pattern must be my lace tablecloths. How accurate can she be! I phone her to thank her. She says it is all a dishonest trade but it could eventually be lucrative!

John, the manager, had told everyone that he had sold his pub, in Cullercoats, on the coast. And he had a half-share here. When he helped himself out of the till, a wad of notes, to pay for the purchase of his pigeons, someone said, "Hey, you did not count this," or, "Put a slip in."

"Mind your own business," he answered. "One cannot steal from oneself."

This was reported to me, "You should know."

My overdraft with the bank had risen to £40,000. The bank manager said he did not think it was large, considering I had just started up and of course I also had the Staleybridge house, no mortgage on either building. I decide the bar is to close at lunchtime, there is so little trade, it is not feasible to pay someone to sit there doing nothing.

A young man from the Tourist Board calls, he said if I would sell fast food I would soon get busy at lunchtime. "Fast food makes you ill, I will never sell fast food," I tell him. "The chippy is open if they are hungry."

"Only trying to help," he says.

There is a half-price offer for smoke extractors, he has a leaflet. "We are not smoky, we have high ceilings," I say, but I buy one.

My dear white witch had said eventually it might prove lucrative. She saw *me* as an oak tree, not the experienced manager.

A dishonest trade, that's what is said. Should I sell the pub? Mandy can't get a job, we have tried the Labour Exchange, only factory work, standing up is available, nothing sitting down, she is disheartened. She was looking forward to running the restaurant, so was I.

I remembered one of my bar customers said, “I have to wise you up, Missus. You’re so new, a baby, listen: first comes the bottle boy, he wants to be bartender, the bartender wants to be a manager, the manager wants to buy a tenancy from the brewery. So what does any experienced manager do? He earns £100 a week on the side if he is experienced. He saves up for a tenancy. We know this is thieving, but they all do it, if they can get away with it. I was shocked: “Surely not all of them?”

“No,” he reassured me, “not all of them.”

I thought there was another way, marry a pub. John Cordell was telling me, “You are a marvellous woman, look what you have done with this old building. Sylvia, I love thee.” He had said this several times. “Marry me, we make a marvellous team together.”

“I don’t want to get married, not to you or to anybody else, not at my age.”

One hears these stories, of men getting married to a woman, or widow, with money. It does not work out, divorce, and he gets half of everything she possesses. Often this happens after quite a short time of so-called bliss. Who is he anyway? I was relieved when John started paying attention to a young woman in the bar, she came in almost every night. I found out she was John Ripley’s ex-wife. He left punctually every day he worked, before the bar opened up for the evening, so as not to meet her.

Meanwhile John Cordell helped himself to my bar takings. My accountant reminds me that April 5th is the deadline for the tax returns, he says let’s do it soon, then you get a better idea of what you are making. I find it tiresome to sort it all out, all those bills the papers. When I had Sylvia Russell (Kensington) my little clerk, Miss Barnes, and later Captain Lewer kept it all in good order.

John is away on holiday, a hired caravan on the coast. He had arranged a replacement bar customer, a regular, William, called Willy, to look after the bar. I think he worked at the Ever Ready factory, Albert, another regular, who is retired, also helps out. When I get the week’s taking, I am pleasantly surprised, Willy has done well, much better than John.

It is a Saturday. My accountant always comes on Saturdays, to drive out from Newcastle would take too much of his time, calling during the week. The result: I have lost £4000 – that is on the bar side. I introduce him to Willy, saying he did me proud. I tell Willy about the missing £4000. "Not possible," he says. "We are always busy." My folder with my papers in is on the table. Willy asks if he could have a look, he would like to know what I paid for the Oak Tree.

"Well, there was the basic price, then fixtures and fittings, and another £3,000 which was supposedly owing. Here you are, have a look."

"Sylvia, why is John not there, I mean his name?"

I answered to the brewery: "The manager's name is not included when you buy a property."

"But he says he owns half of it, he told me, and also my father-in-law who lives in Yorkshire, to look for a pub for when he sells this one."

My accountant laughs, "We have a Walter Mitty." (This was a fantasist from a recent film.) He advises me to have a second till, for exchange, sometimes. He says that would give me better control. Ring up during the evening, and check the takings, saying, "I've brought you more change." The bar is always short of change, people present notes at the weekend. He does not advise me a change of staff, I would not know how to handle the bar. John is popular, he is generous, he sets up the drinks, for all, if anyone in the bar has a birthday.

The Brewery

Recently I got complaints that the beer is not good. Another barrel has to be put on, to change over. I am puzzled. This has happened several times. I go into the cellar to take the number of the barrel, to complain to the brewery. I find that the number on the barrel does not coincide with the number on my bill and statement. I taste the faulty beer, I am not an expert, but it tastes very strange, a bit like orange juice or something. I send a sample to Durham for analysis. They write back, the sample sent is definitely not drinkable, in fact it may be dangerous. They cannot specify what it is, it does contain orange juice, I had smelled this. When I challenged John he said he had signed for the barrels in good faith. I got in touch with Newcastle Breweries, and a manager came to see me. I showed him the report. He said four barrels of bad beer, amazing. He took the tickets off and put them in his pocket, and put new tickets on. I told him our slops go in the garden for the slugs.

There goes my evidence! I was too slow. I did not think John was innocent, he must have done it, together with the drayman. I could not prove anything. The brewery allowed credit for only two barrels, I don't know what the excuse was. I was told that there was an important court case with the Newcastle Breweries some time ago, everyone from managers downward involved.

My restaurant is working well for me. I enjoy myself, cooking. I got good write-ups in newspapers and magazines, one said I was the best 'eating place' in Northumbria. Brake Bros, a firm of caterers, came to supply me. Their quality was excellent, far above average. They also offered fish, fresh-frozen at sea. They came in a large box, different sorts of fish, all sizes, packed in a special transparent plastic. One had to drop it on the floor to separate the content. Their baguettes were baked in France. They had a delicious chocolate sponge, the ice creams came from Italy, had fancy shapes, in small single portions. The quiche lorraine only needed ten minutes in the oven. I extended my menu, cuisine français. And I put on weight.

My accountant, together with Mr Hopper, Director of the Tourist Board, who had become a friend, came to advise me. "What you are earning on the food side, you are losing on the bar." They both agreed: "Unless one stands next to the till, there is nothing much one can do."

Now summer holidays were over, I was back to the serving at weekends only three more years at college, then I would be sixty, could retire.

I notice we had many crates of empties in the cellar, bottled beer, but such quantities of babies, I wondered who was drinking those. I soon found out: the wholesale supplier, Neesham, bought a court case against several pubs, including our manager, but not me. I received a letter stating this. I never found out exactly what happened, I was not told by the police. There was a suspended sentence for my manager John. If you have a criminal record, you cannot hold a license. He had left, I was told, right after the court case, no one was told what had happened. He went to live with his girlfriend, a Mrs Ripley, the ex-wife of my joiner. There were four children, all girls. John Ripley had given her their house, because of the 'four bairns', he did not want them to suffer. John became engaged to Mrs Ripley, who was on social security, as John Ripley's support was not sufficient.

My solicitor arranged quickly for a license for Mrs Hurst. Different tales went around the village. Why had John left? He had been sacked, for what reason? Because Mrs Hurst was jealous when he became engaged to another woman. Some people said they never heard that this Mrs Hurst had been interested in John, it was a business arrangement, but one never knows.

When I arrived on my usual Friday evening, the police called on me and told me to remove the sign from the front door, about John being the licensee. They told me Durham Jail is full, that's why they're put on 'suspended sentences' they were lucky, too much thieving going on.

On Saturday morning more visitors arrived, two persons from the local newspaper, one was a photographer.

Mrs Ripley had contacted the newspaper telling them about the jealous Mrs Hurst, who had sacked John because he became engaged to her. So she knows nothing about a court case? I wondered what he had told her, actually felt quite sorry for the woman, and sorry for her four children. The newspaper people asked me how long I had known him, did we live together? "No comment," I would not talk. The photographer said he had a picture of the engaged couple and four children. Could he have my photograph? "Most certainly not," I replied, "I would not advise you to try it."

"It will make a good story, Mrs Ripley is younger than you are, a love story."

I said, "No comment," again. If she does not know about the court case, I am not telling her, she will find out soon enough.

"Come on," said the other reporter, "tell us, you are a college lecturer?" I repeated, "No comment, please leave now."

They did not get up, we were in the snug, no one was in the bar, to listen or eavesdrop. It was early in the morning. "We must have your story."

"If you must have a story, go to the Stanley Police Station, and now goodbye." I opened the door. "Please go now." They went.

John tried to sue me for wrongful dismissal. When the man came for details – he did not know about the court case, he agreed there was actually no case, the man would not be permitted to work in licensed premises, or be able to hold a license.

A reporter came to my Stalybridge house, saying the paper regretted that I had been harassed by them. I replied, "I would have sued you if anything detrimental to me would have been published, as it is not true." But this was not the end of it. The story about the dismissal because of my jealousy went around Tantobie. Worse still, I had done John out of his share of the Oak Tree, he had said apparently it was because he had nothing in writing, so he had lost his money for the half-share. John and Mrs Ripley got married. Mrs Ripley, who legally owned her house, sold it to John for £20. No kidding. Mrs Ripley's mother had some money, she offered it to them. A loan. Together with the proceeds of the Ripley house sale, they managed to get a tenancy after a few months, in Winlaton.

I don't know what her children had been told, what tales. They threw stones at me, luckily they missed me narrowly. And later on, a burning newspaper was put through the open window of the men's loo, on a tiled floor, and a burning petrol rag through the letterbox of the front door, during the week I was not in Tantobie, I was told that several boys and girls were seen. I contacted the headmaster of the local school, asked him to explain the seriousness of fire-raising to the children. I don't know if he did, I heard nothing.

A new manager was installed. I had a number of applicants, on the next day after John had left, the news had got around very quickly. I did not really like any of them but I was stuck, having to return home, because of my college duties.

I wondered if John's popularity was caused by his generosity. He had 'set the bar up' – free drinks for all present: on the slightest pretext, not only birthdays of a customer, but a win of the local cricket or football team, even the birth of a new baby, to wet his head. Well, he did not pay for any of this.

The new manager lived in Stanley, he came punctually 'on the dot', to open up, and closed on time. It was said that the club across the road watched our premises carefully with a telescope, however I did not know if this was true.

Catering was now easier for me I had bought a commercial large freezer, for the large cellar. Brake Bros called only once a month, so my freezer had three sections.

One for the big box of fish and any of the local salmon, which fishermen brought in. The meat compartment to store my steaks and sirloin roasts, and special cuts for my Boeuf Bourgignon, the favourite. I had found an experienced, old-fashioned butcher, he hung my meat and cut it exactly to my requirements. In January the Forestry Commission culled the roe deer, surplus males. I bought from them a young one, they butchered that for me. Rabbits and hares were sold to me by local hunters. One young, very young man, brought lobsters, mostly quite small, so they fitted in the saucepan. "Missus, what about a rook pie?" the bar customers asked me. I thought they were teasing me, I had never heard of rook pie before. I found the recipe, told the bar if you bring them without feathers, nicely plucked, I will make it. And so I did. I marinated the birds, in red wine and spices, French fashion. There was a write-up in the local papers, then in the national papers, people sent in their grandmothers' accounts of rook pie. It went on, was it a joke, or a novelty? Restaurant customers asked for it. Farmers thanked me, because they got rid of the pest. The editor of the newspaper published, "This must stop now, no more rook pie news!" Actually one only uses the breast and legs. The fridge stored goods bought in quantity, like bread and the patisserie I had made, such as apple turnovers and sponge cakes.

1 – box of yellow fish – RED
2 – meat boxes – GREEN
3 – one green box of bread and patisserie and vegetables – peas, spinach, beans – YELLOW.

The new manager took my bookings for the weekends. He explained we served food continental fashion, not before 7.30, and there was no fish and chips. Fish yes, but no chips.

My excellent cooked meats and bacon were delivered by Tom from Halls of Brockburn. He is still a friend.

Heavy snow

The weather had turned nasty, windy and a lot of snow, much more than was expected. I had bought long-life milk as there were no deliveries. Deliveries to shops had stopped altogether because the roads were closed. The local co-op shop was completely sold out, a notice put up, 'Closed'.

Miners and ex-miners were entitled to free coal deliveries. This caused hardship to many villagers, because the deliveries had stopped. Many of the cottages had a range in the sitting room, the combination was for heating, cooking and boiling a kettle. This was the only heating in the cottage.

The Oak Tree had gas central heating, and we had a coal hole on the garden side for the bar fire. There was no bread in the village, no milk, nothing. I had bought two large sacks of especially nice potatoes, the sacks had a second black cover, to stop the potatoes sprouting.

Albert came in, to sleep, as manager. His cottage was completely snowed in and frozen. He told us some people had to climb out of bedroom windows, the doors were snowed in, frozen.

I found out that the roads from Durham and those from Newcastle were no longer passable. It was not possible for me to get to the Inn. I told Albert – the phone was working – he should offer the old-age pensioners in the mornings free sandwiches, as long as the ham lasted, or free toast with tea or coffee. There was a quantity of bread in my freezer. Jacket potatoes were also offered as the big oven range was in use. Albert enjoyed himself being the host, all given away for free.

Finally, the weather improved. It was now three weeks I had missed. The damage was great. Along the top road the snow plough had taken the roofs off six cars which had been stranded. In the new estate in Tanfield, the roofs of the newly built houses had just 'slipped down the side'. There was flooding. Looking out of the window of the train, I noticed that the train was only inches away from the water, which looked like a lake – covering the meadows, sometimes for long distances. There were water pumps everywhere, this was no good, as the sewers were full.

The wooden railings of my car park had all been stolen, to make fire wood, they had been hacked off.

Tantobie – grants

During the cold spell I had become aware of the plight of the old people. With the roads closed, the coal deliveries had stopped, which the miners and ex-miners were entitled to. Their coal fire/cooking ranges had heated their sitting room, now they were sitting wrapped in their eiderdowns to keep warm. The houses usually had electric lighting, but not power points for heaters.

One of these houses in the main street was up for sale. The locals told me the whole street was condemned. They looked solid enough, built of local stone. Before buying it, I called at Consett Building and Planning Department. Why were they condemned? They assured me they had no plans to pull these houses down, they were on a substandard list, because of lack of amenities. "You can go ahead with your refurbishment. Some time ago we offered the landlords help, but they refused, saying with the £4.00 a week rent they could not afford to modernise." Most of these houses were now owner-occupied, the landlords had 'got rid' of them because the veto of the price increase had not even covered the repairs needed. This had been a war-time measure.

Surely the people would want more comfort, I was certain of this, I told the Planning Department when I called them. "If you are so certain, if you can provide this to us, we might consider giving grants. It needed to be for the majority of people living there."

My architect told me the houses were solid, they had been built by the local co-op, in late Victorian times.

I put a letter into every house, saying refurbishment might be possible, with a grant. There would be a discussion, next Sunday in the Oak Tree, in the room next to the bar, at 11 o'clock. Please come.

It looked to me if as though most did come. I offered coffee. "The Council, the planning department, offers grants, if you want to improve your property. This has to be a majority vote."

They all signed the paper, with their address. Only one man refused, he said he was afraid his income support would be stopped. Then they left for a drink, in the bar.

I went into my kitchen, to cook. I sent my list to Consett, with some old plans I had discovered. The houses had been built 1890, approximately, not all in the same years.

After a short time, the people were advised, individually, that a grant was available. I received a letter from the Planning Department. New kitchens, new bathrooms, power points, and what have you, the work progressed quickly. No one ever said, "Thank you, Sylvia," not one person. I did not expect thanks for my help.

Trouble with the local youngsters

I had stopped selling beer in cans some time ago. The youngsters congregated in the bus shelter, and on the village green opposite. The bus shelter was brick-built, with seating. It was covered with graffiti. A big brush, some terracotta coloured emulsion quickly covered the abusive language.

I went to the little branch co-op shop opposite, "Please don't sell them drink."

The woman replied, "I don't know how old they are, those girls with their make-up and jewellery could be twenty or more." This lady was not helpful.

Well, I thought, the kids have nowhere to go, it's not their fault. One ought to do something for them. A notice had been put up, on a tree, facing the green. That permission had been applied to make a wholesale vegetable market, signed Hall Brown. He was my Saturday supplier. "You can't do that there, it's our green. Why don't you do it in your village? [Tanfield.]"

"It's too residential," he answered.

"Tantobie is also residential," I said. "It would be cheaper. There is a perfectly good industrial commercial estate nearby, why don't you use them?"

"Because it's too dear, what they charge!"

We sent our objections, mine and a few others. We were led by the local school mistress who had a fine house in this village. She said there would be lorries arriving all night and early morning. I was in the process of getting rooms ready, for letting, the noise would make it impossible, disturb sleeping guests.

Hall Brown still supplied me, on my Saturdays. "You can't blame me for trying," he laughed.

The co-op in Stanley and their Tantobie branch closed. It was stated they had become uneconomical, "thieving lots, all of them" was the opinion of my bar.

The former Tantobie Co-op shop was now a supply shop for car parts and other vehicles. This solved the drinking problem of the teenagers drinking. No local supply of booze.

My former coach house in the garden was converted to superior accommodation, two double suites with private facilities, and also a small room with private facilities.

The cottage in the main street also served as accommodation for workmen working in the district. They usually were three or four together. Sometimes it was let for 'Coast to Coast' youngsters on their cross-country bicycle rides, who liked the cheaper accommodation, with bathroom facilities, but having these at a much lower price.

On the roof

My architect said there must be an inspection of these premises, of the properties. "Yes."

"Hm, hm, electric wire with cup hooks fastened to the ceiling? A fire risk!" Climbing through to the loft with him, I was most surprised, one could go from one house to the next, there was an opening, not even a door. One could walk the whole block.

I wondered what these openings were in the loft space of all the houses in the street.

Why were they all connected? Escape routes? Hide-outs? For storing stolen goods before sale? Or was it a smuggler's place for stacking goods?

The architect wrote his report on the village houses:

1) Solid walls.
2) Roofs mostly okay.
3) All the plaster soft, broken off.
4) Heating needed.
5) NEW – Bathroom/kitchen – dismantle outside toilets.
6) Electricity – total rewire needed.

I had understood the co-op built the houses in late Victorian times, in 1880s/90s. The village street is okay, now.

Leave off, Sylvia, nothing to do with you. Stop interfering.

I had been on a 'roof' before , a long time ago – I was a child then.

I remembered my times in Goeppingen. There were three boys on the roofs of the houses, balancing. What for? What did they do there? On the side of the roof of the last house was a sort of tower, more like an elaborate chimney, which had cemented sides all the way up, there were no footholds, to get there, unless one took a journey over three houses.

Storks bring luck, people claimed, children were told, they bring the babies. We also had been told that. Oh, they were going to steal the eggs, perhaps sell them to the man, the fellow with the incubating units for baby chickens. Chickens were a luxury food then. Or to the man with the collection of bird eggs in a glass case. The 'incubating' fellow tried to rear wild birds, it was rumoured. If they were quick enough to be retrieved, he sometimes was successful.

That's not right! I must stop them, but when I called out to the boys, they ignored me. These street boys did not know that I was good at shinning up trees. House roofs were strictly forbidden, I would love to have tried; now I had a good excuse. My satchel got in the way, so I hung it on the fire escape, it was wobbly, I hoped it would not fall off.

I shouted at them, heard them laughing. "This is Know-all – the Fleischer girl."

They shouted, "Know-all, get lost! Scoot!"

Looking down, I noticed people looking up from the other side of the street, to get a better look. Then the owner of the house put a big, thick feather bed on the narrow footpath. In case I slipped and fell off.

With people looking, the street boys could not risk stealing. "Hoity toity, go home, Know-all." I retrieved my satchel from the fire escape, some of the tiles were damaged.

Arriving home, my news had travelled before me, the story of the feather bed was hilarious. Everyone had a go at me, scolding me. "Dangerous, don't you know?" My dress was filthy, so was I.

"Beammerle needs a bath!" Arnold calls. He always called me Beammerle when I misbehaved.

I said to Liesel, "They were quick to report me at home, before I returned."

"That is because you are a checkered dog, everyone knows you."

At dinner even my father had heard about it. "Tell me more of your escapade." I told them, including calling me 'Know-all'. "They call you that?"

Father said, "It must be because of your organizing talent."

"Well no," I mumbled, "more likely because I argue with the teachers." When I knew I was right, I always thought I knew better.

Mother said, "Showing off, not ladylike! Yes, you are showing off."

The Whetborough Court Case

I examine my monthly statements more closely. Butcher in Dipton – ok. Brake Bros – ok. Finefare I paid cash – ok. Greengrocers I paid cash – ok. Electric and gas. How can I check this? It is complicated to read. I have to leave it. It was quite clear, the statements for beer were wrong.

Of course I am suspicious after my bad experiences.

This thieving, this dishonesty is generally accepted in the bar trade. I don't think I will ever get used to it. I will have to be more careful, watching, checking my invoices more critically. I find that there is an invoice which has been duplicated, same numbers. I ring Whetborough at their office, tell them about the mistake. The reply is that it is for two deliveries, two barrels at a time, one signed by L Harrison, the other by Socker Brown.

"Why on the same day?"

"The drayman must have been short, so he had to return."

This had been only three days ago. I check my cellar, there are only two new barrels of Whetborough there, plus the almost empty one, delivered the week before – not FOUR barrels!

In the evening I have a word with Mr Hunter, a regular. He is our local councillor. We had previously talked about the co-op closure, which had stated that there was not enough trade. The bar had laughed about this, saying the little Tantobie co-op was a goldmine. I asked Mr Hunter, "Would you please come into the cellar with me, I want you to see something." I show him my two invoices, plus the delivery notes, from Whetborough.

He says, "I can see only two barrels, not four." I take him outside, there are no empty barrels in the yard, not of any brewery. Mr Hunter tells me he is prepared to vouch for the number of barrels, in writing.

When I pay Whetborough's bill, I deduct the 'wrong' invoice. In due course I receive a court summons to Victoria Court, Consett. I accept it, decide I will defend myself. Why pay a solicitor, when I have good evidence?

The judge asks me, why did those people sign for deliveries? The Inn was not open lunchtime, no trade since the Consett Steelworks closed (and their recompense money ran out). Mrs Harrison is the cleaner, she lives across the road, and Socker Brown has always been there, he sees to the bar fire and sorts the bottles. They can sign when I am out. I submit to the judge my statement for the year, one can see quite clearly I never buy more than one or two barrels from Whetboroughs per week. I also show him Mr Hunter's letter. The judge finds in my favour. When I return to my bar, they cheer me. Taking on the brewery, what a woman! This was the last time I had trouble with the draymen, I think word must have gone around. I only wish I could say that about my internal bar staff.

I have a few regular travellers coming every few weeks. They like to be served in the breakfast room in order to be near the bar. They want an no-itemised bill, dinner and B & B, pay by card.

The manager has left, his family is in Denmark, he joins them. A good-looking white-haired man asked me about the vacancy. He used to work in Consett, but he and his wife own a pub opposite the bus station there. "My better half has always looked after the pub," he said. He offers to work ninety-six hours every fourteen days, would that be suitable? Albert is always there, he is sort of assistant manager, helps out, he just sits in the corner. He is very popular with everyone. I discuss the situation with Albert. He is pleased, he looks at it as a promotion. Relief Manager? Manager proper?

Hollings College write to me to inquire if I could take a trainee. There have been very good reports about my Oak Tree Inn, in the best tourist magazines, including *Staying off the Beaten Track*, The Tourist Board, and in the *Gourmet*. All free publicity. I reply, saying I could offer the bar side, some management, also front of the house for the restaurant, but not in the kitchen, which I do myself, with my daughter. They tell me cooking was never included in the scheme.

A very nice, tall lad arrives from Hollings College. He is twenty-three, this would be his 'practical' for his degree. We get on very well. The bar crowd like him. The manager teaches him 'line cleaning' and also all the 'know-hows' of the trade, such as stock and ordering. I teach him about the vines and the very fine collection in my wine cellar. He drives his own car, offers to help with shopping, at the wholesalers, for spirits and wines. He returns to Hollings for his final exam, after a year, passes with top marks. Now he is assistant manager in a Scottish Hotel.

Hollings send me another candidate, he is a small lad, looks still like a boy. He likes to serve in the bar, but the locals don't take to him.

I get a letter from the Head of the Catering Department, Hollings. The lad had written that the manager works only part-time and he is in charge of the bar. Albert assures me he was there every night, sitting in his corner, supervising our barmaids and whatever. I confront the lad, Albert says he was never absent, and the lad is cheeky to me. "I did not know that Albert was the manager," he answered.

"When you came I introduced you to him," I replied.

"I can't remember that," he says. Hollings write again, they were surprised at the lad claiming to be in charge, that my former trainee had spoken in the highest terms of our Inn, he has now a responsible job, the new hotel was most impressed he could do line cleaning. (This is often done by an outside firm, charging high fees.) I ask Hollings College to recall our new trainee, it will never work. The bar says, "Good riddance."

No further trainees were taken on.

The church next door

The church next door was up for sale. I received a letter from a solicitor to call at their Sunderland office to discuss the matter.

I was intrigued. What did they want? They showed me a yellowed old paper from the Lambton Estate Office. It had been signed by about a dozen or so villagers of Tantobie, giving various small sums of money to purchase the piece of land next to the church.

This was the part of the rubbish dump I had made into a lawn. I told the solicitor my plans showed no boundary line. I had the area cleared because it was a disgrace. This had been my sole interest. "Would your client reimburse me the money I had spent to clean his part?" The solicitor told me that the church could not be sold without the land I had acquired.

Before the Oak Tree was converted into a public house, it had been the Lidell residence of the Cadet Branch of Lord Ravensworth. Lord Ravensworth, formerly a rich Newcastle merchant, had been elevated because he lent King Charles a great deal of money, and then forgot about it. Ravensworth Castle in the nearby wood had been demolished.

I asked the solicitor to send to me a copy of the deeds, assuring him I had no designs on the strip of land. I wondered, why should Lord Lambton own such a small piece of land in Tantobie? I knew small strips of land sometimes belonged to another person, when there was a spring or well on it.

I decided to call at the estate office of Lord Lambton. They assured me they never had any land in Tantobie, pulling out from their large wall containers a huge map. "This proves we have never had land there." I never received the copy of the deeds from the solicitors, had they forgotten?

I went to the Land Registry in Durham. They explained to me, they laughed, there were people who sold pieces of land they did not own, to gullible other people, it had been quite a common occurrence, in those days.

It must have been Lord Ravensworth land before the building of the church.

Paying my monthly bar bills, I was surprised at the quantity of beer which was sold in bottles. I knew cider was popular, because of the Snakebite, which is half beer and half cider. McEwans was the favourite of several regulars, but I was surprised that we sold so much German beer.

So on my weekend visit I had a nice surprise. A handsome Stein, about a foot tall, was sitting on the shelf. "Where did that come from?" I asked.

"It's a pressy," said the barmaid.

"Let me see it."

"Not your pressy, the man said, it's for the manager."

On the lower shelf was one row, that is four bottles, of this German beer. "How many have you sold today or this week?"

"Only one, but I don't know how many the others did."

This was strange, the bills had shown a very healthy trade. I went down into the cellar. The empties were there, and a great number of crates of the German beer and cider. Later on, I opened the cellar door for a delivery, the manager was busy. A young lad stood there; he said, "Sorry, I could not come last week, the road near our club was closed because of a nasty accident." He brought his empties inside, of the German beer and the cider, quite a number of crates.

"Which road was that?" I asked. He was only a delivery boy, I did not think he would be involved in this 'fiddle'. He told me the road. I said, "I have a message, give it to your boss, tell him to find himself a new supplier."

"Nothing for me to take back, lady?"

"No, nothing. Have a nice day." What could I do? My solicitor had told me it costs more to sue than it is worth.

I was busy cooking, the dinner guests were leaving late, after 11 o'clock. The bar was closed. The manager had taken 'his' Stein home. I should have removed it earlier.

"Sylvia, just watch it!"

Setting up the Community Centre

On weekends, groups of youngsters were hanging about in the streets, on the benches in the bus shelters, and also on the little green in front of the Inn. "They have nowhere to go, one should do something about it," said I.

Charlie Spedding and his friend agreed. "Everyone talks, but no one does b-all." "Not many apprenticeships going either." "The army has cut down recruitment."

"What about that old church, next to you, it's still for sale? One could do something with that, a centre. Sylvia, do you know how much they want for it?"

"I am told the asking price was £19,500, it might go for less, this was a while ago," I said.

I discussed our 'good idea' with Mr Kellner, our local area councillor of the Durham Council. Everyone agreed, "Yes, Tantobie needs a Community Centre, the kids deserve it."

"Where? That church is in good nick, it wouldn't cost a fortune to put it right."

I was surprised, I got offers of help from local firms. "When you get started, I can let you have wood, odd sizes of wood, kiln dried, I would let you have it for free." Another man offered rolls of lino. "The colour and the pattern did not sell, but you wouldn't be so fussy." I had received promises of money. Charlie's friends also reported success.

"This is a village affair. We must have a meeting. Best in the Tantobie Club, they have a large room."

I had a flyer made, to put in the house doors, inviting them to the club to discuss a Community Centre. Many people came. I proposed we buy the church, it was central, quite reasonable, the roof was good.

"It's next to the Oak Tree, good for you," a man shouted. "Yes, that's the idea, good for her trade." "Did you know she pinched the land next to the church, the one the old dears had paid for?" "She did that John out of his half-share of the pub, he had nothing in writing." It was noisy. It was getting ugly, very ugly. "Order, order." "Let's discuss the Community Centre."

I had arranged a row of chairs on the platform. I had hoped we would get people willing to act as a committee, to help with this important project.

"We must take a vote, for the four persons you want, write down your choice." About a dozen people came forward. I attached numbers on the chairs. 1-12. These people were well-known, but they stood up, shouted their name aloud, so that the beer drinkers could hear them. I stood up as well, said my name, Sylvia, Oak Tree. The votes were counted. The four highest numbers were called out. Sylvia got two votes, the very lowest of all the votes. I was voted off.

I went home. That was the finish. "Sylvia," I reminded myself, "you stick your nose into other people's business, it's no concern of yours."

I had started it, I'll never learn, I know I am stupid – even though I was hurt, bitterly.

I had been brought up by my mother, "If people are born in a certain position, it is their duty, their privilege to help others not so fortunate." To be a do-gooder, more often they are nosey old twits, that's what my brother Arnold called them. Sylvia, you had your lesson, learn from it!

They lost the support of Charlie Spedding, Olympic Bronze Medal runner, and his Tantobie friends. He declared he would not have anything to do with those people. Sylvia set it up, and then they voted her off.

My friend, Rosemary Black, the retired schoolmistress, lives in Poplar House, on the other side of the church.

I don't know if she gave one of my votes for me, or if she abstained. She keeps me well informed of what is happening.

The purchase of the church was voted against, too near the Oak Tree. Let's build the centre on the Cricket Club lawn. Can we afford it? Rosemary Black got busy and arranged grants from several places. A local builder was chosen. Because he was not aware of new regulations

– I could have put him wise – much of the work had to be redone. There was no road to the building whilst in progress. It made further hold-ups, no lighting for the road, no gas laid, etc. etc. It took years to build because there was no gas.

In a way, I was glad not to have this added responsibility. The only support I give to the Centre is support for their raffles, I am generous. It is a very good centre, serving the community, I am really pleased about this.

The Advertiser, our local weekly paper, gave a report of the meeting, published the names of the committee members, then gave the details. The church purchase was not feasible, because it was too near a public house. The venue at the Cricket Club was considered. No difficulties about land purchase there. The Oak Tree Inn had encroached onto land belonging to the church, the locals said.

I had received a letter from Lord Lambton's Estate, confirming they had never owned land in Tantobie. I put a copy up in the bar.

Not having a good duplicator – I usually had this work done in the office of a solicitor in Stanley – open to public use, for a fee. I stupidly sent his letter to the newspaper, hoping for a retraction. There was a one-line note in the paper, next to the weekly report of the Women's Institute.

"Lord Lambton does not own property in Tantobie, and has never done so." I received no apology. It did not state what it referred to.

I had refused to have anything more to do with the Community Centre, not even when they sent another delegation saying because I had started everything, would I consider joining? No, no, thank you! Too many lies about me.

The Real Ale Campaign had brought in a lot of new trade. This also improved the sales in the restaurant.

Thank goodness, I was now full-time retired, having left college six months ago. I lived at the Inn.

The bar takings were doing better, with Sylvia around, popping in and out, greeting the dinner guests.

Charlie Spedding, the Durham Runner who had received the Bronze medal in the Olympics, came with his friends, so did Brendan

Foster, who was also a bit of a local hero. They were real-ale drinkers. I cooked their Christmas dinner for many years, for about twenty lads.

Mandy had brought her gramophone to the inn. She put on classical music, upstairs, outside the dining room. It made me happy, it pleased my guests.

She was in charge of the dining room. She was waitress, sommelier, and hostess. She looked charming in her Victorian frilled embroidery anglaise apron, which circled around her calf-length. I had managed to obtain non-drip red candles, so I did not have the worry of red candle-wax dripping on my beautiful lace tablecloths. The guests came for the whole evening, we only accepted one sitting. The atmosphere was very friendly, they talked to each other, and also to Mandy, who could explain the French dishes and recommend which wine would go with which food.

"I would like to talk to your mother," said a guest. I was always in my kitchen, having found that I could not employ the 'local talent' to help me. They spoil my food! It was not what they were used to, no chips, no fast food.

I came upstairs. The young man introduced himself and his party, "We are the Quartetto Serioso. I noticed you like classical music. We are looking for a place to rehearse, for a final rehearsal before our performances. How would you like it if we came here? I know your guests would like it."

"What a wonderful idea! Yes please. I could not be more delighted, yes, yes."

"We would come once a month, or more if needed."

The first performance was on 18th December 1982 at 8.30 pm. All welcome. Free entry into the function room upstairs. To the quartello I said, "Please come at 6 p.m., have your dinner downstairs in my breakfast room." That's the name I had finally given the room. I reserved it for them for the night. I cooked for them a three-course dinner, a nice bottle of wine or two. They could relax over a cup of coffee before playing. Mozart, Hayden, Bartok, Paganini.

It was a great success. This is what I had wanted, to go with my Haute Cuisine. Next performance: 21st January 1983.

Christmas decorations were up, Mandy had done me proud, with a helper. Very few of the bar crowd came upstairs.

There were 'the locals' and Sylvia's people somehow it meant two different classes of people.

The dinner guests always ordered wines, which were very reasonably priced. Not those ridiculous prices the hotels charged. I was satisfied with a fifty to sixty per cent mark-up, and my bottles were of superior quality. Everyone ordered wine. We sold little wine in the bar. Only ladies ordered wine in the bar.

We are very lucky, with our new barmaid, Joanne. She is a charming local girl, the daughter of the Hunters' local buses. She is studying for re-sits to enter university. She had been given the wrong syllabus by her teacher. Everyone likes her, she is a great asset. And my bar takings are spot on! She left when she finally got a place at Sunderland University. Rarely do I get bar staff I have a liking for, and can trust. I usually need to watch them. I am told this is general in most pubs.

Everyone was sad when we lost Elaine. She was a cheerful, pretty forty-year-old woman, had a good sense of humour. Her elderly mother became ill, needed care. Elaine was to move in with her. The Social Services gave the mother lunchtime care. Our bar crowd gave her an enormous box of chocolates and a bunch of flowers on leaving. Mandy helps out, she is not quick enough for their liking. "What is the hurry? You have all night," I say to them. My till is right on the penny.

I am not so fortunate with the next barmaid. I am sitting in the breakfast room, which is next to my kitchen. I hear the ring of the till, regularly. I go into the bar because the till needs changing for small coin and silver. The till roll is nearly empty, I change that as well. There are only three takings rung in since the last additions, which was at the finish of last night. The till was opened many times, no sales recorded. That explains the glass with coins, next to the till. "Tips," said the barmaid. "Not in there, not in this bar." They never give tips. I count the 'no sale' – there are seventeen. I say, "Seventeen no sale, please get your hat and coat, leave the glass." Mandy takes over until I get a replacement.

The latest news is discussed in the bar. John Cordell, the former manager, his pub had a fire. No, it's not burned down, but there is quite some damage in the living quarters. "What happened?" "They say he fell asleep, his cigarette burned the bedding, it took hold ever so quickly."

Our bar discuss it. “But he is a non-smoker.” “That’s a new one on me – he made me move from the bar to the corner, when I lit up my ciggies,” says another one. “I said the smoke was bad for his chest.” “A quite convenient fire, he was not doing so well, I am told,” says another. A few weeks later I hear that John Cordell had died of a heart attack.

The new barman has been with us now for three months. He seems satisfactory. The young barman works daytime driving the ice-cream van. He is on the evening shift, from 6 p.m. Three guests are staying with us, they formerly lived in the area, to meet their old comrades. They are not eating in the restaurant, they want to be served in the breakfast room, which is near the bar, to meet them. It’s a sort of reunion. I came to take their dinner order at 7.30 p.m., the usual time. “ Would you like wine?”

“Oh no, we’ve had a belly-full.”

The bar is almost empty – midweek, early. I change the tills, that can’t be right! Only two sales? Pop and McEwans. I go back to the breakfast room. I asked, “Did you enjoy your drink? What did you have?”

“We had your best, I had three pints.”

“I think I had two and a half, I drink them in halves.”

“I had McEwans.”

I change the till roll. These sales are not recorded. “I did not hear the till ringing.”

“Show me the till roll, lady. Well, the lousy bastard!” He points to it on the till roll, nothing showing.

“I’ll give it to you in writing, what we’ve had.” I say to the young barman, “You had better leave.”

“What have I done?”

“You know perfectly well what you have done.”

“Explain it to me,” says the cheeky young fellow.

“If I have to explain it, it will be in front of the police.” He left. Mandy takes over, I phone for a replacement.

This is the young daughter of our lady gardener, a very glamorous, charming girl with long, very long, blond hair.

Thatcherism

I could hear the noise. There was a loud discussion in the bar. What was up? I went in. I listened.

Mrs Thatcher, the Prime Minister, had called the North East 'workshy', and one of her MPs has said 'it was a den of thieves'. He claimed he had received many complaints from constituents. They talked about 'The Great North-East Divide'. Thieving? "There should be more bobbies on the beat. If you can't prove anything – you must have witnesses. Otherwise forget about it." This encourages the stealing, you're kidding, no one wants to be involved. I considered Mrs Thatcher's remark irresponsible, considering the high unemployment of the north-east.

"Workshy? My son has passed his Masters, yes, he is a bright boy, what is he doing now? Delivering parcels, that is all he could get, and God knows how many applications he had sent off, for all kinds of jobs. He is a delivery man now." There are not enough jobs to go around. Those young clerks, at the Job Centre, some are a snooty lot, they do not remove the job cards when the positions are filled, yes, they send several people out when the position is already filled, they send unqualified people with not a chance in hell to be eligible. Job-seekers' allowance, that's a laugh.

Many people found it shameful to go to Social Security, particularly the older generation. The middle-class who lost jobs when the firm closes. Their redundancy was soon used up.

What about the Consett Steelworks, when that closed on 12th September 1980? Some got a packet in redundancy money. "Yes, he bought a house in Spain, and then his missus did not like it. Benidorm, that's just full of booze." 4,500 jobs lost there.

"What does Sylvia think? Here, have your half of a half." The bar found this hilarious. A publican who does not drink (quarter pint of lager was my usual).

I said, "I have something on my cooker, excuse me, I'll be right back." My cooker was my standard excuse, to get out of a conversation, or to cut short a telephone call.

Some people were clever, to fiddle the social security. I had been told of a number of cases. "My boy has to sleep on the sofa, in the sitting room." His bed had been put in the garage. The new divan, still in its wrapper, was sold by them. "The knob on my cooker has come off." "You better have a new cooker," the social offered. This was to one of my staff. I told her, "I take my knobs off for cleaning." "I did not know you could do that!" The Social were generous to the single mother. Being on benefits was rewarding, if you knew the ropes.

There was talk of new industries, of large government grants. When would these be operative? A new Japanese car firm – Nissan opened in production in 1986 in Washington, Tyne and Wear. They gave training to the young men. It is only the large car factory from Japan, Nissan, still in existence nowadays.

Other large foreign firms, such as Siemens, were attracted with huge government grants, and when trading conditions became difficult, closed after a short time of trading. The large factory of Ransome and Marles (Ranson, Hoffman and Pollard), which had opened in 1953, making ball-bearings and parts for the car industry, closed in 1982. 2,000 local people, including Anthony Black, the husband of my friend, the headmistress Rosemary, lost his job. I was grateful for his help and expert advice when refurbishing the small house I had purchased in Ash Terrace. This talented man created for himself a beautiful garden, a joy for everyone to see – even he could not find employment. The Ever Ready Factory lasted a little longer. The unemployment in the North East was rising.

Dishonesty

Why do I get so upset with this constant thieving? If I am honest, it is not the financial loss, this does not worry me, I am told that I should watch the staff and the suppliers all the time. This watching upsets me. Yes, I had been told that the wet trade is known to be dishonest. There is free will, I try to understand this.

I had thought that my EYE stone would protect me. It had not done that, it only punishes the evil doers. Three of my managers had died, within a few weeks of their thieving. Two of the cleaners are in hospital, cancer with removal of breasts, MS (not sure) for the young one. I am also told that the manager of the Midland Bank had died of a heart attack. Surely his death had nothing to do with the Oak Tree? My bank charges were 'enormous'. For my overdraft I paid eighteen to nineteen shillings. For each business cheque I was charged £1.00. I felt I should see if I could use my life insurance, their charges were seven per cent to reduce my overdraft or eliminate it. The Midland Bank manager explained to me that with their exit charges, and other expenses, I would not be better off. He also mentioned that his cousin had been a dinner guest, spoke highly of my establishment, and had told him this Inn was just like the one he was looking to buy. This statement really worried me. Only last week was a detailed account of the Midland's investment disaster in the USA, published in the newspapers. It had gone completely wrong, they had tried to amalgamate with an American company and lost a great deal of money. Now they were calling in money outstanding from debts to reimburse themselves. What would happen to me, if they wanted the overdraft back quickly, or even at once? Could they put the Oak Tree on the market? I check on the bank manager's statement, find out he's been lying, no extra charges, nothing, a very low percentage.

I decided there was no time to lose, I must change banks. I did.

The life insurance I held was not sufficient, but I could 'top up' with a few thousand pounds raised from my own house in Stalybridge, in a new mortgage. I paid off my overdraft at the Midland Bank.

Barclays Bank, here I come! I never looked back. Calling in monies, it did not take long to clear my finances. They did not have a fee for cheques. My bank charges are reduced now. Midland Bank had charged me for every cheque I have used. Why?

I willingly gave money to charity, they call regularly, including the Salvation Army, the Anti-Drink Salvation Army. Jesus Christ said, give your money away, the Essenes lived frugally. But we are not living in Biblical times – and then they also had tax collectors. The undeserving poor – this was before the time of Benefits and Social Services.

A real French restaurant

A real French restaurant, had that been my intention? Reminiscences of child food fare? I soon found out, no one in County Durham or even Northumbria expected the large, full menu. The local hotels offered a much reduced fare, usually offering two to three main dishes.

I made it known that I refuse to serve chips, this is for the 'fast food' trade. I tried to employ local staff, but I had to give this up, they 'spoiled' my dishes, thought the French wine was 'funny'. My dishes were all foreign to them.

Everything is freshly cooked, to order. Mandy explains how it was cooked to the customers.

Three-course dinners are included in the two-day special accommodation – bed and breakfast two nights with three-course dinner. Local people became regular customers. Steaks, Boeuf Bourgignon, Virginia Ham, were always available.

Special dishes are for two persons, marked. *

Starters:	Green soup
	Spring vegetable soup
	Prawn Cocktail
	Egg Mayonnaise
	Smoked Salmon parcels
	Home-made pate, when available
	Quiche Lorraine, from France
Fish:	River salmon, grilled
*	Sometimes fresh lobster (when available)
	Cod, oven baked with tomatoes
Fish dishes:	*Veronique, poached in white wine with grapes
	*Royal Salmon with prawns
Poultry:	*Chicken American, panfried, with sweetcorn and banana
	*Duck to order (three hours)
Entrees:	T-bone steak, garni
	Sirloin steak, garni
	Virginia Ham, garni
Special:	*Steak pie
	*Escalope Viennoise is panfried in butter with breadcrumbs

(*Vegetarian dishes to special order.)

Vegetables:	Fresh, as available.
Dessert:	Choice of dessert or cheese board
	Apple sponge, hot
	Chocolate pudding, hot
	Savarin
	Fresh fruit salad
	Banana in rum butter
	Choice of fresh cream or ice cream.

Mandy laid the tables, replaced the flowers and burned-down red candles. She washed the Crystal d'Arque wine glasses, spotted the lace tablecloths, they did not need completely washing for one spot.

Twice a week, she would go shopping in Stanley, doing the banking at Barclays at the same time. I don't think she missed her college lab job. She had found a new interest – sailing. When the whole flotte came to Newcastle Harbour, she was enthralled. She booked herself for a fourteen-day journey. And afterwards she sailed in the Hebrides and in foreign places. And then there was her photography of the sailing boats.

2,000 sailing boats for an bi-annual meet in Brest and Douanez (France). Mandy was invited by the committee, her photographs were admired, one – a sunset one that had been 'blown up', to cover a wall, like wallpaper. She had two public exhibitions in Stanley, with nice newspaper coverage. Unfortunately Sylvia gets seasick, therefore could never go with her.

During her absence, I served the dinners in the breakfast room. It was a pretty room, situated next to the kitchen. I could manage the work. Actually I enjoyed it, as now I could talk to my customers.

My brother Arnold is an experienced cook. His internee friends, from the Canadian lumber camp have all graduated, with the patronage of the Toronto Jewish people, all in the professions. They are doctors, lawyers, calling themselves, the 'Refugee Mayflower Club'.

They meet once a month, the men pride themselves on practising their culinary knowledge. Women (wives) are not consulted in the kitchen. There is a fancy menu. Arnold writes he has to practise before it is his turn. He sends me a copy menu.

I write back, 'It is too complicated for me, besides I cannot get these ingredients either in Newcastle or Durham.' I am glad the Mayflower Refugee section gives them such a good social life.

Another new Relief Manager

My bar takings had improved whilst the young trainee was with us.

"Your percentage is not right again," says my accountant. "Watch it."

Normally I only go into the cellar to bring up some food or wine required for the restaurant. My cellar part is separate, it also contains the laundry.

I notice all the cellar lights have been left on, the main switch is at the back door. There is a half-barrel standing at the door, containing Real Ale. Strange that, we never buy half-barrels. There is also a crate of mixed babies bottles. I put these forty-eight bottles back in their correct place. I had always thought my good-looking older manager, Sebastian, was all right, honest. I know his wife runs his pub in Consett. Is he supplying his pub from the Oak Tree? A half-barrel fits into the back of a car. I ask him about the half-barrel. He tells me it was supplied in error, it has to go back. I did not mention the babies' bottles to him.

I check my paperwork, no bills for half-barrels supplied – ever. I am upset, because I trusted him. Again, Sylvia never learns, it is human nature to steal, if you can get away with it. His wife phones, two weeks later, says he is not well, needs a rest.

A young man introduces himself, "I am Melville. I hear you need a relief manager." It is surprising how quickly the word gets round in Tantobie.

He tells me he is experienced, has worked 'down south', but is staying now with relatives in Tantobie. "It may be for a short time only," I say to him.

"That's all right with me."

Melville is nice-looking, arrives punctually. He tells me he sings popular songs, I don't like these but I don't tell him that, must not discourage him. Perhaps on Saturday evenings he can sing.

On Saturday, two of his friends arrive to accompany his singing. To my ears the music is horrible, loud, noisy. The bar seems to like it.

The music is so loud, I even hear it in the kitchen. Our barmaid has to catch her bus, on Saturdays, the last one is earlier. I take over in the bar, it is terribly loud, this so-called music. During the night I wake up, I hear a noise, like water running. Have we got a leak somewhere? I check everywhere, even in the cellar and outside. There are no water pipes in the garden, not very deep down. Nothing. I cannot find anything. That is when my tinnitus started.

I receive a phone call. "I have sad news, my husband has died. The funeral will be on Friday."

I don't recognise the voice. "Who are you?"

"I am, I was, Sebastian's wife."

"What a shock, what happened?" "He's had a dicky heart, but before he always recovered, well, he was sixty-four."

I am heartless, I have no feeling. When Melville asks me about his position, is he manager now? I say OK, what can I do, all these staff changes?

Melville asks me to buy a car. "It would save your taxi fares. For your purchases, to Batleys and other shops." I think a car is better than a bus, for commuting to his room with his relatives. Batleys, the wholesalers has an excellent wine buyer. I am most impressed for they stock a French favourite of mine, Chateauneuf du Pape. My other main supplier is Grants of St James, Muscadet sur Lie I get from a Hexham young lady.

Continental evenings in the restaurant

Someone has told Quartetto Serioso that I have 'alternate' music. Are they offended? I am wondering, they tell me that they now have a different place to rehearse, nearer to Durham, more convenient. I am sorry to lose them, I miss them.

To make up for the loss, Mandy suggests we should offer continental evenings. She has made a list. Food, the national dishes. Wine, we have these already in our cellar. Music, she thinks she has most of what is needed on records, if not, she'll buy it.

We start with Alsace-Lorraine: Choucroute Garni, Traminer.

France: Bouef Bourgignon, Cote du Rhone.

Italy: Antipasta, Eggs Florentine, Chianti, no, not pasta! I am not Italian! Plenty of prawns.

Spain: Paella, Rioja.

Hungary: Goulash, Tokay.

Austria: Wiener Schnitzel, Riesling.

Customer can purchase a bottle of wine to take home.

I make flyers, giving the dates, about once a month, and I do hope I can keep to it.

Our evening must not clash with Melville's (I think horrible) bar music on Saturday.

So it will be on Fridays – 7.30 for 8 p.m.

I can seat five tables in the restaurant, the function room can take any additional guests. The record player is in the hall, where the new piano is. The Quartetto insisted I buy a new one. They did not approve of our existing one, which I then put downstairs. I had it tuned. What was wrong with it?

Melville has been with us for three months, he wants a holiday. I must arrange for a relief manager in four days?

"No, I want it right away, to meet friends."

"All right, as soon as possible."

"No, right away." Do we settle for a week? No, right away.

The bar people tell me he has offered a car for sale. The Oak Tree car, he thinks it is his car! The bar people immobilize it, "That will fix it," so he can't sell it. Overnight the car has gone. The auto-part repair shop has helped 'fix it' for Melville.

After two weeks he has not returned, he has gone, he has left, no notice given. His relatives call at the Oak Tree, they tell me Melville has died of cancer, quite suddenly, unexpected, down south. They have no details.

Continental evenings are doing well. Mandy was right. But I preferred the Quartetto.

Mrs Textor, our upstairs cleaner, arrives at 9 a.m. First things first, kettle on, for her tea and toast. She tells me staff always have their breakfast first.

Her husband is a long-distance lorry driver. Our little long-life milk portions and the little butter portions are suitable to take for his bait (local Geordie word). I say nothing, I don't mind, it costs very little.

I notice my large, two-handled frying pan, it measures fifteen inches in diameter, has been put on a shelf. Why? These large frying pans are kept on hooks on the wall, always. My wall clock timer has fallen off the shelf, it is broken, caught on its wire. Who has moved it? These extra-large pans are used for preparing my boeuf en cocotte, on top of the cooker, completely covered with onion slices, for about three to four hours. Cooking on low heat. The meat is almost done, only needs half an hour more to finish off, to make Boeuf Bourgignon, meat pies and Goulash etc. I store it in my freezer until needed.

The Health Bus

The Health Bus is in our village, anyone over thirty years old is invited to have a check for the boobs. I missed this time, because I was busy, but Mrs Textor attended. She tells me she needs a further check in hospital. She is worried.

Why was Mrs Textor's grandson walking through the bar? Is it a dustbin lid that he is carrying? The kids pinch these metal lids, they make 'wonderful drums'. No, it did not look like a dustbin lid. Is it Sylvia's kitchen gear? My information usually comes via the Bar. I better check my cellar, if any meat is missing, or anything else?

Where is my cellar key? I call it a museum piece, it is very ornate, ten inches long, perhaps older than Victorian. It is missing, no longer in my bedside drawer, where I normally keep it. Who knows where I keep it? Mrs Textor hoovers my room, she might have seen me putting the key away.

I need to get into the cellar. I have guests tonight, I need the food. Now I am worried. I ring the locksmith. Two men arrive, they tell me this lock is most complicated, has been made not to be broken in. It took them over thirty minutes, finally they had success. Open, £50 please. "Lady, you're lucky we did not have to break the lock."

I find most of my prepared meat has been taken from the freezer. I put a padlock on. It must have been Mrs Textor, her grandson brought my pan back. Yes, most of the prepared meat was missing at that time. The bar tells me there was an invite at Textors for a family party.

Mrs Textor sends word, she has to go to hospital to have her boob removed. Cancer. My cellar key is still missing, I cannot accuse anyone. I have more than a suspicion. After Mrs Textor returns from hospital, my cellar key returns, miraculously back in my bedside drawer. Also a few small items I have been missing, my orange-handled dressmaking scissors, some special curtain hooks for the heavy curtains, I had to order these specially. I think she is afraid of the 'Eye Stone'.

The people in the bar talked about it when they heard Melville had died, saying "That's the third manager who's copped it. And what about the Whetborough's drayman? A double fracture he got." Was he on drugs as well?

Well, I am glad to have my key back. What about the Eye Stone?

Gwen, a young local girl had taken over from Mrs Textor. Somehow I don't trust her. She cleans the kitchen, is supposed to clean it, all done, she says. Why are my small saucepans missing? "Well, when they are burnt, I throw them out," she says.

"Don't you clean your own?"

"Never, why should I, they're cheap enough."

"Those are good pans," I say. "Leave them for me, there are Brillo pads."

"Good luck to you," she says cheekily. "Enjoy yourself!"

I prepare our takings for Mandy to deposit in the Stanley bank. The money bag is kept in my bedside drawer. Mandy tells me, the money was short, that's the second time it happened. She had counted it with the bank clerk.

I tell Mandy, "Please don't leave Gwen alone, when she hoovers my room, Mandy, stay with her."

"Gwen sent me to get an attachment for the hoover."

I recount the money. Yes, it is £20 short. I had counted it twice, I even wrote down the nominations. I say, "Gwen, we have no bookings, we'll not be needing you for a couple of days. Call me next week, on the phone." She does not call. We both knew the reason.

My red-haired young neighbour calls. Long red hair, gorgeous, like a Rosetti lady. I call her Rosetti, show her a painting. She likes the book. "Do you need a cleaner, Sylvia?"

"Yes I do." Rosetti was with us for years, she stayed until I sold the Inn. She was completely honest, thank goodness. We 'up' her wages, it is hourly pay. Mandy shares tips with her.

Gwen works now in the care homes at Lintz. There was an article in the *Advertiser*, our local paper, about the care home. The old dears complain that their money is missing, has been missing for months now. The manageress is blamed, a court case. Several carers are also summoned. I am not surprised.

I hear that the Midland Bank Manager has died, a heart attack. Again, I am not sorry; he had given me bad advice. Sorry, nothing to do with the Oak Tree. I have been now with Barclays for a lifetime.

When my house in Stalybridge was sold, I bought a village house, dating from 1900, for Mandy. It was what they call a 'shell'. It is now completely refurbished, like a new house, expensive, yes, but a good investment, to give to my darling daughter.

Wind in the Willows

The Wind in the Willows has always been Mandy's great favourite. I told her, when I was pregnant, her daddy read it to me, it was new to me, had not been translated into German. I said to her, you heard the story when you were still in my tummy.

The V & A in their Christmas catalogue had the game, so I ordered it for her birthday, on 3rd January. I was disappointed, it never arrived. My cheque had been cashed. I phoned the V & A, they said they would send a replacement. They were insured for loss.

We discussed the poor Christmas mail in the bar. My customers said it is because they employ so many part-time helpers.

The children of Manager, Panto, sitting in the children's corner, drinking their pop, called to me, "Our dad bought us the *Wind in the Willows* Game for Christmas."

"Where did you buy it, Panto?" I asked.

He answered, "From Fenwick's."

"I need not have written to London for it, saved the postage."

The replacement arrived. Next time I was in Fenwick's I asked the assistant to show me the game. I wondered what they were charging. The V & A one had cost £42 plus postage, it was beautifully made. The assistant said, "Sorry, madam, we don't sell it."

"Are you sure, are you sold out?"

"We've never had it." The buyer confirmed it, saying it was some game they could surely sell, who made it?

What was I to do? Should I pay the V & A? They were insured. Panto had stolen it. Was I dishonestly involved in the stealing of it? I did nothing. I was in a difficult situation. Panto had been employed by Peter Lynch, who was buying the Oak Tree from me. His bank had stipulated, before granting him the mortgage, that he should 'rent' the Oak Tree, the bar part only, as it was his first venture into the bar trade. He had been an insurance agent for many years.

Sylvia continued with the hotel/restaurant side.

So Peter employed Panto, but keeping his agency on, working part-time at the Inn. Should I tell Peter Lynch about the stolen game? I did nothing. Yes, it was a difficult situation.

There was a full, large bag of white Turkish towels missing, ready for the wash, also my beautifully carved, Italian mirror, real gold it was. No proof – one cannot find out, only suspect. The law seemed to protect the thieves!

Hede

Brother Richard visited Europe every year, he usually called here first, in Tantobie, before calling in Goeppingen. I am afraid I still have the shivers when I think of November time.

Our loving Hede darling was still alive, and had sent me a message that she would like to see me. (Hede was our governess, I have written more about her in my first book, *Laugh or Cry*.)

Her son, the family Schwarz had offered to collect me from Stuttgart Airport, and put me up in Gosbach. Gosbach/Ditzenbach is a very pretty village and the Schwarzs' house is of far better quality than my house. Mr Schwarz tells me Hede's story, why my mother sent her home.

I blamed my mother for being stuck-up, that the son of a cobbler was not good enough. That was true. A girl called at my parents' house. She was heavily pregnant. She told my mother if the Sonntage's (cobbler's student) did not marry her, she would kill herself. Hede must give the student up. She knows Hede had a dowry – this was usual at that time. The student did not marry anybody, but became a good Nazi, and the young Mr Schwarz, well-educated with a good job at the Swiss firm in Basel, in a factory with a famous chemical firm, married Hede. Later he was called up, like everyone in Germany. They had two sons. She was a war widow.

Mandy and I have a standing invitation to the Schwarzs' house. Peter and his wife Inge are very generous, proud of their lovely village, and chauffeured Mandy and me around to show the beauty spots to us.

Of ghosts and animals

We had an interesting guest, a Miss Linaham, she told us she was on the North of England Ghost Trail.

The Oak Tree had been mentioned to her. "Are there many places you visit?"

"Yes, hundreds. But I never met a ghost personally."

I told her we had the usual banging, footsteps, upstairs, and no one is ever there. We don't take any notice now. She wanted to know about our ghost.

Our bar customers, several of them, had told me of a gentleman, sitting always in the same corner, next to the fireplace. They say he wears a funny hat, green, others call it a tri-corn. When you try to talk to him he disappears. I have not seen him – I am a sceptic.

There is also my little black cat ghost, I have made her acquaintance. The first time I saw her, I had only shortly arrived. I said to the cleaner, I don't allow cats here, get rid of her. There was a 'whoosh', she is gone. My customers have also seen the cat. When the front door is opened, she escapes outside. "I am so sorry, I let your cat out," says the young man. "I tried to follow it in the road, I called her, but she was gone." The same story, I heard it several times.

I was behind the bar, a lady approached me, "Animals are not allowed in here, I should complain to the Tourism Board about your cat."

I smiled and said, "Yes, do that, please come round and have a look yourself."

"Where is she?" Not here, she couldn't have got out, unless she jumped over the counter.

"It is our 'ghost' cat, she visits often," I say.

We also have the usual knocking and footsteps and so on, but we don't take any notice about that. Twice some people got locked in the loo, but I am critical about this, the lock might have been faulty. It needed dismantling from outside.

Guinea pigs

Talking about animals. A customer says to me, "Close your eyes, hold out your hand." I obey, wondering, "He is a nice man, I am not worried."

There is a little animal, no bigger than a mouse, in my hand. "You would like this guinea pig. Put it in a shoe box until you get a cage." I tell Mr Ripley to make me a nice large cage. He does, a very large one, four foot six inches. Inside is a little house, "Her sleeping quarters, privacy," he says.

The guinea pig food at the store does not look right to me, it has dyed pink bits in it, perhaps it is bread? Guinea pigs like grass seed, I pick for it the oat one, which he likes best. The specialist shop in Consett sells a very great variety of pet food, all sorts, nuts, seeds, etc. I take a scoop of each, I buy a big sackful, mixed. Patch – that is our guinea pig's name, likes everything. She has grown, is more than double the size. The cage is standing on the landing. When she hears me in the morning, she pipes a whistle, but sitting on my shoulder is best, she kisses me, what is that!!

A dinner guest has a guinea pig called Arthur. She says Arthur is very quiet, does not talk, "Yours is lively, she greeted me." We decide on a bit of matchmaking.

Arthur is a prize guinea pig – beautifully marked, cream, copper, in wide stripes.

Patch looks at Arthur, returns to her little house. Arthur sits in the corner. Patch is polite, she lets Arthur have first go at her food bowl. We were hoping for babies, but nothing has happened. Mr Ripley says, "How do you know he is a male, how can you tell?" Arthur goes home.

Mrs Baxter, our upstairs cleaner's granddaughter received a guinea pig from the same litter as ours, at the same time. Mandy asked if she can see it. When she gets to the garage where it is kept, Mandy gets a shock. The animal is half the size of ours, has lost about a third of its fur. Mandy asks, "What do you feed it with?"

"She likes cardboard and also chocolate biscuits."

Mandy says, "I would like to buy it. Is it a she or a he? Would you accept £5?" Mandy does not know they usually cost £2 – £2.50 at the pet shop. She is put in the cage with Patch, who recognizes her and whistles.

I say to Mandy, "You spend a lot of money."

Mandy says, "I could not possibly let her stay in the cold garage, starving, eating cardboard. Anyway, it's my money!"

After a month, Mona (for money) has grown to the size of Patch, her fur is nice and glossy. She loves Mandy, takes no notice of me, not even at food time. When Mandy comes, she puts her little hands out, wants to touch Mandy, her paws looked like hands. She knew who had saved her life. Mona only lived for four years. I was told she had a rough time as a baby, that may be the reason. Patch lived seven and a half years. That is supposed to be exceptional. When Mona died, I bought a little guinea pig from the pet shop, almost identical markings, to be company for Patch. Patch knew the difference, it was not her sister, she was a stranger.

Miss Mogg Parky

On the windowsill outside the breakfast room sits a cat, looking in. She sits there a long time.

It is a beautiful animal, looking half feral, half Egyptian Mau, with a three-cornered little face and very handsome markings. She must be smelling the food.

I put the left-overs from breakfast – I give very large portions, guests say 'too much' – on a plate, on the steps outside the kitchen door, which is right next to the breakfast room.

It is accepted, with several purrs. This becomes a daily procedure. Cat does not like vegetables, she leaves the tomato. Mandy calls her Miss Mogg Parky.

Where does she live? No collar. The weather has changed, it is getting colder. I find that cat has now slept in our coalhole. I buy a cat basket, put some blankets in, there is room in the large coal hole. When in November it gets really cold, I move her basket into our beer cellar, into a protected corner. There is always a small barred window open in the cellar, for ventilation. Miss Mogg Parky has found her basket, she is sleeping soundly. I see her when I go into the cellar to fetch something. She never comes into the bar, the breakfast room, or my kitchen, she knows this is not allowed, but she found my sleeping quarters. The wide windowsill is nice and warm because there is a radiator underneath. She sleeps on the window sill. My bed is next to it, almost. After a while, Miss Mogg Parky sleeps on my bed cover, near my feet.

It is Mandy who plays with her, cat games, with string or ball. They get quite rough, she scratches Mandy deeply – I am sure it was an accident – but Mandy smacks her, the cat runs away. We don't see her for days. Mandy goes looking for her, calling her name, she walks around the streets, it is a week now that she has been missing. Some children tell Mandy that the boys (teenagers) ran over a cat in our own car park. "We put it in a box and buried it next to the chapel." We retrieve the box, bury it in our garden under a rose bush, say a prayer. I did not realise it before, how attached I was to her. I grieve for her.

Years ago in London I had lost my cat, Wednesday, I grieved for her for a long time, and even now, years and years later, I have almost tears.

Orange Boy, a cat with totally orange fur, is a cat known to the bar crowd. It sits outside my kitchen door. The bar people tell me that Orange's owner is in prison. Orange boy looks for food. It is winter now, less hotel guests, not much leftover food. I have to buy cat food, I had never done that before. After a while, Orange Boy comes several times a day. That is not normal, the chemist says, "Must be worms." I add it to his food. It works, after five days he is back to once a day. His master is released from prison, good behaviour. Adieu Orange Boy.

We have another guest, a beautiful "Heinz-57 variety dog". I save the dinner leftovers, every evening. The dog cleans the plate so thoroughly, it looks like it has been washed. He comes punctually 11 o'clock, every morning. Mandy calls him Hoover. He answers to Hoover. His mistress has a small-holding across the road. She has horses, chickens, and there is another dog, Lady. Why does he come to us for food? The bar says, "Your restaurant food is more to his liking!"

The Slug

A summer weekend, were fully booked only couples.

Mandy coped very well, considering she was also the sommelier.

The large hors d'oeuvres were used as a 'main', more interesting than a salad. This gave me extra work, to assemble all those diverse items.

Mandy told me she had to instruct a customer (almost) forcefully, explaining that the red wine they had ordered was too strong, would kill the delicate items on their 'main'. They accepted the Muscadet sur-Lie, perfect with seafood.

These customers wanted to see me, they sent for me to come from my kitchen downstairs. What did they want? The people had eaten most, the wife's plate was clean.

"Look at that!" the man said quite loud. "What am I looking at?" He pointed with his fork. "Oh my God," I was shocked. A very small slug was wriggling on a lettuce leaf; about one and a half centimetres long, with tiny black horns, like black dots.

I whispered, I did not wish the other restaurant customers to hear our conversation. "I am terribly sorry, sir, we did not see it." Well, with all these different food stuffs, salads, I had missed it. I tried to take the plate away. He stopped me. "I am reporting you to the Tourist Board. And furthermore, when I put my bedside light on, I got a nasty shock. No, I don't want the pudding, I am put off my food."

His wife shouted, with emphasis, "We are leaving."

Everyone in the restaurant looked up. "I won't charge you," I said. "We are leaving now."

He had put the lettuce leaf with the slug on it in an old used envelope he had pulled from his pocket. "This is my evidence, I'll need this."

"Mandy, dear, please quickly replace their bedside light, whilst I look up their reservation."

Received cash, £30, no receipt required, we are travelling. The signature was unreadable. His deposit, the £30, went on the mantelpiece in his bedroom. "We must find another hotel," they said, they packed a small suitcase, and left.

Next morning their bedroom door was left wide open. They

had used the room after all. I realised it would be hard to find accommodation after 8 p.m., so they had returned.

We heard nothing from the Tourist Board, but we did hear from the TV. The slug, fly, or ant, story was an old trick originating in the states (USA). My brother Richard, who lived in the States, laughed. I often phoned him. Overseas phone calls were cheap at that time. He explained they do this trick on small places, who value their goodwill. Copycat in England.

How had this man carried our slug? Perhaps in a match box.

Complaints: Tourist Board Inspection

I was told we would have an inspection; there had been a serious complaint. Two ladies and a gentleman from the Tourist Board arrived at 10 a.m. Most of the guests had left by that time, breakfasts were available from 7.30 a.m.

I offered coffee and croissants which were accepted. "Where is the cellar?"

"This is the staircase down to the cellar, but you can reach it from outside, from the garden."

"There is pest control available, for infestation," I was informed by the Tourist Board man.

"Miss Mogg Parky, my lively cat, lives in the cellar." I introduced her. I laughed, "I have not seen a rat in years."

"Do you have mouse traps?"

"No! Miss Mogg Parky is a half-feral cat, she comes in when it gets cold." The man departed, saying he had another call to make.

"Where would you like to start?" I asked one of the ladies. They worked on a clip-folder. "Bedroom 3, the single one, a full length mirror is missing. Bedroom 4, no curtain at the door over the fan-light," they said.

"Anything else?" I asked.

"Oh yes, old newspapers in the drawers, newspapers are not permitted."

"Window sills are very dirty, full of smuts."

I thought, "Surely they are nit-picking."

1) Regarding the full-length mirror, the oak furniture usually has a mirror on the side of the door, as mine had in bedroom 3.
2) Surely you don't need a curtain for the fan light – the doors are six foot eight inches. You cannot see in!
3) I must apologise for the newspapers, the date was over a month old, I could not understand why they had been left so long. It came to me later they had been left by the Antique Dealers who had visited the Hexham Market, and had used the newspaper to pack their purchases.
4) The smuts on the window-sills – very careless of us.

The kitchen fridge. Packets of bacon were in the wrong place – I was told bacon must be treated like 'fresh meat'.

My main fridge was in the cellar, a large one like in the supermarket. I had decided on three compartments. Red for meat; Green for veg; Yellow for desserts – such as ice cream. The ladies approved.

I asked about the 'massive complaint'. It was anonymous, in the strongest terms. I was told later by my bar customers that the complaint was made by the boy "you barred from the premises, he said he hoped to get you into trouble". It did not work.

The smuts on the windowsills, they were burning rubbish in the smallholding next door. One serious complaint, I was told to replace a shower curtain. It was a new curtain, a guest's Wellington boots had mud splashes from the rain, no replacement was needed once it was washed down.

I was not on good terms with the Tourist Board, who wanted me to change my menu to include fast food. I told them 'Fast foods make you ill, I will not sell it! I don't want this trade and I will not sell chips!!" etc. etc. They resented that I did not want their advice.

"There surely is a mistake on my bill," said one of the guests.

I had a look. "It seems to be correct."

"You charged me £11 for the wine! It stated that the wine is free."

"Yes, sir, one glass of wine is free, per person. I have deducted £3.00 from your bill. You had chosen Chateauneuf du Pape, appellation controllé, cost £14."

"You should not state that the wine is free, this is misleading."

"Surely, Sir, you did not expect a bottle of the most expensive wine to be included? The bill is correct." The customer grumbled, but paid up.

Refurbishment

The Tourist Board seemed very interested that I wanted to refurbish The Oak Tree Inn, including a good restaurant. They told me that grants were available and I did finally receive a grant for £700. I was encouraged to advertise in their north-east brochure and also in the new brochure, to establish afternoon tea for the area. This proved to be a failure. The Beamish Restaurant's tea was considered poor, I was told by customers. Sandwiches with curled edges, salads with browning lettuce leaves. I had some pastries in reserve, sponge cake, but I never had to use them – not once. No one called for afternoon tea. I was told later that Beamish Restaurant improved their fare.

My overdraft was £40,000 which was for building work. The £700 I was awarded paid for the advertisement. To my great surprise I found that I had been given the cover picture for the next few issues. It was a nice cover picture, full colour, whether it brought me customers, I did not know, I was not told.

Staying off the Beaten Track. This publication was most popular. I had usually relied on personal recommendation.

The Japanese Room

Taking orders for the evening meal, Mandy told me room number 2 must have left, there is no luggage, the key was left on the desk. "They must have gone during the afternoon."

"I turned a couple away," I said, "I could have re-let the room."

A few days later I received a letter asking for the return of their deposit, as they had not used the room. I wrote back that cancellations are accepted, if made on time. So they complained to the Tourist Board, stating that the room was unfit for occupation, had flimsy walls, some even made of paper. The bedlinen was dirty.

When the Tourist Board phoned me, I explained they must be

referring to the Japanese Room. "Well I never," said the Tourist Board lady. "That lovely room." However, she suggested that as a gesture of goodwill I return the deposit.

There had been a Japanese exhibition in Newcastle which Mandy and I had attended. We were most impressed with the very large lacquer screens. "Now we can make an en-suite in the corner. Bedroom 2 is very large," said Mandy. There is matching fabric, cotton/satin. The screens looked like eighteenth- or nineteenth-century copies with exotic birds and many trailing flowers, very oriental.

I bought black furniture to match, including a large writing desk. Our Japanese room was much admired, had been mentioned in brochures. It had even been written up in my Visitors' Book. This was for favourable comments – thank-yous – wonderful food – lovely four poster bed, etc. etc. A book to be treasured, this visitors' book.

On these lacquered screens, copies of eighteenth- or nineteenth-century, the ivory for the birds was now in plastic, but the painting of the flowers was exquisite on the black background. Our number 2 bedroom could now be en-suite. Matching satin/cotton fabric was on offer, even the paper/bamboo extension to reach the ceiling. We purchased the black furniture for the Japanese look.

The Tourist Board is always on the customer side – for the good will, even when nothing was wrong.

We had 'created' our Japanese room after visiting the Japanese Exhibition, where we were much impressed by the high standard of artefacts.

Coast to Coast

There had been a couple who had left, secretly, without paying for their weekend in the Coach House, room number 3. I sent the outstanding bill – minus their deposit – to their home address. They wrote that the accommodation was substandard. They said the Oak Tree was empty, no cars over the whole weekend – no bookings in the restaurant, the breakfast room needed cleaning. They came late for breakfast, shortly before 10 o'clock.

My coast-to-coast party, five doctors and medical staff, had arrived early. Their bicycles had been stored in the cellar for safety. For their Celebration Trip they had asked for a private dining room – explaining they might get noisy. They had Real Ale and French wine.

My coast-to-coast guests, all nine of them, all wanting different breakfasts, had left early, to visit Durham Cathedral on their two-night stay, also the Botanical Gardens – with a medical herb section. We tidied up the breakfast room after they left. To see my customers content and happy gave me much satisfaction. Some even wrote thank-you letters, promising return visits, and recommendations to friends. I even received Christmas cards from some of them.

My commercial travellers stayed regularly, this was not only profitable, but pleasant.

On the second day they visited Beamish Museum, returning home via Newcastle by train.

The number 3 party did not pay, but wrote to the Tourist Board with their complaints: no porter on arrival, no telephone in room, poor general standard of cleanliness, dining room empty, no hand towels (not necessary as three large bath towels were provided).

I sent a copy of the booking sheet – we were showing fully booked – to the Tourist Board, also stating we give only porterage to the elderly and people with children.

In this case the Tourist Board were on our side – they send their brochure to them which gave the list of facilities offered to the various grades, and with costs. We were three crowns, but charged less than was usually charged.

The customers did not pay, did not reply. A free weekend with good wine – not worth suing for.

Hold-up

A late customer. I explained that the main building was fully let, but I could offer accommodation in the annex, very reasonable, it was en-suite.

He said, “I wanted to stay in the main building.”

“Sorry, sir, this is not possible.”

He was a strange looking man, very pale, a very smooth, pale face.

"You will find the room satisfactory."

"No I won't, I don't want it." He pulled out a revolver, and put it to my head.

I heard Mandy on the staircase. I shouted, screamed, "Get back upstairs, to the dining room, don't come out."

The man grabbed the phone, pulled it out of the socket, still pointing the revolver at me. A bar customer ran to the public phone in the road to call the police, who arrived in minutes. The man ran off.

"Can you describe the man?" the police asked.

I replied, "He had such a smooth face, it looked like a mask."

"What did the gun look like?"

"I don't know, it was grey, it had a long barrel, I don't know anything about guns."

The phone box was found, broken and empty, in the garden. I got a replacement phone within days. I insisted the phone be placed now in the vestibule, to be reached through the door leading to the staircase.

The Tourist Board insisted that the phone must be placed in the bar, if I wanted to retain my three-crown grading.

I refused, saying it was dangerous for me.

They said, "All the phone calls must be free, no charge made to customers. If you wish to retain your three-crown grading." This was not fair, some of the customers took advantage, made long distance calls, not one, but several.

Breakdown of the boiler

Regarding the breakdown of the boiler, that is the third time the boiler is on the blink. The fellow from the Gas Board says he cannot find anything wrong, perhaps it is 'old age', you say you have had it nearly thirty years, or thereabouts, it needs retiring! My brother, Richard, he was in the building trade, blames the small bore copper they had used for supply, pipes, advises me to insist on a larger gauge if I renew the heating system. The small ones may clog up.

We decide on a new boiler. The engineer of the heating company tells me that small bore (15) is the norm.

I decide to buy my own copper pipes (22), large bore.
We have three heating systems:

The bar fire with back boiler
The dodgy one in the cellar
The Worcester at the Coach House accommodation.

Our accommodation side of the Inn is quiet in winter, mainly relying on our regulars, the commercials. The Coach House has two double and one single bedroom, all en-suite, this is sufficient. We can use an electric fire in the dining room.

So I have bought the large bore copper pipes, 22, advised by my brother, myself. The engineers take a photo of the reading on the old meter, before ripping out the old system, standard practice. I am called to the cellar.

"Mrs Hurst, you must see that! Unbelievable!" The man shows me our system was connected to the outside pipes with Gorilla Tape!! "It is surprising it has lasted that long." Apparently now the bad weather, the wind, "gets in".

"It should have been bolted and soldered."

Tantobie labour, I am not surprised.

My new supply, the copper pipes, are running on the cellar ceiling. The work is ready before Christmas – they have taken long enough! Over two months. It cost less than I expected, I got wholesale prices from suppliers, both for the boiler and the copper pipes.

Gas bill

Our Leek Show was exceptional this year, we got second prize locally. There are photographs in the *Advertiser*, our free weekly paper, with our giant leeks.

Mandy suggest we invite all our regulars for the special festivities, free buffet. For the Christmas Grand Raffle we put on for the Yellow Brick Road. I have bought a four-foot teddy from the wholesalers, I have 'treasures' in china and glass from the various 'bring and buy sales in the village, it is surprising what people throw out, good stuff.

The bar is very busy. Mr Lynch is happy, so am I, this will be our last year here. I will be seventy-five years old in March.

When the bills come in, in January, I have a shock. My gas bill is enormous. How come? We only used gas in the Coach House, Worcester, this is separate. I had paid my September bill. Our old meter was discarded. I got a copy of the photograph. I got a new one installed in December numbered from zero.

I telephoned the supplier and tried to explain, but I can only leave a message. After repeated attempts, I give up, I write. A further demand arrives, then a warning notice of a court case. I send a further explanatory letter, by recorded mail. I receive a court summons. This is crazy. I decide to attend court myself, with the photo of the disconnected meter and the bills for the new combi-boiler, the large copper pipes, the installation charge.

This is a preliminary court hearing in Consett Court, so I am told. I tell the judge I do not owe anything, I give her my papers, which I had itemized. The judge addresses the young lady solicitor for the Gas Supply Company. "I would advise you to withdraw your case."

The young solicitor answered, "I have been instructed to continue."

My case is transferred to the main court in Newcastle. I have to pay £50 fee. I submit my papers to the judge.

"Why was this case brought here? Dismissed."

I forgot to ask the judge for the return of my £50 fee. There is a solicitor not connected with our case, he explains to me that people settle out of court, because they are afraid of court and solicitors' cost. A sad state of affairs, they take advantage of it! He asked my age. "Seventy-five? That may be another reason."

On my return my bar crowd cheers me. That calls for a drink all round." Free beer for the bar."

"Cheers, Sylvia, good for you."

Because I am hoping to sell the Inn, it was essential that the heating supply is in good order.

A poor barbecue

Peter Lynch had asked me to put on a barbecue, in August. "Snacks would do, I don't expect a full meal, I like to charge no more than £1," he said. "That's up to you," I replied. "A sausage in a bun, a hamburger, I'll put a bit of salad with it."

In previous years I had given what amounted to a very full meal, for £2.50, steak and ale. Miss Rosetti my assistant, helped me. She said, "Sylvia, he has come back three times." Peter had taken the money at the door. £1 a go. "Help yourself to sides." No way, I went twice into my kitchen for replacement because we had run out of food.

Well, never mind, it was the last time.

Moving across the road

Mr Black, husband of the retired schoolmistress had been working, off and on, on my house, across the road from the Oak Tree. The services were working. The new cooker was very efficient. I lit the candles for our first meal – a rib roast, to celebrate.

Mandy laughed, now we are petit-bourgeois.

Sunday roast, Monday cold cuts, Tuesday meat and veg stew, Wednesday Shepherd's Pie.

The Millennium

There were many articles, in most of the newspapers, about the forthcoming Millennium Dome. It was to be a very grand affair in London, built on a loop of the River Thames. How much cement was needed to stabilize the sand? Many millions of tons of cement. It sounded so commercial, all of it. Where was religion? Forgotten? It was Jesus Christ's date!

Melvyn Bragg had a 'much publicised' interview on 28th January with the Archbishop of Canterbury. His Grace expressed his wish for a display of the story of Christ to be included in the Dome.

When I retired from teaching in 1982, I had transferred my art work into the small terraced house I had bought opposite the Inn. My outsize Christmas Cards I had done in Hollings College for the good of my soul, 'GOOD WISHES TO ALL', to counteract 'Alles Raus'.

I had an idea. It would become the 'Story of Christ', by adding further sections. It was to give me peace, solace. I had felt compelled to work, to draw, not knowing why. I had been told it was to be executed in white glass. Who told me? In my head, in my heart? Engraved white glass? I had A4 copies made of my Story of Christ, I sent them to the Archbishop.

Who could make the panels in white glass? Wilhelm Von Eiff had invented a sort of dentist's drill in order to etch into large panels of glass, plate glass, very durable. He was very famous, internationally famous. He had lived in Goeppingen before moving to Geislingen an der Steige, to the important WMF –Wurttembegische metallwaren fabric, who produced much artwork. He had married a Jewish lady from Ulm. The Nazis put great pressure on him to divorce his wife, which he finally did, when he became a professor of art in Stuttgart. I remember my father telling me- he knew him well – that von Eiff should have emigrated, he surely could get another professorship abroad.

Who could do my work in Northumbria? Perhaps the Glass Museum in Sunderland could help, advise me. I had looked around myself. The work I had seen was not to my liking. I thought the drawing was poor, Modern Art.

When I showed my cartoons to the Sunderland Glass Museum, the man (Mr Alex Thirlaway – the curator?) called his colleagues to view it. He said, "This work must not be lost. There is no one here good enough to do it. I will introduce you to a London firm." So I took my large folder – the sketches were thirty-two inches by twenty-three inches" – on the train to London. I booked into a small hotel opposite Kings Cross Station.

I had envisaged my panels to be set in large stand-up wooden frames, six to seven foot high, to be connected with hinges. Making a dodecahedron or if all of the eleven panels could be used, or eight in number, or even two, three to six, any number, according to the time of year, Christmas, Easter etc.

To be movable, for exhibitions or display. I phoned Goddard and Gibbs, the glass firm. "We will see you in an hour, at your hotel. This will be easier for you."

White glass – the story was easy to see, not like the stained glass in churches, where the eye has to absorb the message.

I had spread my sketches out on the large double bed.

The man said, "Oh yes, we certainly would like to do this work. White glass, yes, treble strength. We can paint on this, transfer your work." He gave me the prospectus of Goddard and Gibbs. I was more than surprised. This firm had done a window in Westminster Cathedral, several Royal Mosques abroad. They were the premier glass firm in England. And they considered my work good enough. I was astonished. "For the Millennium. Yes," he said. "May I suggest we execute a sample first, should it be the manger scene, or the Pietra? Perhaps the manger, it is near Christmas."

What would be the cost? For the sample – £2,000 for the whole work? "We have to discuss that later, what is involved. Yes, not more than £2,000 for the sample."

"I can pay that," I said. He left. He took my folder, I was glad I had brought a duplicate set, made for me by the firm in Carliol Square, Newcastle.

My next call was Church House, London to meet a representative of the Archbishop of Canterbury, Reverend Lynas I had asked for an interview, in answer to his Grace's comments to Melvyn Bragg. I had enclosed an A4 copy of my piece of glass.

When I arrived at Church House, I was glad the taxi found it, in spite of my incomplete instructions. I was given a visitor's pass. I had to wait a long time before I could show my work to Reverend Lynas. Several other clerics saw it, they said nothing. I was given tea, twice. Then, "That is very interesting, what about funding? Goddard and Gibbs, you said. Excellent firm."

"I don't know about founding," I said. I had never thought about the founding. The papers were full of the huge amount of money which was spent on the Millennium Dome. I said,

"Perhaps my bank, Barclays, might be interested."

"Madame Eva Juricna is in charge of the 'Spirit Level'. This is purely a suggestion, nothing else. Do you understand?"

"Yes."

"Here is her card."

There was a telephone number; I received an interview for next morning, when I explained I was staying only two days in London, from County Durham. Madame Eva Juricna is an attractive middle-age lady. Whilst she looked at my etching, I told her that I had studied comparative religion, with Dr Walter Johanes Stein in my youth, that I was non-denom and came from a multi-religious family.

I explained that I had visualized a dodecahedron of about 14-16", Dia, made of 11 white glass panels, set in wood from about 7 foot high. Slotted together. I showed my plan. A wooden door – Christ said, "I am the door." It was to be lit from the inside.

The people walking around on the outside – hopefully in large numbers – could absorb the Christian story immediately – this would not be possible in stained glass.

We know now more about Biblical times, much has been discovered with archaeology.

Madame Juricna said, "Your work is exactly what I want, it will fit in well in the 'FAITH', with the building." (It was called Spirit Level before.) I told her about how Messrs Goddard and Gibbs are making a sample glass at present. The cost complete with erection, might be £50,000. "A very good firm." She seemed pleased. "Keep in touch."

"I will, thank you." I was happy. To be in the right place at the right time.

Reverend Lynas at Church House had asked me about funding. I contacted the Head Office of Barclays in Newcastle. The lady there seemed interested, said she would speak to the directors, she would let me know.

After a few weeks I phoned her, her secretary was evasive, no contact, I phoned several times, and then gave up.

There had been ugly rumours in the newspapers about misappropriation of funds. Contractors not getting paid. I had a short note from Mme Juricna, it said the project was on hold. Best wishes. Then a young man from Goddard and Gibbs called at my house, in the evening, delivering my sample glass, nicely framed in gold. He said, "One of our directors called at the admin office of the Dome, about the funding. When he finally spoke to someone in charge, he was told the project was in abeyance." "Thank you for letting me know." I found more ugly stories in the newspapers.

The Millennium is over the whole world, not only London.

My daughter Mandy told me about a glass artist in Consett. He gave lessons, twice a week in their studio, mornings and evening. I phoned, was told they were fully booked, but I was welcome to see what they were doing. I went. Very interesting, stained glass panels, lampshades copying Tiffany, small window frames. "It is a question of table space," I was told. "We are full up." It was a class for housewives, nice ladies.

Mr Ramsay informed me, "I am putting on another class because of my waiting list." So I enrolled. I chose the simplest glass picture, I did not trust my arthritis in my hand, and my trigger finger, lately much improved. The class was very well organized. The lesson for the class was, first one chose a design, then decide the colour of the glass to be used, which had numbers. By the next lesson, the various glass items had been delivered from their large store of glass.

I asked would it be possible to paint on glass. On stained glass windows in churches the faces were usually painted. Could I learn this? "If you can draw, you can." I told them I was a designer all my life. To prove this, I brought in my St Francis Talking to the Birds drawing which I had made for an embroidery teacher at Hollings College, over thirty years ago.

The glass was very thick, was laid over the drawing. I purchased the special pens and brushes, outline in black. Pastel colours from little bottles. I enjoyed myself, my arthritis in my hand had gone completely. .

My St Francis was a success. I never knew I could do it. Could I do my Christian story? "Why not? Your drawing is excellent. But there is a snag. Our kiln is not big enough."

"Oh, they are all about, in use, like in Sunderland Glass Department. But there is a further difficulty. The glass pictures takes three days in the kiln – to be cooked, and there is the cooling time. It must be sole occupation of the kiln." The kilns were for general use, everywhere, for every student.

"How much cost for a large kiln?"

"It would be £3,000, plus vat, plus transport."

I decided to go ahead and order one, pay up front, as requested. The money from the sale of the Oak Tree, what better use for it? Delivery was quoted in approximately two months. I went every day to the Ramsay Studio to paint my story. It was time-consuming, slow work. I ordered real gold wire to enhance the glass, for halos etc. Also I had managed to find tinted glass in a pale multi-colour for St Michael's robe for the Annunciation. An angel must look different from humans.

The time needed in the kiln would be three to four days per cartoon, therefore I could reckon about two months, after installation of the kiln. Mr Ramsay said he was able to do the woodwork needed himself. I ordered the wood for the panels from Renpye in the Hobson Industrial Estate. They supplied at cost. This was very kind. The man, I addressed him as Mr Pye, said it was his contribution. Thanks again. I ordered the wooden door from Treen Woodcarvers in Smithfield.

Jesus Christ had said, "I am the door."

The entrance glass was to be lit from the inside. There had been much publicity about the forthcoming Millennium, 2000 AD, of Jesus Christ. There were arguments about the date of his birth, some factions claimed it had been in September, and transferred to fit in with local usage to coincide with the pagan-established New Year, new birth. After all, the Queen had her birthday on a convenient date. The Christmas date of the Catholic Church was generally followed, they had 'taken over' the 25th December. The Resurrection was discussed, did Jesus survive? The Christians in India claimed he did, and so did the Moslems and the Gnostic factions.

I felt, if a great number of people pray together, worship together, earnestly, this may create a momentous force, this force may become a real fact. This would explain the wonderful Holy feeling we get, and feel, at Christmas.

I remembered, I was helped in 1963 when I had been very upset by the unfair treatment I had received in Hollings College, by the healing I received when I drew my outsize Christmas card – my trypticht – Goodwill to All Men, in answer to 'Alles Raus'.

My glass work was on display in Stanley for the Millennium and is now in safe storage. The wood has been oiled, therefore it is quite safe.

The Holy Shroud

The Holy Shroud had been given by the Italian King Victor Emmanuel of Italy, to the Pope. Was it genuine? Was it a fake? Learned Bodies brought scientific proof. Shroud societies were established. When I called at the Louisa Centre, they did some duplicating for me, Mr Halls, the man in charge, said to me, "And what does Sylvia think about the Shroud?"

I answered, "I know nothing, I have never thought about it." In my religious studies, many years ago, we had never talked about the Shroud, the burial cloth of Jesus. I had to remedy this, the best book was by Wilson, I purchased it. We discussed the Crucifixion, Joseph of Arimathea, his reputed uncle, him asking Pontius Pilatus for the body, Pontius Pilatus saying, "You can have the corpse." The Centurion Leginus, the experienced soldier, surely he knew where the heart was situated, on the left side, not the right? Very few of the painters of antiquity drew the wound on the left side. Art was copied, over and over, that is where the right side wound may have been established. They copied the existing painting.

For many a night I thought, I felt, about this most important event. Jesus Christ was given Refreshment, what was it? A sponge on a stick? He died soon afterwards. Was it poison? Surely not. A painkiller? I thought something, perhaps a sedative for pain? No, he was lifeless – something which put him in a deep coma or death? What was known about coma? Very little. There were stories of dead people 'waking up', even in coffins, after days.

When the Spirit left His body, the sky went black, the sun hid, there was thunder and lightning for hours, for days.

The Spirit had entered Jesus at the Baptism in the Jordan. The

Spirit left him at the Cross. The body of Jesus was left behind, a much damaged body – cruel flagellation.

In the Jewish religion, relatives were allowed to bury their dead. If it was a violent death, all of it, the body, everything must go into the grave, you are not allowed to wash the body, according to the Jewish religion.

When we read the Bible, we found there are different versions in the Gospels. It is not about belief – I want to know what happened. Longinus at Pilatus declared death, he was no doctor. Who were the doctors at that time? Doctors of Antiquity, Hippocrates, Paracelcius, Galen, there no mention of coma, of suspended animation.

I researched the first century. I found Dioscorides, a Greek doctor with the Roman army. He had written five books on all the medications available at that time, their uses. His books are still available, now translated. No coma, but treatments of wounds, how to treat sepsis. I am not surprised there are plenty of wounds to be treated, plenty of wounds if you are with the Roman army.

Joseph of Arimathea was a rich and powerful man. The new tomb he had created for his family's use had never been used. It had been protected with a circular stone (there is a photograph of the tomb of Herod with a circular stone available). Tombs had a large slab in the middle, for the preparation of the dead person.

There were stories, legends, hopes, of a Messiah rising from death, could there be a chance of truth, a possibility?

Washing the body was not allowed, at least we can soak the main cloth, the sindon, in disinfectant, the silver nitrate in use at that time (silver nitrate was in use generally until the nineteenth century, and is used even now). The cloth was large enough to cover the top and underside of the body, as the wounds were on both sides.

The weather was horrendous, never had one known such lightning, such storms.

The story of the empty tomb is well-known. Figures in white garments had been seen. Angels? Essenes?

If Jesus survived the coma, he must be hidden. He was under sentence of death by the Romans. Was Joseph of Arimathea his uncle? He could arrange that.

The Holy Shroud. I felt it was true, real, powerful. The image, there was no painting, no photograph. An explanation came to me, a simple explanation.

I remembered reading that one had to be very careful if using silver nitrate, because it stains, causing bad stains. My doctor, my friend, Dr Quigley, gave me some silver nitrate for experiment. Not having a dead body, a chicken leg with skin would suffice. I possessed a nice piece of old linen cloth, hand woven, very fine threads. I soaked it in the silver nitrate, placed it over the meat. No lighting was available, but the strongest light bulb I could find would have to do. We discussed if chemical processes continued in the body during a coma.

Yes, there was a black stain, showing all details, including the pores. Permanent? I boiled the cloth for two hours. The stains became even more prominently black. Never faded.

Many tombs have been excavated. An archaeological party from USA have been working at a site in the ancient Ascalon of sixteen family graves having the same pattern. They all had ventilation shafts in the centre. The walls have niches to contain the bone boxes, containing the skeletons, after the flesh has rotted away, of the bodies which had been laying on the central stone slab. Above this slab is a wide central shaft for ventilation.

I assume Joseph of Arimathea's tomb was of the same or similar pattern, with a central shaft, to enable the light to enter. This, with God's help, created the shroud. Was this the way?

The stain on my small piece of linen has not faded. In 2001 I sent it to the Pope (the Polish one), name Paul. I received a letter from him, dictated, where he thanked me for my gift, sending best wishes. The piece of linen was returned to me by his office – no address. It looked as if a little had been cut off.

Twice I have had a water flood in my house, the last one was whilst I was in hospital. Neighbours tried to help. I have difficulties to find my papers, my books are in disarray, many had to be discarded. I am too tired to care. That is not true, I do care, but I don't have the strength to see to it, I am now ninety-three years old, at the time of writing,

I visited the Millennium Dome in London in early 2001. Mme Junicna had used many coloured large posters for the various religions. She had no funding. I admired her. My own work was shown in

Stanley Civic Hall for four months, Christmas 2000 until April. It is now stored in a shed in our garden.

I was surprised to find out that the details of the Christian story, which I had portrayed instinctively had been proved by extensive excavations.

There were no inns in biblical times. Families kept their cow, their ox, their donkey, in the ground floor room of their house. The floor was usually tiled, it could be hosed down every day – this prevented the milk from turning sour. The translation of the Bible was often questioned, especially about the Virgin, it should read young women, of Royal descent, born in Sepphoris, the Ornament of Galilea. Ancient Hebrew and Aramaic were difficult. Translations were difficult, they vary. The Catholic Church chose to portray Joseph as an elderly man. How could he, leaning on his stick, walk Mary and baby Jesus the 330 miles to Egypt, on the Nabatean Trade Route, a feat for a young man, or a man in his prime? Much information was lost, when the Roman Caesar Constantine called the Council of Nicea 335 AD. The various Bishops selected the Gospels, everything else was declared heretic, to be burned, discarded. The Gnostics had to worship in secret. The Christian Church was now the state religion – officially. Luckily some of the other Gospels were saved in Naghammady, in a jar in Egypt, discovered in 1945.

Constantine had declared himself Head of the Mithracan Sun Cult, he was only baptized on his death. He worshipped both religions. My mentor, Dr Walter Johannes Stein had told us in a lecture that the Christ Spirit which entered Jesus at the Baptism in the Jordan was the Sun Spirit.

History

The Co-operative Society was the first in England, in the Lancashire town of Rochdale. I had given details of this to my students in Hollings and Ashton College. I was very surprised to be told by proud villagers in Tantobie that their co-op was the third one in England. Whilst I was unable to get confirmation, historically about this, there was evidence that Tanfield Leigh and Annfield Plain sought the advice and help of the Tantobie Co-op, which was closed in the 1990s.

The chapel next to the Oak Tree Inn was erected in 1876, possibly on donation of land given by the owners, formerly the Liddell Family (Lord Ravensworth).

I had spare time for the first time in my life. Mandy was away sailing, hopefully the weather would be good in Brest and Dauvarnez, where she was attending the Meeting of the 2000 Sailing Boats.

Sorting my books on the shelves, I am no Dewey, I came across my manuscripts – I should say typescripts. I had not touched these since 1950, I had put them away when I had been told, by the best publishers, "The time was not right, the book might create anti-German feelings – we want to forget about that." Myself, I read my own manuscript, I enjoyed it, even if I said, it myself, it was good, well written.

I received a long letter from Amina (wife of a French cousin, Denis). Their new house was ready, the work had taken much longer than she expected. "This is an open invitation for you and Mandy. I thought you were retiring this year, you're seventy-five now?"

She was correct, I had told everyone that I would sell the Oak

Tree and retire when I was seventy-five. A regular customer had approached me, last year and asked if he could have first refusal. He was an insurance agent, had no experience of the wet trade, so his boss, who had offered the mortgage insisted on a six-month trial period. That saved me the hassle of advertising the Inn. He agreed to the valuation – which was on the low side.

For the trial period – the bar side only – Mr Peter Lynch had offered a month rent-free.

My side of the Inn, the hotel side, is doing fine, Mandy does a great job looking after the restaurant. More than that, she does the shopping, banks the money, supervises the laundry. We wash our bedlinen – short wash – but send the white aprons out. Contract.

I did the stocktaking myself. Not to include the wine cellar. I needed the wine for my restaurant.

Our cousins, Denis and Amina Gril lived in Aix-en-Provence. Denis was a professor of Ancient Arabic Languages. Amina had studied Oriental Art, mainly Middle Eastern, Islamic and Mogul. The new house was most impressive, there was an atrium, several trees had been planted, growing in the centre. "I had trouble planting these," admitted Amina.

Three walls were lined with bookshelves, reaching to the ceiling, with a moving ladder, like they have in libraries. "You must have several thousand books," I said.

"We have not counted them. Denis is considered a great expert on religion in France – you know we are Moslems, so the publishers send him all the newly published books, when they come out. The French government 'loans' him, abroad, all over the place." Seriously, Dr Denis Gril travels a lot.

All the bedrooms are upstairs, there was a gallery. Ingenious, wonderful. What an unusual house!

Provençe is a very nice place for a holiday. We did not like the Mistral, blowing sand everywhere, most of the time we were there. Mandy adored the local market, open every day from 6 a.m. until past lunch time. Every morning she fetched the newly baked croissants and the dark rye bread. Her French was much improving.

Aix-en-Provençe is only half an hour away from Marseille Airport, direct flights from Newcastle are mostly for package tours, so we had to change planes in Paris, to different airports. Never mind. It was a wonderful holiday.

What had brought me to Tantobie, County Durham? Simple, the price I could afford for a purchase. I was not buying these plastic pubs, low ceilings, smoke ridden, blaring pop music!! I would rather start from scratch, as long as the building was solid.

I was living now in the Land of the Prince Bishops. I always had been interested in local history. So I attended lectures in Newcastle and Durham. I found the village of Tantobie far more interesting than I had expected and wanted to make myself familiar with my new surroundings.

William the Conqueror had appointed Earl Walcher in 1071 as Bishop of Durham, to the troubled See of Durham. He came from Lothringia (now called Alsace-Lorraine), together with his cousin, Gilbert de la Leigh, who was appointed by Walcher in 1071 as secular administrator. Gilbert lived in South Leigh Tanfield Farm, Tantobie. Horses were bred in Wester Leigh (still breeding horses today). Earl Walcher had brought craftsmen from Lothringia, for the large castle he was building, which had a moat of sixteen yards long, nineteen yards wide, six yards deep. He was not popular with the local former Saxon aristocracy. He was murdered outside a Gateshead church on 14th May 1080, when attending a peace meeting, together with Gilbert and a hundred of his retinue of French and Flemish men (according to the Anglo-Saxon Chronicle). Bishop Walcher was buried in Durham Cathedral. William the Conqueror responded to the killing of the Bishop by sending his half-brother Odo, Bishop of Bayeux for reprisals.

Bishop Odo of Bayeux was reputed to have commissioned the famous Bayeux Tapestry, 1066 and all that. In my costume history class in Hollings College it was a spectacular teaching aid. I had enlarged a section of the tapestry, the students enriched the A4 copies with the silver paint I had supplied.

There is a great deal of information about the ecclesiastical story of the area, especially about the married clergy and the learned publications. I did not research this.

My own interest in the Bishop Walcher/Gilbert de la Leigh story was that my family originated from Alsace Lorraine, I had a family tree from 1690 of our Sephardic Jewish-French family.

I had read that the two sons of the attainted Earl of Northumbria (he had his head cut off) had been placed in Leigh Farm, Tantobie. Unfortunately, I cannot remember, where I had read it – I am researching. At a later date they were transferred to Stanley. They received their inheritance when the Queen came to power.

Ette and Liz

I am in touch with Margaret (Ette) Duisberg in Goeppingen. The Duisberg nursery was adjoining our property. Ette was two years older than I and I particularly remember her for her gift to speak in verse. To celebrate Grandmother's seventy-fifth year, our theatre performance of *The Suitcase Exchanged in Error* was put into verse by her. Every Christmas I sent a present from England to her. She kept me informed about local news – if there was anything of interest.

She was in touch with Mr Meyer-Rubner, who arranged the Stolpersteine, and the extensive write-up college students gave to the Fleischer family. It was the work of the year 3 history students.

I was wondering what the archives might contain about my father, his gifts regarding nature cure, bearing in mind everything had been conducted in secrecy.

Whilst I was hoping to finish my book, *Laugh or Cry,* I realised I needed help before approaching publishers. I always wrote in longhand. All my life I had a secretary, and I considered myself computer illiterate! I took my longhand letter, in German, to Stanley Library, where a charming young lady I had not met before, offered to type it for me. The letter was my enquiry to the Archives in Goeppingen. I was most surprised this lady was able to do this, to type in German. She was the private secretary to Patrick Conway, Director of Culture and Leisure, who also oversaw arts, libraries and museums in County Durham. She worked Saturdays in Stanley Library, as she, like myself, has a great love of books and literature.

There was not one single spelling mistake. That clever girl! No wonder she was secretary to one of the top directors in County Durham. Somehow I felt very close to her, as if I had known her for years. She told me she felt the same. This was the beginning of a deep and lasting friendship. She was to become my honorary daughter!

Liz helps me to tidy up my part-manuscript, part-typescript for my book, *Laugh or Cry*, and it was through her introduction that the launch of *Laugh or Cry* happened in Stanley Library, where Patrick Conway did the honours. He was a most important man in County Durham.

At a later date I wondered how she had managed to type my letter in faultless German. It became clear to me that she knew no German, and very little French, and I had to correct words later used in these languages. But on that occasion there were no mistakes. Who helped her, and me? Who wanted us to meet, be close? Later on many things just occurred to me, I seemed to be 'told' what I was to do. I was directed to do certain work.

Publication of Laugh or Cry

I had approached Messr Holzbrink of Stuttgart regarding publication of my book. They wrote, by return, that they were not publishers, but would send my manuscript to Macmillan in England. At that time, Macmillan had started a new department, "Because so many good new authors" were falling through the net. The Macmillan lady told me it would take at least two years. I suffered at that time from frequent palpitations which was later cured by a pacemaker, but at that time I didn't know how long I would last on this earth. I told her I only had six months. I thought she had turned down my manuscript , rejected it. I was milling as to whether or not pay for the publication of my book out of my own resources. The book I am working on presently is nearing completion, and I am wondering whether or not to contact Macmillan for publication of this one.

Book Guild was advertising for authors. They thought six months was okay for publication of a book. So I signed up with Book Guild.

People who had read my book passed it on to review. I had over twenty good reviews.

The Jewish papers did not give me any reviews. Not one!! Was it Ashkenazim versus Sephardic?

Mandy is admitted into hospital

In December, 2008, I booked for New Year's Eve a table at Derwent Manor Hotel, Allensford. They had advertised an all music-dance evening. The table allocated to us was rather small, but because Mandy danced every dance, all evening, it did not matter. The food was poor, considering their charges.

At the beginning of January, Mandy and I left for Llandudno, Wales. This hotel really looked after its guests very well. The food was excellent and every evening we had entertainment. The two bands were good, played alternately. Mandy danced all evening. She looked very pretty in her silver/black lace outfit. She was never short of a partner. The Conga chain was enormous. The return journey by bus took rather longer than we had hoped. Too many stops. This was uncomfortable, and made Mandy late for her insulin.

By now Mandy had a urinary infection. She became delirious, paranoid about cleanliness, everything had to be soaked, put in water, even pictures in frames.

She refused to eat, saying she was not hungry. Would not take her medications, Metformin and Insulin.

I called Dr Quigley, who said she must be admitted to hospital. I consented, not realizing that it was a mental hospital. They were taking her by ambulance.

Mandy objected, Mandy fought the nurses, Mandy became wild. Her antibiotics prescribed by Dr Quigley had been thrown away.

A psychiatric drug was given, a large dose.

I visited every day. "She needs her antibiotics," I said.

"No, she does not. We know what we are doing. Her blood sugar is very high, almost thirty."

I said, "She never has these high blood sugars, please don't give the large puddings, Christmas pudding, please look after her diet." They claimed she was a mental case and she was given a variety of psychotic drugs.

I am shown the diet chart, everything is allowed for D. This means diabetics, except the treacle sponge and marmalade pancakes. I am surprised all of this is allowed.

This was 28th January 2009.

The treatment given to my daughter was very detrimental; we never got to travel together in our retirement as we had always planned, especially to visit family in France.

Gerald Durrell

Gerald Durrell was one of Mandy's favourite authors. There were direct flights from Newcastle to Jersey.

Mandy told me that the Jersey Zoo had outstanding animals, apes and Aye-aye, which had been reared from birth, a sort of re-establishing program.

We travelled there together. Unfortunately the transport plane was an old tin can, I was twice very sick into the extra strong paper bags. The kind hostesses replenished them for me. Mandy was not affected by this.

I was so pleased when we arrived, thank God that was over!

Gerald Durrell had provided a warm in-between house to acclimatize guests in his collection. If it started to drizzle, the animals went into their half-way houses, which were well heated. The silver-back ape was playing with his son, or was it his grandson? He played hopscotch, he had learnt it very well – "We all fall down". It was a copy of our own play.

Mrs Aye-aye sat on the top most branch with her small baby. "He is lovely," said Mandy. "But I cannot see the baby, not properly." Mrs Aye-aye sent her baby down to stand in front of Mandy, it twirled around, twice, before ascending back to Mama! "He understands English, he learnt it from birth."

Mandy decided to stay there, just in case there were anymore displays, however I needed my beauty sleep. We had only booked a weekend, could not stay longer.

I bought a nice jersey creamer jug to take home with me, I use it sometimes when we have visitors.

The animals were allowed to wander freely around the town. There were notices everywhere, DO NOT FEED THE ANIMALS. The restaurants knew what to give them, they must have had an arrangement with Mr Gerald Durrell.

There were also ring-tailed lemurs, they lived outside in the trees near the halfway house.

The refugee situation

I myself have been a refugee, and am aware of the refugee situation at present. I feel the following may be a solution.

The Gulf of Aqaba is a major tourist attraction.

There is the Egyptian side with hotels. There is the opposite side, with nothing, not in use. Formerly, in Biblical times, it was used by the Nabatean Kingdom. Their water problem had been overcome, terraces, condiments etc. were well maintained.

Lack of care? Why? A result of the Nabatean Princess being divorced from King Herod, in order to secure his marriage to Herrodia? A climatic change? No, with good will, more than that, yes good will, inspired by God, we could recreate the Hanging Gardens of Babylon.

Bromeliad, the pineapple type plant could grow there, it grows on rocks. A visual feast. Hotels could provide rest stops for the Moslem pilgrims on the way to Mecca-Medina.

Sorghum could grow on the plain for the needed food supplies of the labour force. Which labour force? There are millions of refugees looking for a home. I am sure Israel could help. Cheaper than war!! It would help and support the refugees, including the families with small children.

Everyone would be glad to create rather than destroy. The Refugee problem: the land is there, the climate is begging to be developed. A great asset for the Arabian owners, not political, but the will of Allah.

The refugee problem a plus, not a minus – a joint venture for the whole world. Allah is non-denom.

President Obama of USA has had a meeting with the Saudi princes, perhaps between them they could arrange something.

This area could become a loyal and very productive province, possibly under the supervision of one of the princes. Constructive, not destructive.

I hope the refugee situation will be resolved sooner rather than later.